Smallmouth
Strategies

Smallmouth Strategies

Complete Angler's Library®
North American Fishing Club
Minneapolis, Minnesota

Smallmouth Strategies

Copyright © 1990, North American Fishing Club

All rights reserved.

Library of Congress Catalog Card Number 90-62350
ISBN 0-914697-32-3

Printed in U.S.A.
10   11   12   13   14   15   16   17   18   19

Contents

Acknowledgments

Illustrations in *Smallmouth Strategies* were created by David Rottinghaus. The authors provided many of the photos in the book. Additional photos were contributed by Janet Bean, Darl Black, Soc Clay, Paul DeMarchi, Doug Hannon, Dan Johnson, Kitty Pearson, Tom Rodgers, Kurt Sleighter and Lyn Verthein.

Special thanks to our friends at Alumacraft Boats, Arkansas Game and Fish Commission, Lund American Boats, Smallmouth Inc., Billy Burns, Otto Fajen, Charlie Huskey, Mike Johnson, Bernie McBride, Fred McClintock, John Phillips and Stan Sloan.

This book was made possible through the efforts of the staff of the North American Fishing Club: Editor and Publisher Mark LaBarbera, Managing Editor Steve Pennaz, Associate Editor Kurt Beckstrom, Editorial Assistants Amy Mattson, Jane Boers and Susan Peterson and Layout Artist Dean Peters. Thanks also to Vice President of Products Marketing Mike Vail, Marketing Manager Linda Kalinowski and Marketing Project Coordinator Laura Resnik.

Jay Michael Strangis, Managing Editor
Complete Angler's Library

Foreword

Anyone who has ever encountered a smallmouth bass is first impressed by its fighting ability. Dr. James Henshall explored many of North America's waters during the Nineteenth Century. In 1881 he wrote: "He is plucky, game brave and unyielding to the last when hooked. He has the arrowy rush of the trout, and the bold leap of the salmon, while he has a system of fighting tactics peculiarly his own. I consider him. . . .the gamest fish that swims."

Some would argue that Henshall's words were directed at black bass in general, including largemouths. And there is no denying the largemouth's fighting capabilities. But to disciples of smallmouth fishing, there is little doubt which fish is the subject of this praise. When measured for pure tenacity and heart, the smallmouth swims alone.

At home in his underwater world, the smallmouth will tackle any meal it can force down its gullet. This fish will charge to the surface for a bug, slash through the shallows to tear at schools of baitfish or jam its nose into a narrow crevice to pummel a hapless crayfish. And with equal abandon, the smallmouth will throw itself at the angler's lure.

These traits endeared the smallmouth to the anglers of Henshall's time, and continue to endear it to millions of fishermen today.

Come along with the experts in this book and learn more about smallmouth bass fishing than has ever been compiled in any one source. The NAFC has gathered these experts from all kinds of smallmouth waters to bring you an encyclopedia of smallmouth fishing. The authors have not only caught smallmouths for years, but they have solved many of the mysteries of smallmouth fishing.

Some 40 years ago, Samuel Eddy wrote in his enduring book *Northern Fishes*, "It is impossible to give explicit directions for catching bass because only the individual bass knows what it wants and what it will do. Both smallmouth and largemouth bass are capricious, and many fishermen remember the nice big bass that was not interested in any of their fancy lures, but that snatched up the worm on the handline of the small boy sitting in the stern of the boat."

That may have been true four decades ago, but it is certainly not true today. Sure, the smallmouth still seems whimsical in its choices at times, but improved equipment, experimentation and the combined observations of millions of modern anglers have turned bass fishing into a science. And the eleven authors of this book have condensed that wisdom into the most thorough book of its kind, just for NAFC members.

Whether you prefer the beauty of wading a mountain stream, the solitude of traversing a wilderness lake or the pleasure of high-tech boats and equipment, smallmouth fishing offers it all. And, as you will understand once you have read this book, smallmouth fishing is getting better all the time.

Perhaps you have seen photos of hundreds of smallmouths taken in great-grandpa's era. "Those were the days," the old-timers would say. And Henshall probably was glad he did not live so long to see the destruction by pollution and erosion of some of the best bass waters in North America. But there is another side to the story.

Today, smallmouths are more widespread than ever before. As a matter of fact, some of the largest smallmouths and most abundant smallmouth populations now swim in waters that contained no smallmouths in Henshall's day. This fish is fast becoming one of the most popular anywhere, and deservedly so. The smallmouth's glory days are yet to come, and NAFC members will be a part of this fishing action, and the most informed, thanks to this book.

After you have learned how to find and catch smallmouths, turn your attention to the last pages of this book. Besides reading about the world record smallmouth and the best smallmouth waters in America, note the outlook for the future. It is here that the bright waters lay for smallmouths, and it's largely due to the regard held for these fish by anglers.

No other group respects its quarry like smallmouth fishermen do. Catch and release is thriving, and the results are dramatically improving your chance of catching a trophy smallmouth, or even a new record fish.

Whether you're a seasoned smallmouth fisherman, or just beginning, you'll want to keep this book handy. It's all you'll need to catch the most exciting fish—anywhere!

Steve Pennaz, Executive Director
North American Fishing Club

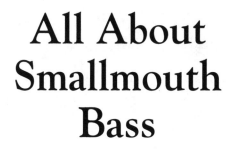

All About
Smallmouth
Bass

1

Tiger Of The Sunfish Family

With its pounding strikes, skyrocketing leaps and determined runs, it is not surprising that the smallmouth bass is fast becoming one of the most popular fish in North America. Smallmouths are found in nearly every state, and, pound-for-pound, their fighting abilities match or exceed those of any fish found in freshwater today.

Anglers who stalk this broad-shouldered dweller of the deep call it brown bass, bronzeback, redeye bass or just plain smallie, depending on their locale. Scientists call it *Micropterus dolomieui*. But whatever smallmouths may be called, they are best known as the "gamest of fish."

The smallmouth's propensity to jump completely out of the water when hooked, its preference to stay in and use the current to its advantage in a fight, and its dogged style of battling to the last, make it the ultimate sportfish in the eyes of many angling enthusiasts. Anyone who has ever watched his line go limp as a smallmouth bass skyrocketed out of the water, long remembers the thrill.

The appearance of the smallmouth only heightens its standing among those who seek this rugged fish. Its natural camouflage consists of vertical bars or stripes. And because of its tendency to lie in wait in shadows in order to ambush prey, and its strong fighting ability, many anglers liken this aquatic dynamo to another fierce animal of the wild—the tiger.

Few freshwater fish compare with the smallmouth bass when it comes to fighting ability. Their tendency to rocket to the surface when hooked has won over the hearts of many anglers.

Tiger Of The Sunfish Family

Smallmouth, brownie, bronzeback, brown bass—by any name the smallmouth's vertical bar shading, seen so well on these fish, can help set it apart from the largemouth or spotted bass.

Identifying Smallmouth Bass

Smallmouths are members of a group of fishes that are generally known for their hard fighting abilities—the sunfish family. While this tiger of the sunfish family is easy to separate from most members of the clan such as bluegill, redear or crappies, occasionally it may be difficult to tell the difference between smallmouth and its two closest relatives—largemouth bass and spotted bass.

Coloration would seem to be a logical way to tell the difference between the smallmouth and the other two basses, and often the marked difference in appearance immediately sets them apart. Smallmouth bass usually have vertically-barred or plain bronze or brown sides, whereas largemouth and spotted bass generally have whitish flanks with a horizontal line on their sides. However, water chemistry, bottom type, variety and extent of aquatic vegetation, depth of water the fish are inhabiting and the magnitude of light reaching the fish may affect their coloration.

Smallmouths can be distinguished from largemouths by the distance the jaw extends behind the eye. In smallmouths, the jaw does *not* extend behind the back of the eye. The largemouth's jaw extends far behind the back of the eye. This holds true for all but

Characteristics Of Common Black Basses

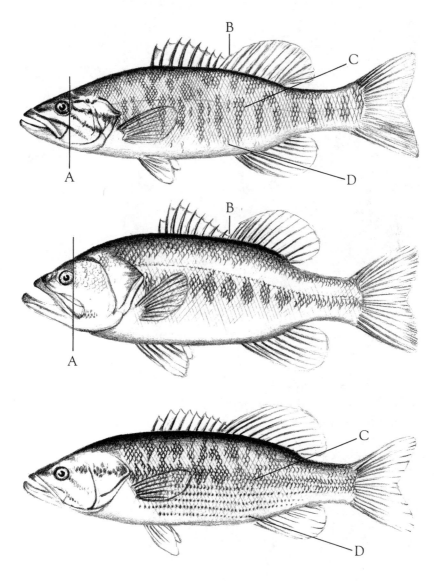

Smallmouths (top) differ from largemouths (center) by the distance the jaw extends beyond the eye (A) and the depth of the notch in the upper dorsal fin (B). The smallmouth's vertical bar shading (C) differentiates it from the spotted bass (bottom), which has diamond-shaped markings. A series of dark connected spots forming lines is visible on the lower sides of the spotted bass (D). The smallmouth's lower sides are without spots.

Not all smallmouth bass you will catch display vertical bar markings. Some have almost a solid bronze or brown coloration. However, note that the jaw does not extend beyond the eye.

the smallest fish since the bass' jaw structure does not form completely until after it is several inches long.

Spotted bass, or Kentucky bass as some people call them, have a series of dark connected spots forming lines on their lower sides, whereas smallmouths have plain sides or have a series of vertical bars on their sides.

How Hybrids Occur

While the three black basses may seem different in appearance and have different habits and food preferences, they are actually genetically similar enough that hybrids of the three have been produced. Hybrids are the offspring of parents of different species. A hybrid commonly known to man is the mule: a cross between the horse and the donkey. Illinois biologists have produced a smallmouth x largemouth hybrid called the meanmouth bass that has been studied in experiments in ponds and lakes. It has not been found to occur naturally in the wild, but another hybrid, a smallmouth x spotted bass, has.

Numerous examples of this hybrid have been documented in streams within Missouri. The hybridization of the smallmouth and spotted bass in streams that previously were blue-ribbon smallmouth streams, is generally believed to be due to habitat and water quality degradation. The change in water composition allows spotted bass access to streams in which they were not historically found. Hybridization between these two species causes a dilution of genetic material in the smallmouth bass population in that particular stream. Fisheries' biologists believe that this hybridization has the potential to be a major problem.

Water quality brings up yet another reason that so many anglers are endeared to this fish. Smallmouths are inhabitants of clean, clear, well-oxygenated water whether it be a lake, reservoir, pond, stream or river. The ever-increasing group of people who proudly call themselves smallmouth anglers spend little time around stagnant, scum-covered ponds where you might find a largemouth lurking. Nor do these fishermen frequent low gradient, silt- and sand-bottomed streams that harbor spotted bass. Rather, they pursue their challenger in crisp, cascading mountain streams, loon-patrolled ponds with 30-foot water visibility, high bluffed Ozark float streams, large northern glacial lakes and deep, southern hydropower reservoirs and tailraces.

Habitat degradation on a smallmouth stream allows less sensitive species like spotted bass to become established. Hybridization would be harmful to the smallmouth population.

Smallmouth waters not only hold exciting fishing opportunities, but are scenic in themselves. This pristine headwater stream represents an excellent smallmouth fishery.

How Do Smallmouths Measure Up?

How can we measure the popularity of smallmouths compared with other freshwater gamefish? One barometer might be angling effort versus take-home. Let us look at a few of the most popular freshwater sportfish species and use this criterion to evaluate the effort expended versus the payoff.

Sunfish (bluegill, redear, green, pumpkinseed, etc.) fight well for their size, and getting a good "mess" of fish is normally not a problem. Keeping sunfish or bream is the norm and, in many lakes, is "the right thing to do" because they are prolific spawners. The effort/take-home comparison is similar for crappies.

Now, consider walleyes. Except for some organized walleye groups, most anglers will admit to pursuing walleyes for one purpose only—to get the fish off the line and into the skillet. Walleyes are extremely difficult to beat in the eating department, and that is where the payoff comes. Trout undeniably have more history in the United States than most other fishes, and there are catch-and-release programs throughout the country, but there are also put-and-take fisheries everywhere. Many strains of trout have become so domesticated that you can do as well, or better, fishing for them with commercial trout pellets as with a Royal Coachman.

What about largemouth bass, you say? Well, yes, there is an enormous group of people who expend a great deal of effort fishing for largemouths; many fishing for meat for the table, several practicing catch-and-release fishing, and a great many going, quite literally, for the payoff—competitive fishing and the prizes and cash that go along with it.

Now let us look at smallmouths and smallmouth anglers. There are some people who go smallmouth fishing for meat for the table, and in recent years, even smallmouths have been pursued by tournament anglers. However, most smallmouth anglers behave this way: they spend a great deal of time floating, boating and wading in lakes and rivers, streams and ponds in order to hook into this gamest of fish. They do this so that they can feel the strike, see the head-shaking jump, play a game of tug-of-war with the savage slugger, and then they release it so it can fight another day.

What? Is that the payoff? Darn tootin' it is, and it is worth every second and even millisecond that it lasts! Catch and release is practiced more among smallmouth anglers than any other group of freshwater anglers today. The thrill of the fight is what makes it *all* right.

2

Smallmouth Distribution

Historically limited to a native range comprising only a portion of North America, smallmouth bass can now be found across the United States and in much of southern Canada. This fact attests to the smallmouth's popularity, and it is interesting to trace the expansion that followed the angling public's fascination with this great gamefish. Smallmouths held the second-widest native distribution (behind the largemouth) of the six black basses (largemouth, smallmouth, spotted, redeye, Suwannee and Guadalupe) originally found on the continent. The southern limit of its native range ran from northern Georgia and Alabama to the Ouachita and Ozark Mountains of western Arkansas and eastern Oklahoma, with a noticeable gap in the delta area of the Mississippi River.

The Appalachian Mountain range was the eastern limit of its original distribution.

The western limit of the smallmouth's range was eastern Kansas, Missouri, central Iowa, Minnesota and a small corner of South Dakota.

The smallmouth's northern native range extended from Minnesota across Michigan, Wisconsin, Quebec and Ontario in Canada, to New York in the northeast. There are areas within this large range in which smallmouths were not originally found due to unfavorable water temperatures or migration barriers caused by glacial impasses.

Native And Expanded Ranges Of Smallmouth Bass

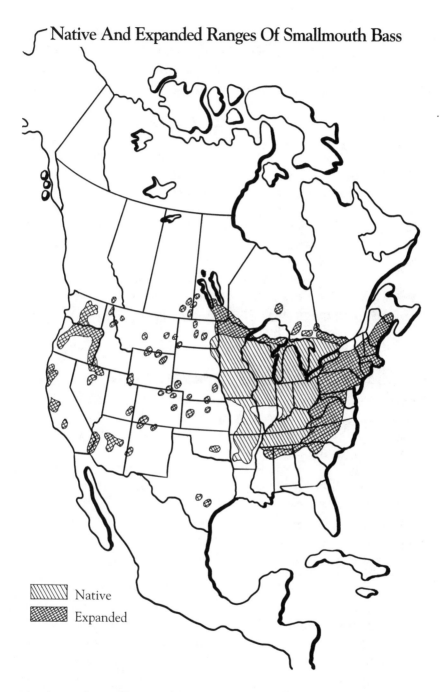

Native

Expanded

Map showing the original, or native, range of the smallmouth before widespread introduction to new waters by both fisheries personnel and enthusiastic fishermen.

Within the fairly large area described above, smallmouth bass thrived. This hard-fighting fish was as much at home in the Great Lakes as it was in the large rivers of Kentucky, the Canadian Shield lakes or the streams and rivers of the Ozark mountains.

Stocking Smallmouths To Extend Their Range
Stories of the fighting abilities of smallmouths date back to the late 1700s so, evidently, many of our forefathers were as impressed with this fish as we are now. This explains why the original range of the smallmouth bass has been so widely extended. Stocking to extend the smallmouth's range occurred at a much earlier time than that of the other black basses. This is attributed to a consensus among anglers that smallmouths were the superior sportfish of the black basses.

Records of the stocking of smallmouths date back as far as the early 1800s. These early stockings took place on the eastern seaboard in Virginia and North Carolina and in the Appalachian mountains. By the mid to late 1800s, smallmouth bass were dispersed throughout much of New England, and introduced populations were expanding rapidly.

States west of the Mississippi River did not begin transfers of smallmouth until the late 1800s. As can be expected, California was one of the first far-western states to receive smallmouth bass, but the majority of western states did not get on a serious stocking schedule until the early 1900s.

Introduction of smallmouth bass into non-native waters across the United States and southern Canada has grown throughout this century. Originally found in 23 states in the United States and two Canadian provinces, smallmouths are now found in at least 24 additional states and six Canadian provinces. The only states where smallmouths do not occur are Louisiana, Florida and Alaska.

Large-scale expansion of the range of smallmouths has been possible for two reasons. First, in many areas there existed suitable lake and stream habitat not naturally accessible to smallmouths because of physical barriers. Secondly, a number of new reservoirs have been constructed in recent years, providing fisheries biologists with new, "two-storied" habitats, especially in the South. Smallmouths can now be introduced into locales historically unacceptable from a water temperature perspective.

Tailwater areas below southern reservoirs have become fine smallmouth bass habitat in many cases. This river is at low flow, a condition that periodically occurs between water releases.

A good example of this has been the success of smallmouth bass stockings in Oklahoma and Texas. Extreme eastern Oklahoma streams are native smallmouth habitat, but the Sooner state's *lakes* never saw significant numbers of bronzebacks until the 1980s. In both Oklahoma and Texas, smallmouth stockings in reservoirs of arid regions have created new fishing opportunities in what were traditionally "largemouth waters." In other parts of the country, tailraces below reservoirs have created new, prime smallmouth bass habitat where smallmouths have exceeded expectations of sportsmen and fisheries managers alike.

In subsequent pages of this book, expert smallmouth bass anglers from across the country will tell you where and how to fish for the king of fish. The following is a general guide to what makes up good smallmouth water, with some specific examples from some of the significant smallmouth fisheries from around North America.

Smallmouth bass habitat can be described in a number of ways, but the obvious, primary classifications separate smallmouth waters into either flowing-water systems like creeks, streams or rivers, or relatively static or slow-moving systems such as lakes and reservoirs. Variations of these two types of habitat are discussed in depth in chapters 13 through 20.

Characteristics Of Good Smallmouth Waters

Whether in a lake or stream, good smallmouth waters always have a number of components present. These requirements include good water quality, adequate forage base, desirable spawning substrate and a variety of cover. The quality of a smallmouth fishery, of course, depends on the perception of the angler. Whether you consider a lake or river to be good smallmouth water depends on your idea of quality smallmouth fishing. Is quality fishing catching a smallie weighing more than 4 pounds, even if you catch only a few fish per day? Or is it the opportunity to catch dozens of smallmouths per day in a relatively undeveloped setting, even if the average smallmouth is not that large? It makes a difference.

Trophy Smallmouth Waters

If large fish are your forte, trophy smallmouth waters run the range from the Great Lakes to the man-made lakes and tailwaters of the southeastern United States. These lunker holes meet all the requirements of good smallmouth waters, but usually have one outstanding component such as abundant forage, a long growing season, lack of intense fishing pressure, or a combination of several of these. Without a doubt, the hottest lunker-producing area in all of the smallmouth's range is also the warmest in average water temperature. The mountain lakes and large main-stem river reservoirs of Kentucky, Tennessee and Alabama produce the largest smallmouth bass caught anywhere. The combination of abundant forage, or food fish, for the bronzeback and the longest growing season in North America's smallmouth range, gives this area an advantage for producing enormous smallies. The most impressive mounts and stringers of trophy smallmouths ever assembled were on display at a recent International Smallmouth Bass

Rocky outcroppings on a Southern impoundment can produce trophy bass like this one. Smallmouths have thrived in the deep, clear waters of many of these types of lakes.

Smallmouth Distribution

Small rivers throughout the smallmouth's range, especially in mountainous regions, can be a jewel of a find for the angler willing to do some exploring.

Symposium in Nashville, Tennessee. The numbers of smallmouths weighing more than 9 and 10 pounds at that show were incredible. The vast majority of these lunkers had been caught in Center Hill, Norris, Ft. Loudoun and Cherokee lakes in Tennessee, Wheeler and Wilson lakes in Alabama, and Dale Hollow and Cumberland lakes in Kentucky.

Ever heard of an area that grows double-digit smallmouths where these same fish are considered a liability by some? It's the Pacific Northwest, and the unwarranted suspicion of smallmouths wiping out the trout and salmon fisheries in some waters has some salmonid anglers hot under the collar. The Snake and Columbia rivers are just two Northwest haunts of huge smallmouths. One real plus about this area is the lack of heavy angler competition as is so often found in other parts of the country.

Clear water, nice scenery and a lack of fishing pressure mean quality smallmouth fishing. For many anglers a scene like this may be closer to home than they realize.

The oldest of the trophy smallmouth waters are the Great Lakes, which have produced many a lunker smallmouth from shallower, warm-water areas. Even though these massive lakes are near large population centers and some areas receive heavy fishing pressure, their enormous size often makes long boat rides necessary to reach some of the better bass bays and islands. This keeps fishing pressure low enough in some sections of the lake to allow bronzebacks to reach trophy size.

These areas contain the best-known lunker waters, but lakes and rivers in many other parts of the country grow smallmouths from 4 to 9 pounds, and they all qualify as trophy waters to those anglers fortunate enough to have caught a big 'un. If you know of trophy smallmouth waters that are a well-kept secret, maybe you ought to keep that secret to yourself and enjoy!

Canadian Shield lakes that make up the best smallmouth waters often contain extremely clear water. Little or no angling pressure on these lakes makes for super fishing.

Constant Action? Aesthetics? Fish The Shield Lakes

If quality smallmouth fishing means catching large numbers of ꞵmallies in an aesthetically pleasing environment, then the lakes ꞵnd rivers you fish may be quite different from the ones we just talked about. While the rocky, remote islands of the Great Lakes might fill the bill quite nicely, the man-made smallmouth reservoirs and tailwater areas below the dams in the deep South would never meet the criteria of these "purist" smallmouth anglers. This breed of smallie angler is more in his element on the St. Johns River in New Brunswick, the James in Virginia, the Buffalo in Arkansas, or the St. Croix, which forms the Minnesota-Wisconsin border. The epitome of this type of smallmouth fishing can be found in the remote Canadian Shield lakes of northern Minnesota and northwestern Ontario, where literally thousands of lakes and thousands of miles of streams are teeming with smallmouths. Obviously, these waters produce fewer trophy fish than their southern counterparts. However, due to the lack of fishing pressure on many of the lakes and streams, catches of 50 smallmouth bass a day are not unusual.

Other lakes and rivers less remote than tne border waters, but containing relatively high numbers of smallmouths, include the Kennebec River in Maine, Cayuga Lake in New York, the Vermilion River in Minnesota, the Susquehanna River in Pennsylvania, the Gasconade River in Missouri, the Maquoketa River in Iowa, and the Russian River in California, to name but a few.

Quality, of course, is a little like beauty—it is in the eye of the beholder. Whether you pursue trophy smallmouths, constant action or magnificent panoramas, quality smallmouth waters are out there to be found, explored and appreciated. Don't remember what defines quality for other people—get out there and experience it for yourself. Only then will you really come to know the tiger of the sunfish family—the smallmouth bass.

3

Senses

Because we live on land, it is often difficult for us to understand how fish function and survive in an aquatic environment. We may often wonder what a smallmouth bass perceives when a sinking minnow-imitating lure is thrown into its watery domain. What things do anglers do that might hamper their chances of catching a nice brownie? A smallmouth's perception of its liquid world depends on its senses. Senses, of course, are any of the functions of hearing, sight, smell, touch and taste. Most of these are important to smallmouth bass just as they are to man, but often in a different way. There is also at least one other sense a smallmouth possesses, which will be discussed later in this chapter.

Sight—A Smallmouth's Most Important Sense

All things considered, sight is the most important sense to smallmouth bass. From the time the fish is a small fry until it becomes trophy size, sight not only is the primary sense used in finding food, but it is also used when avoiding becoming food. The relative importance of sight is a function of the type of water, both stream and lake, in which smallmouths have evolved over the years. Smallmouth bass water is typically clear, or at least clearer than the environments of many other freshwater fish. The reliance on eyesight to avoid predators and obtain food is naturally enhanced by the location of the eyes on many fish. The photographic term, "fish-eye lens" refers to a camera lens that brings a

A smallmouth's senses may be keen, but that does not mean it cannot be fooled. Note the lateral line and nostrils, or nares, clearly visible on this dandy bronzeback.

wide-angle picture of almost everything in front of the camera into focus, rather than the narrow field normally in focus through standard lenses. This lens does not exactly imitate a fish's eye because a fish can scan 180 degrees or more on each side of its body. This "wrap-around" vision helps fish like the smallmouth elude danger and ambush prey by allowing a near total view of what's going on around them without having to move constantly to take in the surrounding area.

Understanding several other aspects of a smallmouth bass' vision can help the serious angler. Unlike some warm-blooded mammals, most fish are not color-blind, and various experiments have shown that fish in general, and bass in particular, have fairly good color differentiation. That is why different colored lures work better some days and in some waters than others. While the jury may still be out on gadgets such as color meters that advise the use of certain colored lures in different situations, the theory behind this idea is sound.

As a fish moves from the surface to deeper water, water becomes darker due to the absorption, scattering and reflection of light rays. Since water absorbs the longer light rays first (i.e. the reds), the deeper a fish descends the more the shorter rays (blues and greens) make up the remaining light. The deeper you go in a body of water, especially a clear one, the more blue-green everything becomes.

Does this mean you should change from a red-colored lure near the surface to a blue, green or a combination thereof when you are probing the depths for a strike? Not necessarily, since that red lure at 20 or 30 feet will appear black, which may make it more readily seen by a smallmouth at that depth than one that is blue-green and blends in with the surrounding water.

As you might expect, anything that causes the water to be muddy, or less clear, decreases the depths at which colors are transmitted. So color is important to the angler trying to catch smallmouths, and the varied colors of lures on bait shop shelves are there for reasons other than to simply catch the eyes of fishermen.

It is commonly known that fish do not have eyelids. Eyelids lubricate the eyes, and since fish are in water, they do not need a lid to do this.

Another difference between a smallmouth's eye and that of

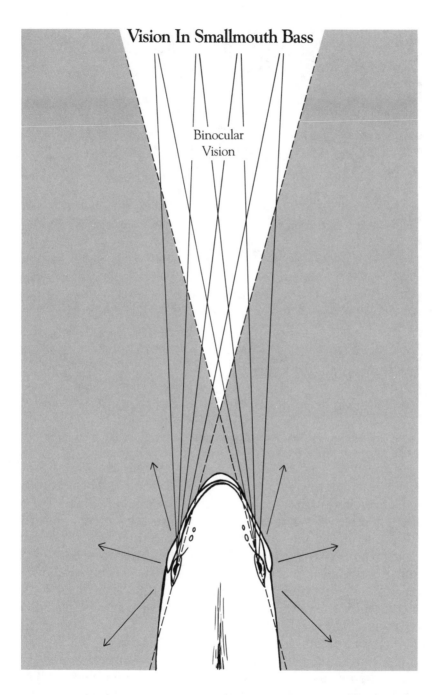

Vision In Smallmouth Bass

Binocular
Vision

A smallmouth bass does not have to move to take in the surrounding area. It can see almost 180 degrees with each eye. A narrow field of binocular vision gives depth perception.

The normal clarity of a smallmouth's environment makes eyesight its most important sense. Notice the brownies finning in the current at the tail end of this pool.

man is that our iris is similar to a camera diaphragm. The iris opens and closes in response to the amount of light entering the eye. A smallmouth bass' eye, however, has a fixed iris that cannot quickly adjust for the amount of light shining into the water. They can make adjustments in their eyes to handle different levels of light, but it is not an instantaneous process by any means. Rapid increases in light intensity, or extremely bright days, often force smallmouths to use the depths or shade near boulders and other cover as a light regulating-process.

What importance does this information have for the average angler going after a bronzeback? For one thing, on streams and in lakes where you expect smallmouths to be in relatively shallow water, use a cautious approach when fishing so you do not scare the fish before you have a chance to catch them. Novice anglers may like to be able to walk up to a stream and actually see the bass they are after, but chances are if you can see the fish, it can also see you, greatly decreasing your chances of catching it.

Generally speaking, although both largemouth and smallmouth bass are "sight feeders" and depend on sight more than any other sense, a smallmouth's environment usually has greater water clarity. Use smaller, natural-looking lures when fishing for smallmouths. The structure of a smallmouth's eye may explain why bluebird days might seem like better days to fish than to catch fish. This does not mean that you should forget these beautiful, bright days, but rather, if you want to improve your chances of catching many smallmouths, and perhaps a large one, make sure you are out on your stream or lake of choice during one of the two low light conditions, dawn or dusk.

Hearing And The Lateral Line System

Next to vision, the smallmouth's most important senses are hearing and the lateral line system.

It is important to be especially quiet when wading in a river and to make sure not to drop a rod in the boat or throw an anchor

Sensory Features In Smallmouth Bass

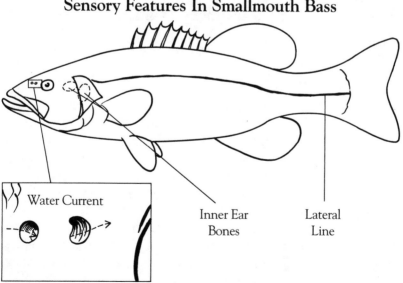

Smallmouth bass use hearing and the lateral line most when darkness or murky water impairs their vision. Nares, passages located in front of the eye, are used to pick up scent in the water.

Rain may cause muddy runoff to enter a stream or lake. At times like these, smallmouths rely more on their lateral lines to locate prey. Baits that create vibration would be a good choice here.

overboard instead of quietly lowering it down into the water. Sound travels several times faster in water than in the air. This is true whether the water is clear or muddy. While vision is restricted severely by muddy water, sound transmission is not, so an accidental dropping of a can of bug spray in the boat may spook every wary smallmouth in a quarter-mile area around you. In contrast, a poorly retrieved bait in murky water may only spook the one or two fish that can see it on its way back to the boat.

Although you may not see them, smallmouth bass have ears. There are no external openings giving away their presence, but they are located on both sides of the head, close to where you expect them to be if you consider the position of your own ears. Fish do not need ear canals because sound is transmitted in water through the skin, muscle and bone to the inner ear.

Complete Angler's Library

Understanding the sense of hearing in smallmouth bass can help you discriminate between lobbing a large topwater bait directly in front of a good-looking boulder or throwing it past and working it back to the cover. If tricky river currents force you to pinpoint cast right to the boulder, it might mean going one size smaller in the same lure pattern to avoid spooking the fish. Other situations might call for crankbaits with internal noisemakers to give the bass something to home in on from a distance. Remember, noise can be an advantage or a disadvantage, depending on the degree.

A sense equally as important as hearing to smallmouth bass is the lateral line: a network of tiny pores that begins at the head and extends down each side of the fish all the way to the tail.

Up and down the lateral line, sensory hairs containing nerve fibers send signals to the fish's brain when the hairs are pushed one way or the other. The lateral line responds not only to sound vibrations but also to water movement. For example, sound waves from a nearby boat will be sensed by a smallmouth's lateral line but so will the vibrations and water movement made by a nearby minnow or lure.

Because a canoe rides low on the water, it can help you slip up on wary smallmouths in clear water. Carpeting on the floor and rails can help you avoid making noise.

At night, vibrations are probably as important as visual cues to smallmouths. A plug that rattles or vibrates, or a spinner blade that thumps, will attract smallmouths.

Anglers can use the smallmouth's lateral line sense to their advantage not only with lure noise, but also by using lures that create water movement. In mountain streams and rivers, it is often difficult to catch smallmouth bass in the low-flow summer months when water may be gin clear. A summer thunderstorm may add just enough color to the water to get smallies out of their "wary" pattern. With the water a little dingy, bass may have a hard time seeing a lure long enough to hit it. Spinnerbaits work well at these times because the blade produces vibrations and moves the water in such a way that the bass' lateral line detects this disturbance. Although its vision may be limited, the lateral line directs the bass within striking range. While the lateral line cannot detect sound from as far away as the fish's ears can, within a limited range of a few feet a bass can "find" another fish or lure and inhale it using only its lateral line. Resourceful fishermen have found ways to capitalize on the smallmouth's sensory abilities, especially in off-colored water or when fishing at night.

The Sense Of Smell—Less Important

The olfactory system, or sense of smell, is well-developed in many fish and is, in fact, extremely important to their survival. Catfish and sharks use the sense of smell to find food. Pacific salmon use this sense, at least partially, to locate spawning streams not seen since their days as smolt.

Smallmouth bass use their sense of smell to augment other senses as they locate prey, but they do not rely on this sense to the degree that freshwater catfish do. This, of course, has a bearing on an angler's decision to use commercial scents on lures. Frankly, the best policy may be, "If it works for you—use it!" Confidence may be an intangible thing, but having it in a particular lure combination may lead you to fish harder and more effectively, thereby leading you to more fish.

4

Smallmouths' Favorite Forage

Historically, veteran anglers examined the stomachs of freshly caught smallmouth bass to determine what the smallmouths were eating. In recent years, however, the trend of releasing smallmouth bass to fight again has made dissection less practical. In addition, years of study by state conservation agencies monitoring the food habits of smallmouths in all kinds of waters have shed more than enough light on the matter of diet.

Why should an angler be overly concerned about what smallmouths are eating? Because knowledge of the feeding habits of smallmouths is almost as important as knowing where to find them. It may be the major difference between becoming a consistently successful smallmouth angler and one that more times than not leaves a stream or lake with little action that day.

Studies conducted on hundreds of lakes and rivers across the country in every region where smallmouths are found have shown that, with a few isolated exceptions, smallmouth feeding habits are fairly predictable.

What They Eat

Freshly hatched smallmouths feed on zooplankton, microscopic animals in the water that are the staple of extremely young fish of most types. Once smallies reach an inch or two in length, they switch to a diet comprised mainly of insects, but they also feed on any small crayfish or fish they can catch and swallow. The

Complete Angler's Library

Using a kick net in riffles can reveal the kinds of insects and crayfish found in a particular stream. Hold the net downstream as you dislodge gravel and rocks.

Smallmouths' Favorite Forage

first feeding shift of interest to anglers occurs when smallmouths reach adult size.

Adult smallmouth bass feed primarily on crayfish, small fish, insects and tadpoles. Adult smallmouths feed more than 70 percent of the time on crayfish and fish. In fact, depending on the season and the body of water in question, crayfish may make up 70 percent of the diet by themselves. This affinity for crayfish is due to many factors, but is definitely tied to the preference both smallmouths and crayfish have for rocky areas and outcroppings.

On the other hand, in the Tennessee River reservoirs and tailwaters that grow the most trophy smallmouths, super-abundant shad are what puts the weight on those fish. Smallmouths are opportunistic feeders, utilizing the forage that is most abundant and easily accessible.

Insects, both terrestrial (like grasshoppers) and aquatic (like mayfly and dragonfly nymphs), are an important part of a smallmouth's diet. They may make up as much as one-third of a brownie's item selection during some seasons. Even though they may eat large numbers of insects, the weight or volume of insects in a smallmouth's stomach, compared with crayfish and fish, is relatively small.

Tadpoles can be a locally important part of a smallmouth's diet and may be preferred for their soft consistency and lack of spines or a shell. Their abundance in a bass's diet is, of course, seasonally related and normally occurs in the spring of the year.

Keep Seasonal Considerations In Mind

The makeup of a smallmouth's diet not only depends on the lake or river in which both the fish and forage are found, it also depends greatly on the season of the year.

In the spring, if all four of the major food groups listed above are found in the same system, smallmouths might feed heavily on young, newly spawned fish and developing tadpoles. As the summer begins, young fish are still abundant, insect nymphs have developed enough to become a desirable food item, and crayfish are growing and abundant. In the fall, crayfish and fish make up the majority of an adult smallmouth's diet, because tadpoles have developed into the more difficult-to-capture adult frog, and insects are being thinned out by numerous other small and large fish of all kinds, including panfish, bottom feeders (i.e., suckers,

The average size, and especially color, of crayfish indicates which lure to select when fishing a body of water. Matching these as closely as possible can improve your fishing success.

redhorse and catfish) and opportunistic predators.

Winter is the slowdown feeding period in most climes, and a smallmouth's feeding intake is generally limited to small numbers of crayfish, fish and a few winter stoneflies or the ever-present diptera larvae (nymphs of the midge family). Exceptions to this winter slow period do occur, especially the farther south you travel. A hard freeze in some southern areas will cause mass die-offs of threadfin shad, followed by gorging on these excellent forage fish by a number of predators, including smallmouths.

One axiom to remember when dealing with fish or most other living creatures is that there can be exceptions to any rule. The angler who is ready for every possible feeding pattern is the one who can adjust to the exception.

An example occurs during late spring when burrowing mayflies may hatch out in droves in your favorite lake or river. These large nymphs can average an inch to an inch and a half in length and are strong swimmers that start from the bottom when hatching, undulating their way to the top to hatch out and fly away. A feeding frenzy occurs during these hatches, and smallmouths take advantage of this ready food source. If you don't think a 3- to 4-pound smallmouth would bother with inch-long immature insects, consider the fact that not only have large smallmouths been documented to fill their stomachs with them, but so have 25-pound striped bass.

Normally, you match the size of the bait with the size of the fish you want to catch. But when nature throws you a curveball, the angler ready with a small, light-colored jig or fly pattern can really take advantage of an insect hatch while others are throwing lures too large for fish that are selectively feeding.

How To Select The Right Lure

Just what is the size and kind of lure for smallmouth fishing? Generally speaking, use a slightly smaller lure when fishing for smallmouths than when fishing for largemouths. Smallmouth water is often crystal clear, and a smaller bait may tease more strikes than a larger, more splashy lure.

The above discussion brings us around to matching lures with natural foods. Jig and pigs are a good choice where crayfish are abundant. Soft plastic imitations of crayfish, hellgrammites and other creatures can be very effective smallmouth baits. There are a number of lure companies that make plastic and balsa crayfish imitations that are so real-looking it makes you want to twist the tail off one and try it yourself. Color is important and the best way to find the proper colors for your crayfish imitations is to be observant. Turn over a few rocks the next time you are on your favorite smallie stream or lake and grab one or two of the crayfish before they scurry away. Match that color as closely as possible. The same holds true for crayfish grub lures.

Fish imitation lures are a little more difficult to select than crayfish lures because, not only do you have to worry about size and color, shape is important also. Smallmouths feeding on darters (a small cousin to the walleye with the same torpedo-shaped body) are not as likely to go for a thick-bodied sunfish imitation. The best advice is to use some common sense and be open-minded. If you are traveling from Illinois to Tennessee, for example, take along your favorite lures, but ask questions at bait shops near the smallmouth waters you are going to fish. The hot lure in a foreign locale may bear little resemblance to the favorites that slay them at home.

Another trick to remember is the use of a short minnow seine, where legal, to take a quick look at the baitfish in a body of water. A few short seine hauls in your waders or sneakers in riffle areas or along shallow shorelines can tell you what your minnow imitation lure needs to look like. Matching lures to natural food items in a given body of water is an age-old technique developed by trout fishermen using flies.

This brings us to the use of flies and nymph imitations for smallmouths because they are very effective at the right time.

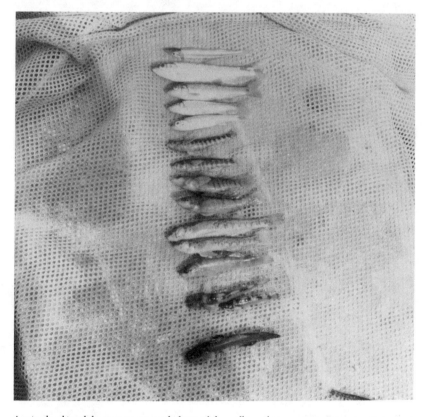

A seine haul in a lake or stream reveals forage fish smallmouths prey upon. It is not as important to know the species of baitfish as it is to know their appearance.

These crayfish parts came from the belly of this smallmouth. Unfortunately, if you are going to utilize this forage identification technique, it means killing one of the first fish you catch.

Complete Angler's Library

Normally, smallmouths are not as finicky as trout concerning fly pattern and size. Matching the lure to the prey item is important, and every effort should be made to improve your chances of getting a strike from a feeding smallmouth. While dry flies and popping bugs get a lot of the press because they lead to savage topwater strikes by smallmouths, most aquatic insects that brownies feed on spend 90 percent of their life cycle underwater in the nymph stage. That is why nymph patterns and streamers are important in the fly fisherman's fly box.

The importance of nymphs in a smallmouth's diet need not be overlooked by the non-fly fisher, either. Small jigs and grubs make fine nymph imitators and are easy to throw with light spinning gear. Hellgrammites, those large, fierce-looking larvae of the dobsonfly, are great smallmouth baits, whether caught and used for bait or imitated by a small grub or jig.

Above All, Experiment!

Stay out of a rut when it comes to thinking about what might appeal to the appetite of a smallmouth. Don't be caught always using the same bait, even if it doesn't work, because that is what you have always used in that particular stream or lake. Adapt, modify, meet the challenge of finding out what those smallmouths are eating in the water of your choice and get ready for some rod-shakin' fun from those brown bruisers.

5

Habitat Preferences

Smallmouth bass prefer the same type of outdoor habitat that most smallmouth anglers would prefer, even if it were not the home of the brawling brown bass. The best smallmouth water is cool and clean, whether lake or river, and much of it is found in rugged valleys, rolling, mountainous terrain, or backdropped by wild, northern forests. The quality of the surrounding scenery is matched by the quality of the water itself, which is usually grade AA.

Perhaps the easiest way to outline the preferred habitat of the smallmouth is to provide a chart like the one in this chapter, which includes the major physical, chemical and biological measurements associated with a good smallmouth fishery.

Remember, this chart represents preferred levels. There are streams and lakes outside of this range that have smallmouths in them. Now, let us begin looking at how these variables affect smallmouths.

Preferred Water Temperature

Water temperature plays a major role in determining what constitutes good smallmouth habitat. Smallmouths do not survive long in water that stays cold enough for trout (65 degrees) on an annual basis, nor will they tolerate excessively hot water temperatures (84 degrees).

Various life-cycle processes of smallmouths are dependent on temperature. In the northern part of their range, smallmouths

Water type and quality determine where smallmouths can live and reproduce. Within those parameters, they will seek out the biological and chemical elements that most fit their needs.

Habitat Preferences

Smallmouth Water Preference

Water Temperature	
Spawning	59° – 68° F
Feeding	50° & 78° F
Summer	68° – 75° F
Dissolved Oxygen	2.5 ppm
pH	6.9 – 8.0
Turbidity or Water Clarity	Minimum 18-inch visibility
Water Depth	
Rivers	2 – 20 feet
Lakes	1 – 60 feet
Stream Gradient or Drop	7 – 25 feet per mile
Current	0.3 – 1.3 feet per second
Bottom Type	Gravel, rubble, boulder, bedrock

Smallmouths prefer cool water, at least moderate clarity and a moderately fast current.

become lethargic during the winter months when water temperatures drop to 40 degrees or lower. They look for deep crevices and cover to lie in, moving and feeding little until the water warms. Even low levels of feeding do not usually occur until the water warms to 50 degrees and their metabolisms increase.

At 55 degrees, mature male smallmouths begin nesting activities, seeking out a gravel or cobble bottom if available, and fanning out a nest 2 to 3 feet in diameter. When the water temperature nears 60 degrees, the female smallmouth spawns, releasing anywhere from 2,000 to 7,000 eggs per pound of fish. The male guards the nest, fanning the eggs with his fins to keep the water oxygenated and prevent silt deposition. Depending on the water temperature, it may take from three to 10 days for the eggs to hatch.

The newly hatched smallmouth fry remain among the rocks of the bottom for three to four days. They enter the "black fry" stage and are guarded by the male until the school breaks up.

Temperatures during the summer affect the activity of smallmouths, especially in southern climes. Preferred summer temperatures for smallmouths are from 67 to 71 degrees, and if an angler can find water of this temperature in a smallmouth lake at or above the thermocline and near some cover, the fish he seeks should be present.

Dissolved Oxygen And pH

Measuring the temperature can often provide an angler with clues that will help catch fish on that particular day. Although water quality measurements such as dissolved oxygen and pH are important, measuring them on a specific day will probably not help the angler much.

Unless a particular body of water is highly fertile either naturally or due to incoming pollution, dissolved oxygen levels in most smallmouth waters are normally adequate. The same holds true for pH, even though recent increases in acid precipitation in North America have ruined miles of rivers and acres of lakes, killing thousands of fish, including smallmouths.

Water Clarity

Water clarity or visibility is related to the amount of precipitation received in a watershed, but after this runoff has lessened, lakes and streams of fairly high water quality, like smallmouth waters, should clear up. If you can't see at least 18 inches into a lake or stream during a period of little or no precipitation, there is a good chance the body of water has either too much clay turbidity or is loaded with too many nutrients to be a good smallmouth bass fishery. There are exceptions to any rule, but smallmouths and murky water do not usually coexist well for long. One of the main pollutants impacting smallmouth fisheries today is the amount of sediment coming off roads, farms and silvicultural (forest) areas and ending up in streams and lakes.

The Importance Of Proper Depth

There are few quality smallmouth waters, either lake or stream, that do not have a fair amount of deep water somewhere in the system. In the dog days of summer and the ice storms of winter, smallmouths will seek out deep water to get away from

Unlike largemouths and spotted bass, smallmouths must have fairly clear water and a firm, clean bottom. During dry weather, streams and rivers exhibit these characteristics.

these temperature extremes. Absolute numbers here are a little misleading because of the varieties of smallmouth water found in North America. Most smallmouth fisheries that produce adequate numbers of fish and good-sized bass have a deep-water habitat component.

Gradient And Current

These two measurements are directly related to each other. Gradient is a measure of the amount a stream drops as it winds its way downstream. Current, or the speed of water, depends on the vertical drop of a riverbed over a horizontal distance. Optimal ranges are listed in the accompanying chart and you can see that smallmouths prefer streams with some current but not the cascading, high-gradient streams preferred by trout, nor the slow, meandering sloughs inhabited by largemouths.

From experience, the smallmouth angler gets a feel for the kind of current smallies like and can just look at a river and know whether it is right or not.

Logging operations, farming and other shoreline activites often disrupt good smallmouth habitat, causing siltation of the streambed. Continued activity can destroy a fishery.

Bottom Type

One of the most obvious preferences smallmouths have is their association with bottom type. In most cases, smallmouths will select the rocky areas of lakes or can be found in high numbers in streams that have a lot of gravel, rubble, boulders and bedrock, as opposed to mud, silt and sand.

Spawning is almost always done on gravel/cobble bottoms, and when you think about the smothering tendency of silt when it covers sensitive fish eggs, it's not hard to understand why. When fishing for smallmouths, a good diversity of bottom type is best. Long stretches of gravel, without other types of bottoms, are never as good as gravel interspersed with larger rubble and with numerous boulders nearby for escape cover.

Preferred Cover, Not The Same As Largemouths

One of the last areas to cover under habitat preferences, but certainly not the least important, is not even listed in the above table because it is difficult to measure. It is cover and it takes a lot of different shapes in different water, but it all means the same thing for smallmouths—protection, escape and ambush.

With experience you can learn to judge the proper gradient and current of a good smallmouth stream or river. The best ones have a moderate current.

Complete Angler's Library

Cover is an essential component of any smallmouth lake or stream during all life stages of the smallmouth bass. When young, some type of cover is needed to escape predators, which are many during their first year of life. Even when they become juveniles and adults, they still need cover for escape from avian and terrestrial predators and, of course, the ultimate predator, man. However, the aspect of cover most anglers are concerned about is that used by smallmouths to ambush food.

Generally, as the term is used here, cover is some type of physical feature in a lake or stream such as a log, root wad, boulder, bedrock ledge, undercut bank or any other feature that can hide a fish. Deep water and the amount of surface disturbance can also qualify as cover, so don't forget about these two less-publicized types of cover.

Spawning and cover are almost always tied together when talking about smallmouths. In several studies conducted by state conservation agencies, more than 95 percent of observed spawning smallmouth pairs spawned near cover. Other studies have shown the attraction of smallmouths to cover, especially horizontal logs, boulders and root wads. The next time you are fishing in your favorite lake, chart one of your special smallmouth holes. Nine times out of 10, some type of cover will be found holding those smallmouths on the spot.

In rivers, the importance of cover becomes even more obvious, because most of the cover is visible either at or from the surface. The really good river smallmouth anglers do not waste a lot of effort in areas devoid of cover. Even if it means wading or canoeing a quarter-mile between casts, they know that the smallmouth/cover connection is a strong one and fishing long stretches of gravel without some break caused by a log, boulder or root wad is generally unproductive.

This discussion brings us around to placement of cover in smallmouth waters to increase your catch. In streams, cover placement is inadvisable because channel formation and maintenance flows in the winter and spring will generally blow out all but the best engineered and anchored structure. In lakes, however, there is some real potential for this type of habitat addition. When planning on some type of habitat placement in your favorite lake, the first step is to obtain permission from the managing agency or owner of the lake. Research has shown that with smallmouths,

The cover smallmouths associate with may seem open to an angler who usually pursues large-mouth bass. River cover is normally more obvious than smallmouth cover found in lakes.

thick, horizontal log sections are favored more than thin, spindly treetops; so just sinking a stack of Christmas trees may not be as good as having some large and dense woody debris out there.

One of the best ways to approach fish cover projects is to contact your state or provincial fisheries professionals and discuss your objectives with them. They can often provide support in habitat placement and construction. Having experience in this type of technique, they can also give you an idea of the amount of manpower needed, and the logistics of moving the structures out on the lake. Fisheries biologists are working for the same goals that we as anglers are, an improved fishery, so you might be surprised at the interest they show in your project.

6

Growth

One of the most often-asked questions smallmouth anglers bring to biologists concerns the length of time it takes their favorite fish to reach a certain size. Normally, just a simple answer will do. In reality, it is not that simple.

Smallmouth growth varies from region to region, whether the body of water in question is a lake or river and even how far up the river the fish lives. Often the area of a river the fish inhabits has a major impact on its growth. Growth can and does vary from year to year in the same lake or river depending on weather and abundance of forage or food organisms available to the smallmouth.

Regional Differences

As anyone might expect, a lake or river location in respect to the range of the smallmouth has a major impact on how fast a smallmouth can grow. This chapter contains a table comparing growth of smallmouths as one travels from north to south and east to west in North America.

Growth trends differ as you go from north to south. The difference in growth in the first year alone is 3.8 inches between a lake in Ontario and a lake in Alabama. It is not too hard, looking at this information, to understand why some of the largest smallmouths caught today come from the southern part of the smallmouth's range. However, the growth rate is really not as clear cut as it might appear.

It may take six to eight years to grow smallmouths like these in southern waters. In the northern part of the range, these fish would probably be more than 12 years old.

Growth   55

What northern smallmouth bass might lack in amount of growth per year, they make up for with a longer inherent life span. This same phenomenon is seen in other animals that occur in a range from far north to lower south. In other words, smallmouths may live more than 15 years in the northern part of their range and therefore reach almost the same size as their southern counterparts that tend to die at earlier ages. The warmer average water temperatures and longer growing seasons in the south create a higher metabolic rate and faster growth, causing fish to reach maximum growth potential at a younger age.

Factors Limiting Smallmouth Growth—Forage

A primary factor influencing smallmouth growth is a pretty obvious one—food. We have already talked about primary foods

Smallmouth Growth
Length (in inches)

Age	2	4	6	8
Lake Openongo Ontario	5.2	9.1	12.1	14.5
Big Lake Maine	5.8	11.0	14.8	17.1
Lake Michigan	6.3	9.7	13.2	15.8
Siloom Springs Lake Illinois	7.0	13.0	–	–
Hiwassee Lake North Carolina	9.1	14.0	–	–
Pine Flat Lake California	8.9	14.7	17.9	–
Pickwick Lake Alabama	10.7	16.6	20.4	21.6

As you travel northward, smallmouth growth is slower but life expectancy is greater. Both water temperature and available forage can be growth-limiting factors for these fish.

Genetic differences as well as the availability of forage can affect the size of same-age smallmouth fry. These youngsters are old enough to have begun a diet of insects and fish.

Growth

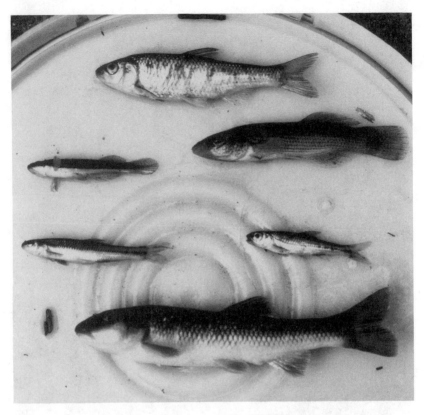

Having a variety of forage on hand enhances a smallmouth's chances of growing at an optimum rate. If one forage type becomes limited, the fish can turn to another food with little effort.

of smallmouths (Chapter 4). Normally, the greater the variety of food organisms available to smallmouths, the more stable their food base and the chance for optimum growth rate.

One of the reasons smallmouths get so large in the Tennessee River impoundments is the variety of food available to them. Admittedly, the number one food for smallies down there is shad, which are super-abundant, but in the event of a poor year-class of shad, smallmouths can switch over to a great variety of minnows, sunfish, crayfish and aquatic insects, just to name a few.

The study of animals always has exceptions. At a recent smallmouth bass symposium in Nashville, Tennessee, a report was given about a population of smallmouths in Idaho that was stocked into a lake that had few fish or crayfish in it. The number one forage for these smallies was the large zooplankton found in great numbers in the lake! Zooplankton are small, simple crustacean organisms that live in every lake, stream or pond. Generally, they form the first food that any young fish feeds on when first hatched from the egg. In most predatory fish, the fish quickly switches from zooplankton to insects, crayfish or fish as they grow larger and need a higher caloric intake. In this particular lake in Idaho, however, smallmouths did not have the diverse food base commonly available to them in many other lakes and had to do the best they could with what was abundant. Surprisingly, they have done well in this lake (Brownlee Reservoir) and, in fact, length-at-age data compares well with those in similar geographic areas.

Smallmouths can sometimes overrun their forage. When this happens, it is possible to have a large smallmouth bass population, but a shortage of food. In a case like this, reduced growth, or stunting, can occur since the numbers of fish have outgrown the productivity of the system. Most lakes and rivers have a certain level of nutrients available in their watershed and in their soils. Fish populations, over time, usually stabilize around these productivity levels. This is commonly the biggest limiting factor of smallmouth growth potential for any aquatic system.

Habitat—A Growth Rate Limiter

Habitat can influence the growth rate of smallmouths. Usually, lake smallmouths grow faster than river smallmouths, even if they are in the same area. There are several reasons for this, but one of the main ones is that rivers are harsher environments than lakes. Smallmouths living in rivers must handle current, which means expending more energy to maintain their positions in the water column when feeding, spawning or traveling. Of course, smallmouths are not always in direct current, and in fact, the larger they grow, the more they tend to stay out of the main current. They do, however, stay close to the current because of its food transport capabilities. When storms pass across a stream system and runoff increases, a gently flowing stream can be turned into a raging torrent in a hurry. In this situation, smallmouths have to be able to summon the extra energy needed to fight strong currents.

Lake smallmouths, on the other hand, live the good life, since lakes, as an aquatic environment, are much more stable, change

Fisheries personnel use an electronic shocker to momentarily stun smallmouths. The captured fish can be measured and weighed. A scale is removed from the fish to determine age.

less quickly and offer safe refuge only a short swim away should a storm blow in. Productivity of lakes can be higher, and forage easier to come by for smallmouths.

Within lakes, especially in large ones like Lake Ontario, sub-populations of smallmouths that inhabit the inshore portions of the lake grow faster than those living in open-water areas. Shallow areas hold more food than vast, deep-water areas, explaining this more rapid growth among shoreline fish.

In rivers, the lower reaches of smallmouth waters often have faster-growing fish than the upper reaches or headwater areas of the same stream. This is related to several processes occurring in both upper and lower river sections, but is due primarily to the greater amount of energy, and therefore food, available to smallmouths in the lower reaches.

Growth in fish is often quite different for males and females. In most fishes, females are larger at the same age than males. This is not the case with smallmouth bass. Numerous studies have shown that males and females grow at about the same rate. If you observe a large female smallmouth on the nest with a smaller male, it is probably because that male is a younger fish.

For the average angler, it may seem difficult to determine what stream or lake might hold larger-than-average smallmouths. The easiest way to determine this is to contact your local, state or provincial fisheries biologists and see if they have information on smallmouth growth rates of lakes and streams in your area. This information is usually readily available. Or, contact nearby bait shops and tackle stores for information on where the big ones are being caught.

If you are the more adventuresome or do-it-on-your-own type, there are other ways to gain insight into whether or not a smallmouth stream might have the potential to grow nice-sized smallmouths. Be as observant as you can be when visiting streams. Riffles or shoals are the production areas of a stream; that is, where most of the insects are produced that feed the minnows and other forage that ultimately feed the bass. Since smallmouth streams are usually pretty clear, it is not difficult to see below the surface at normal flows. Stop at several places along a stream where there is a riffle and just stand watching for signs of forage fish activity underwater. A pair of good polarized glasses will help.

A good rule of thumb for stream fishing is that streams that have a lot of riffle minnows working an area are often productive smallmouth streams. While you are at it, keep an eye out for crayfish and notice their abundance and as already advised in a previous chapter, note their color. The more observations an angler makes, keeping his eyes open for what nature has to reveal, the better that angler will be in mastering smallmouth fishing.

Equipment

7

Rods And Reels

Upon first glance, it may seem that bass tackle is bass tackle, regardless of where it is used or for what species. While there is a category of standard "bass tackle," there are exceptions depending on species, water type, water conditions, size of fish and size of water fished.

Part of the difference between smallmouth and largemouth bass tackle is based on the species themselves. Largemouths typically grow larger, are found in warmer waters and live around woody or weedy cover. That cover often requires heavier line and a powerful rod to horse a fish out of, or away from, obstructions.

Smallmouths favor rocky areas, gravel bars, boulders and rock-strewn streams. This more open water often allows fishing with lighter line, more flexible rods, and greater finesse than what is required for most largemouth fishing situations.

Smallmouths prefer cooler water and have a higher tolerance for current than largemouths, which leads to a food base of minnows, crayfish and insects—fare that is often smaller than that attacked by a largemouth bass. The smaller mouth of the appropriately named smallmouth also dictates smaller lures (covered in Chapter 11), which in turn require lighter tackle and line for effective casting.

Conditions That Dictate Tackle Choices
Smallmouth anglers generally try to match their equipment to the fish and the situation in which they may be fishing.

The right rod and reel for smallmouth fishing can be mostly a matter of personal preference. You might want ultra-light gear for the ultimate battle, or heavier gear for that ultimate fish.

Rods And Reels

Locales known to have trophy-sized smallmouths (see Chapter 31) require anglers to use heavier rods, reels and lines to successfully land these fish. Waters with lots of medium-sized smallmouths can be fished with light or ultra-light tackle and lines.

Usually, the size of the fish will also dictate the size of the lure. A fish that can be wolfed down by a 6-pound smallmouth would probably compete for food with a 10-inch smallmouth from a smaller stream. Lure size will in turn dictate the size of the line and power of the rod used to effectively cast and retrieve the lure.

Retrieving the lure with a jigging motion requires a stiff rod. A similar rod is required for working topwater lures, particularly the stick types that are worked from side to side. Soft-action rods are often preferred by anglers fishing crankbaits, based on the theory that the soft-action tip prevents tearing holes that might allow the fish to throw the bait in a frenzied jump.

As stated above, most smallmouths live in open areas. Even so, habitat plays a role in tackle selection. Fish in boulder and rock-strewn rivers might require a larger line size to lead them to open water. A deep-water, canyon-lake smallmouth can be played in open water using light line spooled on light tackle. Similarly, smallmouths found around weeds, woody cover or brush, or any place where they can hang a line, require heavier tackle than open-water fish.

Selecting Spinning Tackle

Spinning tackle is ideal for smallmouth fishing on most waters, since outfits can be matched to the conditions. The ease of using open-faced spinning tackle allows for a wide choice of lures or baits. Standard spinning tackle might include a medium-sized spinning reel spooled with 8- to 12-pound test line matched with a 6-to 6$^1/_2$-foot rod suitable for casting $^3/_8$- to $^5/_8$-ounce lures.

Reels should have wide spools for long-distance casting, with smooth comfortable handles and quiet gearing. For lure fishing, almost any reel in this standard freshwater size range will do, but for bait fishing (see Chapter 12) consider one of the newer reels that have a standard "front" drag, with the addition of a "rear-bait" fishing drag. In a nutshell, a front drag is a series of discs that provide resistance when the reel spool turns. A rear-bait drag, on the other hand, works against the shaft rotation. Rear-bait drag

Spinning reels like these from Abu Garcia, Zebco and Shimano offer a rear drag to allow the fish to take line with the bail closed. A lever engages the front drag for fighting the fish.

has far lighter settings than front drags.

In use, the front drag is set to the preferred fighting drag while the rear drag is set to allow a smallmouth to run with the bait without resistance with the bail closed to prevent line tangles or loss. Flipping a rear drag lever locks this drag, engaging the front drag for setting the hook and fighting the fish.

Lighter spinning tackle is often preferred on open western waters or shallow rivers where smaller fish are found. For this type of fishing, choose the same reel, or one a size smaller, but spool it with 6- to 8-pound test line. For the lighter line, and presumably lighter, smaller lures, choose a slightly lighter 6-foot rod with a lure range of $^1/_{16}$- to $^3/_8$-ounces.

To catch hammer-handle smallmouths (small, 10 inches or so) choose ultra-light tackle with one of the tiny reels spooled with 2- to 6-pound test line and matched to an ultra-light rod of about 5 to 6 feet designed for casting tiny lures in the $^1/_{32}$- to $^1/_4$-ounce range.

This type of fishing is usually found on very shallow rivers or small headwater streams.

Choices for downrigger fishing with spinning tackle should

include longer rods with flexible tips. For straight-line trolling you can use shorter rods if they are not too stiff.

Making The Most Of Casting Tackle

Commonly called baitcasting tackle, revolving spool reels are basic to any freshwater fishing. Casting tackle lacks the range of reel sizes and rod lengths found among spinning tackle, but can still be broken down into standard and light categories. A typical smallmouth outfit would consist of a standard-width or narrow-width reel, either of which will have suitable line capacity for smallies. Many casting reels have special features such as flipping switches, anti-reverse switches, special drag systems (in addition to the standard star drag found on all casting reels), thumb-bar versus push-button spool release, magnetic cast control (found on most casting reels) and even instant-change spools.

While some choices have to be made (magnetics or no magnetics, thumb-bar or push-button spool release) it is important to get only those features that you need in a reel. If you are planning to use the reel for flipping as well as casting, choose a reel with a flipping switch to best perform this technique.

These baitcasting reels offer magnetic cast controls that can be set to match the weight of the lure you are throwing. The resulting spool control makes for trouble-free casting.

Complete Angler's Library

Baitcasting reels offer various kinds of push-button, thumb-bar spool releases. Wider line capacity displayed on some reels is not necessary for most smallmouth fishing.

For most casting techniques, the reel should be spooled with 10- to 15-pound test monofilament. A matching rod could have a pistol grip or the increasingly popular straight or trigger-grip style of handle. Most standard casting rods are 5 to 6^1/$_2$ feet long, with foam or cork skeletal grips. Most rods in this range are ideal for casting ^{3}/$_8$- to ^{3}/$_4$-ounce lures.

Such an outfit is suitable for catching smallmouths almost everywhere. It is ideal for casting all but the lightest lures and is a standard in many smallmouth boats.

A lighter-weight version of this outfit would include a slightly lighter, smaller reel spooled with 6- to 10-pound test monofilament. Some smaller reels have been made for light-line fishing, but the limiting factor is clearance between the spool and side plates to prevent trapping light line. Six-pound test is about the minimum that can be used on most baitcasting reels.

Lighter rods match better with light line to cast lures ranging from ^{3}/$_{16}$- to ^{3}/$_8$-ounce. Most of these rods are labeled with similar lure-weight ranges.

Lighter outfits are best for any fishing where lighter lures are required or for getting the maximum fun out of small fish. They

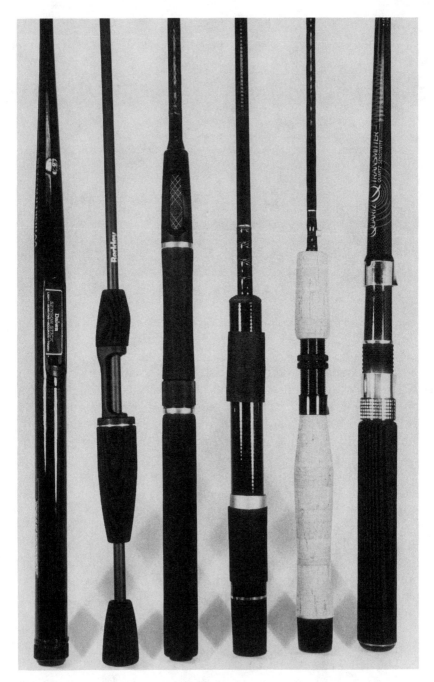

Assorted styles of rod handles and reel seats. Many feature skeletal style in which the reel sits on the rod blank or on a hard spacer to provide maximum sensitivity when fishing.

Complete Angler's Library

Typical spincast reels include (rear) underspin styles that hang under the rod and have a trigger release. Others (front) display standard spincast features.

are not the best choice where trophy fish are encountered.

Choosing Spincast Gear

While not as popular as spinning and casting equipment among experienced smallmouth anglers, spincast tackle works well. Spooled with the right size line, or bought that way (spincast reels are often pre-spooled at the factory), spincast gear will take smallmouths on everything from large reservoirs to tiny streams.

Spincast rods look similar to baitcasting rods although some have an offset reel seat that will better hold the bulky reels for easier palming and day-long fishing. Most rods are about 5 to 6 feet long, and in addition to the offset reel seat, sometimes have a slightly larger butt-guide ring, along with a slightly softer, more parabolic action. Most have lure ranges listed on the butt section for ease in matching the rod to the lure and fish.

Choose a spincast rod that will match the water. For big fish, a rod that will cast $^3/_8$- to $^3/_4$-ounce lures is most appropriate. Choose one fitted to $^3/_{16}$- to $^3/_8$-ounce lures for lighter conditions, smaller fish, shallow rivers and tiny streams.

Reels may vary in size from smaller styles that are easier to hold—particularly for women and children—to larger ones with heavier line and more line capacity. Many smaller reels are spooled with 6- to 8-pound test monofilament; larger ones with 10- or 12-pound test.

The Fun Of Fly Rodding For Smallies

Fly rodding tackle is not as popular for smallmouths as it should be, given the fact that it is one of the most enjoyable ways to take a lot of smallmouths. A fly rod allows you to cover a lot of water easily and get the maximum fun out of any fight. A wide range of fly tackle can be used for smallmouths, ranging from large outfits for big water and big fish, to light, trout-like gear for small streams and shallow rivers.

A standard outfit for big water fly fishing would include an 8- to 8¹/₂-foot-long rod matched to a weight-forward 7- or 8-weight line. If undecided, choose the 8-weight outfit. A weight-forward line is a must for maximum distance and to double haul and shoot line to get to faraway fish.

Since standard fly lines are only 90 to 105 feet long, it should be spliced to 50 or more yards of 20-pound test Dacron backing,

An assortment of fly reels for river or lake fishing includes (top) simple, single-action direct-drive reels and (bottom, l. to r.) multiplying, slip-clutch anti-reverse and single action.

Complete Angler's Library

A multiplying fly reel (left) and single action reel (right) shown with an assortment of flies and poppers for bass fishing. Choose fly size to match the fish you are seeking.

that in turn is tied to the spool arbor. A 7- to 9-foot leader is a must, tapered from a thick butt section to a tippet matched to the fish and fishing. For most smallmouths, a tippet of 6- to 8-pound test is ideal. One alternative would be to use a shooting head of 30 feet matched to a running line, in turn tied to Dacron backing for steelhead-style maximum distance on big smallmouth waters. This combination uses a flexible, braided Dacron backing line to hold big fish tied to a stiffer running line. This running line is much like a thin fly line, and is used in the cast to get the short shooting head, leader and fly out to the fish. The shooting head has the bulk and weight (like that in the forward part of a weight-forward line) to allow casting the fly.

Both single and multiplying action reels are ideal for smallmouth fishing, with the less common multipliers preferred for their quick line retrieval. The reel should be of a diameter to hold the line, but not so large that it cannot be filled with standard lengths of line.

While most smallmouths can be handled with lighter fly out-fits, larger sizes are necessary on lakes and rivers so that the line and leader will properly cast large bugs, streamers and flies. These outfits are ideal for boat fishing because they allow for long casts with the line coiled on a front or rear deck. If you pursue big smallmouths or want to throw big flies and bugs, choose the same outfit, but switch to a 9- to 9$^1/_2$-foot rod. The extra reach will also help to make up for the distance lost when wading ankle- to thigh-deep in current. Standing low in the water—closer to the surface—requires a longer rod to hold the false casts up.

In most river and stream fishing for smallmouths, smaller bugs, nymphs and flies are standard (see Chapters 11 and 21).

For a lighter outfit, first select a weight-forward line that will throw the flies and bugs you choose. Hook size alone is not all to consider here because the mass and air resistance of the fly also enters into this rod-reel-line formula. A size 6- or 7-weight line matched to a rod and a single-action or multiplying reel works best (reel manufacturers all list their reel models by line size and backing capacity to make the right choice easier). The rod can be the same 8- to 8$^1/_2$-foot length you might use for boat fishing or should be a longer, 9- to 9$^1/_2$-foot model for wading.

Notes On Rod Selection

While rod choices are made based on the criteria mentioned .above, there are certain characteristics that are germane to all styles. First, choose rods with the best materials possible.

Good graphite rods will increase casting distance, improve sensitivity (important when fishing bait, worms or jigs while spinning or casting, and flies with fly tackle) and be lighter in weight than glass rods. Composite rods of graphite/glass are a good compromise if price is a factor.

Rods should have plenty of good guides of aluminum oxide, silicone carbide or Hardloy styles. Cork or foam grips are fine for all but fly rods where cork is a must for both casting ease and sensitivity. Foam grips on a fly rod will not properly deliver the "punch" of the forward cast for a narrow loop and reduced shock waves.

Skeletal reel seats on casting, spinning and spincast rods help maintain sensitivity and transmit lure and strike impulses to your hand.

Action and power in rods are often misunderstood. Power refers to the strength of the rod, or resistance to bending. This resistance to bending is often expressed in the lure range, since a stiffer rod will only bend, or "load," with heavier lures and a light rod will

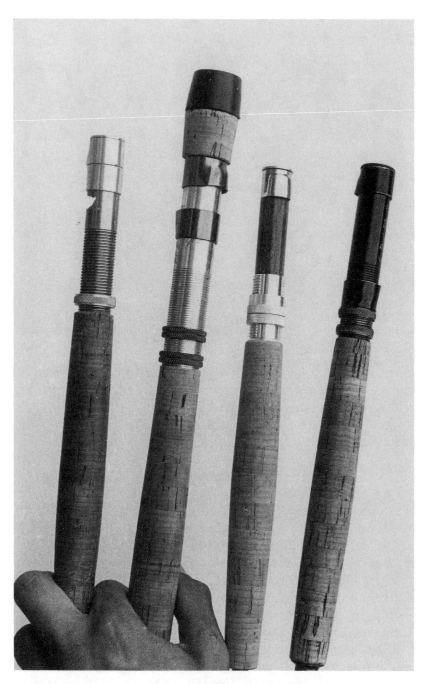

Cork handles are a must when choosing a fly rod for smallmouth fishing. Both plain aluminum and wood-insert reel seats are available. Double locking rings prevent slippage.

Monofilament line is the best choice for smallmouth fishing. Most is suited for either spinning or casting, but the Magnum 7/20 (lower right) works only with revolving spool casting tackle.

do the same with lighter lures. A light rod will be overloaded or strained with heavy lures; a heavy rod will not flex enough to cast light lures far enough to fish them effectively.

Action refers to the way in which a rod bends. Typical actions include fast tip, in which the tip bends and the rest of the rod is stiff, and parabolic in which the rod bends evenly down to the butt and sometimes even into the handle.

Notes On Line Selection

Monofilament line is almost universally used with small-mouth spinning, spincast and casting tackle. Important characteristics include a blend of factors such as tensile strength, shock strength, knot strength, abrasion resistance, limpness, etc. Provided they are the right test strength, most lines can be used for both spinning and casting. Some flat mono lines can be used only with revolving spool casting reels.

Line color is important in some fishing, since the bright fluorescent lines are ideal for fishing bait, jigs and worms that require line-watching to signal a bite. In addition, there is increased interest in night fishing for smallmouths in some parts of the country.

Here, black, or ultraviolet, lights mounted in the boat will cause fluorescent line to glow (see Chapter 24) making it possible to fish effectively under the darkest conditions.

Braided nylon or Dacron is sometimes used for trolling for smallmouths, using the same tackle as above, and with a 5- to 10-foot nylon mono leader spliced to the end.

Similarly, fly lines vary in style and weight. While floating lines are standard, a variety of sinking lines (with different sink rates or density) are available along with lines that have different lengths of sinking tip sections, followed by a floating line to make it easier to pick up for the next cast.

Floating lines are ideal for most stream and shallow river fishing, but the sink-tip style is good to get slightly deeper.

The pure sinking lines, while harder to pick up at the end of the cast (an aerial roll cast is best) will get down very deep in both current and still-water situations for schooling smallmouths or those holding on a breakline.

Because fly lines are very thick (it is the line that is cast; the fly just goes along for the ride) and visible, a length of tapered mono leader is a must to separate the line from the fly.

8

Boats And Accessories

J ust as the fish and water conditions dictate the type of tackle used for catching smallmouths, so do these factors influence boat choice. All smallmouth fishing is in freshwater, but that freshwater can range from the smallest rivulet you can float a canoe or pocket boat on, to the Great Lakes, where rough water is often synonymous with serious fishing.

Since smallmouths are often rocky river inhabitants, care must be taken to choose a boat that will not only be suitable for the fish and the river but will also survive the rocks and boulders. As with most fishing, choose your boat and accessories based on the water you typically fish.

Canoes: The Portable, Shallow-Water Craft

A good canoe will float on a heavy dew, can be portaged and will hold an assortment of light tackle. It can also be used as a base for wading shallow water. Canoes are fast and quiet and move quickly with paddles, small electric motors or tiny outboard engines.

The best canoe sizes range from 15 through 18 feet with the former getting the nod from most anglers on small, shallow streams. Larger canoes are best suited for extended trips and back-country smallmouth fishing. Both double-end and square-stern canoes work well. Use the latter with a small outboard for long trips to the fishing grounds.

The choice of aluminum, fiberglass or one of the plastics such

The boat you choose for serious smallmouth fishing should match the water. Choices range from canoes and inflatables for shallow rivers to large, high-powered craft for big lakes.

Boats And Accessories

The shallow draft of canoes makes them ideal for fishing shallow, rocky rivers, and their light weight makes them portable enough to get to otherwise inaccessible waters.

as ABS can be a personal one, or one based on the water conditions. In shallow rivers, aluminum or ABS is best since the rocks will tend to chew up fiberglass. Aluminum tends to hang up on rocks, ABS tends to scratch and gouge, but both bounce back for fishing and are easier to repair than fiberglass.

A disadvantage of a canoe is that space for tackle is limited and during all-day fishing they can become cramped.

Conquering Fast Water With Inflatables

Inflatable boats are ideal craft for fishing fast sections of rivers that might otherwise be impossible to reach. Large, tough inflatables with multiple chambers and durable fabric allow anglers to reach spots too dangerous for any other type of craft. Inflatables will bounce off or slide over rocks and, with a drag anchor, allow

Inflatable rafts make it possible to fish in smallmouth rivers impossible to navigate with hard-hulled craft. The result often means access to fish others never reach.

you to fish deep pools most other fishermen never reach. You can get wet in an inflatable, so they require special waterproof bags or boxes to hold spare clothing, cameras and similar delicate equipment, lunch and spare tackle. Although the best inflatables are heavy and require trailers to transport, they are the only type of craft that will get you to some river smallmouth spots.

Enjoy Shallow Water In A Johnboat

Originally designed as river craft, johnboats have seen increasing use in lakes and reservoirs. Most are made of aluminum, have a square prow and range from 10 to 18 feet in length. The larger models incorporate heavier-gauge aluminum hulls and are often used by commercial fishermen or guides. Smaller, lighter models are easily car-topped for dropping into likely spots.

Some call johnboats the "poor man's bass boat," but they have been around a long time. The johnboat's design endures because of its shallow draft and stability as a fishing platform.

Johnboats can be poled in rivers or used with appropriately-sized outboards. Since they are wide and spacious, larger models are ideal for carrying two or three anglers.

Some johnboats can be purchased with livewells, some have side consoles for steering-wheel boat control and most can be equipped with a bow-mount electric motors for positioning while fishing. These are not high-speed boats and are thus no substitute for higher performance bass or bass-style boats.

Because most johnboats have a low freeboard and a square prow, they are not good for rough water. Some designs incorporate a modified v-hull. Because of their versatility, johnboats are ideal for bass fishing of all types. They have good stability, plenty of storage space, and are ideal for the rivers and streams that are often the best smallmouth waters.

Johnboats can be purchased with modified v-hulls and custom-rigged with floors, rod boxes, livewells and other comforts. With their wide, flat bottom, they will handle shallow water.

Boats And Accessories   83

The semi v-hull represents one of the most widely popular fishing boat designs in use today. Constructed of aluminum or fiberglass, these hulls handle waves better than johnboats or bass boats.

Getting There In A V-hull Boat

U-hull and semi v-hull boats are commonly constructed of aluminum, although fiberglass and ABS-type models can be found. They are good, all-around fishing boats that fall between a johnboat and a true bass boat.

While these versatile boats range between 10 and 18 or more feet in length (like johnboats) the pointed prow and semi v-bottom create less usable space. Some anglers add floorboards (if the boat does not come equipped this way) to make for level tackle storage space, particularly in the bow area. As with johnboats, they can be customized for individual use and tackle storage by imaginative anglers.

Because they have a deeper bottom and pointed bow, v-hulls are well-suited for cutting the waves and for high speed travel on bigger, rougher waters. They are also ideal for slow trolling with lures and live bait, and backtrolling with live bait and bait-walker rigs.

Boats Made For Catching Bass

True bass boats are designed specifically for bass fishing— regardless of the species sought. Most range from 15 to 18 feet, are wide, stable and have a v-hull. This type of hull gives a deeper draft for fishing in shallow water and more stability at high speeds in rough water.

Most fishermen equip their bass boat with the maximum outboard engine size, anywhere from 100 to 150 horsepower depending upon hull length and type. The v-hull provides the high-speed performance necessary for tournament bass anglers who may run up to 50 miles one way on big lakes if they believe the fishing possibilities at the end of the trip warrant it.

Bass boats typically have a side console, two or more riding seats, two fishing seats (one each on the forward and aft storage decks), one or two aerated livewells (two for separating anglers' catches for tournament fishing), rod lockers, tackle storage and large gas tanks for extended travel. A bow-mount motor and one or more depthfinders complete the rig.

Getting To Smallmouths On Big Waters

Large lakes become rough quickly and require big boats for deep-water smallmouth fishing. These boats typically run 16 feet or larger, are wide, stable and made of aluminum or fiberglass. The best have high sides, deep v-hulls and high transoms or splashboards to prevent following seas from landing in the boat. In short, they are designed for serious fishing in big water such as the Great Lakes where rough water is often encountered.

Fitting Your Boat With Accessories

Rigging your boat just the way *you* want it can greatly enhance your smallmouth fishing. Endless numbers of gadgets are available for these purposes, but only a few are real assets to the smallmouth angler. Here is a short summary of some of the most practical.

Electric trolling motors are ideal as the main propulsion of small craft in quiet water or as a positioning motor for bigger craft. They are also good for slow trolling or backtrolling with live bait

Bass boats offer the ultimate combination of speed and stability. They are designed to hold high-horsepower outboards, yet, while at rest, they make a steady fishing platform.

86   Complete Angler's Library

or slow-working lures.

Bow-mount electric trolling motors, like those commonly seen on bass boats, offer the convenience of foot-pedal controls. Stern-mount electrics, sometimes used for backtrolling, are typically just pulled straight up when stored for high-speed running rather than being swung flat the way bow-mount trolling motors are stored.

When choosing an electric trolling motor, consider its power or pounds-of-thrust rating to best match the size of your boat.

Electrics are better than outboards in controlling the boat at slow, trolling speeds for continued periods since continued slow speeds tend to foul the plugs of outboards.

Protect Your Outboard In Shallow Water

For running shallow, rocky rivers where rocks and riffles can quickly chew any prop, some anglers protect the lower units of their motors with arched, metal "forks." Similar to the tines of a pitchfork, these prongs are mounted on the lower unit and completely cover the leading edge of the prop area to help slide the outboard up and over rocks. Most forks must be individually fitted based on their shape and the brand of motor. They are commonly clamped on the lower unit or bolted to the cavitation plate.

If making a set, be sure to select tines from a thin-tined pitchfork, rather than the wide blade spading fork. Some fishermen prefer homemade forks, designing and mounting the devices themselves.

Enjoying The Benefits of Rod and Lure Racks

Rod racks are a must for serious smallmouth anglers because they allow instant access to rigged rods. Racks can be purchased or homemade, but should be designed to hold all the rods that you wish to carry or can legally use. Rod racks should be distinguished from rod lockers, which limit instant use and are designed for storage of spare equipment. Homemade rod racks can be easily constructed from two-inch PVC pipe to hold rodtips and a platform or hook to hold reel handles.

On bass boats, rod holders are often nothing more than specialized hook-and-loop straps designed to hold a collection of tackle while the boat is running. While fishing, rods are usually lined up on one side of the deck. Commercial rod racks typically

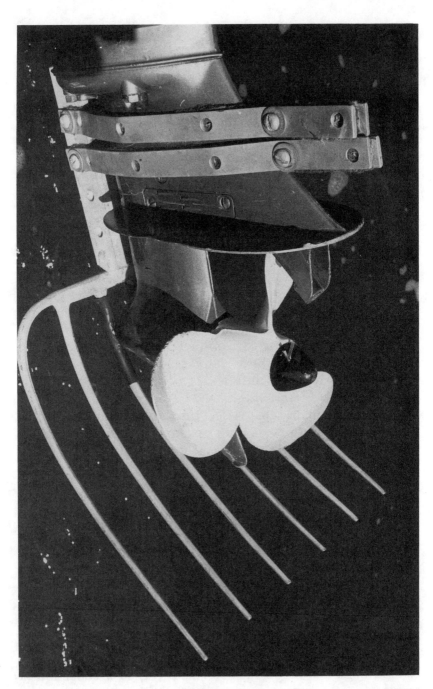

For running shallow rivers a clamp-on fork like this is a must. Be sure not to block the intake of the lower unit and to use only the narrow-tine pitchfork, not the wider tine spade.

You can customize even a canoe to fit your smallmouth bass fishing needs. The possibilities include lure holders, rod racks (or tubes), carpet, storage boxes and more.

include hole-and-hook arrangements that will hold from two to four rods.

In addition to rod holders, some fishermen choose to use lure racks that are commercially available and designed to hang lures of all types. Some lure racks offer compartments for pork rind jars, scent bottles, tools, etc. They are easily mounted on the inside hull of any boat. Make sure that any mounting allows room for all the lures you want available and does not interfere with normal movement while fishing.

Choosing The Best Anchor

An anchor is a must when fishing over a bar or in deep water where you want to hold position after locating a spot on your depthfinder. In fact, every boat should have an anchor anyway.

Lake And River Anchors

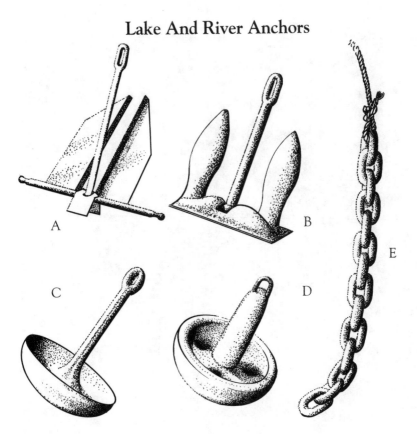

Popular anchor styles: Danforth (A) Navy (B) and two styles of mushroom (C & D). Drag anchor (E), for floating rivers, consists of a heavy chain attached to the end of an anchor rope.

What constitutes a good anchor depends on the boat size and bottom type. Danforth-style (thin fluked) anchors perform best on sandy bottoms. Navy-type (heavy fluked) are designed for gravel and rocky bottoms. Mushroom-style anchors are a good choice for small boats.

An anchor that is not manufactured, but performs exceptionally well when river drift fishing is called a drag anchor.

Drag anchors are nothing more than a length of chain on a short piece of rope. Hung from the bow and dragged along the bottom, this anchor is not designed to stop the boat, but only to slow it enough to allow thorough fishing and to keep the bow pointed straight into the current.

The length of the drag anchor should be chosen based on current strength and boat size. Often, anchor length will match boat length so that the engine can be run while the anchor is out with no danger of having it tangle in the propeller.

Boat Poles

For propelling a boat in very shallow water, a push pole can save many hours of frustration. Poling can be done from either end of the boat, but often greater control is maintained from the bow. Boat poles range from 8 to 16 feet in length and are usually constructed of wood or fiberglass. They can be racked on a boat with a special boat-pole holder, a U-shaped rack made of strap aluminum fixed to the inside or outside of the craft. The best poles have one pointed aluminum end and one Y-shaped or duck-billed fork for soft bottoms.

Storage

Storage space, if not already built in, is easily added using picnic coolers. The many sizes available can be held in place with bungee cords to hooks mounted in the deck. If working with bait, or filleting fish where legal, bolt or glue a piece of plywood to the lid as a cutting board. Protect cameras or binoculars in plastic bags before placing them in these coolers and be sure that they have some cushioning for protection against shock.

=====9=====

Sonar For Smallmouths

Many have said that smallmouth bass are as hard to catch as they are to find. And, finding them is never easy. Anglers who consistently catch smallmouths, however, know that mastering the use of a quality sonar device can mean the difference between success and failure. In fact, the majority of them would list it as their "most important tool" when it comes to catching smallmouths. Sonar is an angler's "underwater eyes."

Generally called depthfinders or fishfinders, four types of sonar units are used by sportfishermen. All work on the same principle.

Whether you are an NAFC member who chooses to use a liquid crystal display (commonly called an LCR), paper chart recorder, video or flasher unit, the serious student of sonar can master the basics of operation and interpretation quickly and easily. Unfortunately, many dedicated smallmouth anglers utilize sonar only for determining the depth of water, not for finding fish or studying their habitat.

The astute know that smallmouths are generally found near structure in the mysterious and wonderful underwater worlds of lakes and streams. Some anglers reason wrongly that sonar instruments cannot detect fish in such close quarters. They also express that the instruments "look" complicated, when they really are not. Learning to use sonar to your advantage is like learning to read. The more proficient you become, the more you can visualize

Whether you fish the Great Lakes, reservoirs or any other type of lake, sonar can help you catch smallmouths. Not only do these electronics monitor depth, but they can spot fish.

Sonar For Smallmouths

places you have never been. In this case, that means the sometimes mysterious underwater world of the smallmouth bass.

Sonar Reading Improves With Experience

Most depthfinders are truly also fishfinders, capable of revealing many of the secrets of the underwater world. Even state-of-the-art units—those that are fully computerized and resemble the control panel of a spaceship—are really quite simple. The keyboards on some chart recorders and liquid crystal graphs, for instance, are easy to operate despite their appearance. Properly used, they can be a smallmouth angler's dream.

Consider, for example, that the smallmouth's favorite food is crayfish. Both fish and prey prefer to live where there are rocks, gravel, bluffs, ledges or riprap nearby. Sure, the fish are hard to find in such places, but the task is greatly simplified—and the catch rate increases considerably—for the studious sonar user.

At the same time, becoming an expert requires a degree of experience, too, like becoming a good fisherman. It takes time, research, concentration and practice.

The beginner, in fact, is well-served to learn sonar interpretation before tackling the other many and varied tasks in becoming a master smallmouth angler. Following a few simple rules will allow him, and the veteran operator as well, to master the basics.

A sonar unit is the only product in the angler's arsenal that can find concentrations of migratory, suspended, schooling and nomadic smallmouths, and pinpoint their unseen habitats.

How Sonar Works Its Magic

How and why sonar instruments operate as they do is immaterial to most anglers. However, you should know a few of the technicalities in order to understand the many facets of interpretation.

The word "sonar" is an abbreviation of *so*und, *na*vigation and *r*anging. The first cumbersome tube-type units were developed by the U.S. Navy during World War II as a means of tracking enemy submarines.

Modern units are small and compact and consist of four main parts—a transmitter, receiver, display and transducer. The transmitter fires a short burst of energy (from a 12-volt electrical source) into the transducer. At the same time a mark is made on the display at the zero location. It signifies the surface. The

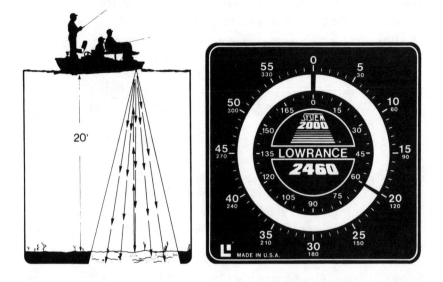

The screen of a flasher unit reveals a blip at 20 feet indicating bottom. Like all sonar, a sound wave is bounced off the bottom and converted into a visual signal.

transducer converts the electrical energy into sound waves, which are transmitted into the water in a cone-shaped pattern that resembles a megaphone or light beam.

Sound travels through water at approximately 4,800 feet per second—four times faster than through air. When it strikes an object or obstacle, it rebounds. The returning sound wave is called an echo.

When the echo strikes the transducer, it is converted into electrical energy. This electrical impulse is then transferred to the receiver, amplified, and sent to the display. Since the speed of sound in water is known and constant, the time lapse between the transmitted signal and the received echo can be measured and the distance to the object determined. The depth of the object causing the echo can thus be read by comparing its location on the display to the depth scale provided on the face of the sonar unit.

Select The Proper Transducer

Transducers, like the display units, vary in size and function. They are the most important part of any sonar installation, and must, above all, be installed properly. A particular type is made for every kind of boat and hull configuration. Precise instructions on installation are provided by manufacturers and should be followed carefully.

For smallmouth fishing, a transducer with a 16- to 22-degree cone angle is best and will give the finest detail.

Determining exactly what is below the boat and being able to positively identify various underwater objects, is a skill within itself. Identification of some objects is easy, while others may be quite difficult. Beginner and veteran alike can profit, however, through "trial and error."

First, remember that a quality sonar instrument, installed properly, does not lie and is capable of providing vast amounts of valuable information. Keep in mind, however, that the sonar device is reading three-dimensional sound waves, while you view it on a flat screen or dial.

Study To Get The Most Out Of Your Electronics

Before you launch for the first time with a sonar unit, spend at least an hour or so reading and reviewing the instruction booklet, even if you are a veteran sonar user. If it's a new model, it likely has many features with which you are not familiar.

Read it thoroughly! Look at the drawings and photos! Study it and put it in your boat and take it with you on a "shakedown" cruise.

Once you are on the water, motor to an area that is large and open enough for the boat to drift free for some time. If possible, select a place known to have varying bottom contour with rock, ledges, drop-offs and channels. Start in water that is relatively shallow—about 20 feet. If you can, pick a quiet day, or select a calm cove or inlet for the trial run.

Turn off the motor, turn on the new unit and forget the fishing rods for a while.

If the unit is a flasher or chart (paper) recorder, set the depth range on 0-60 feet and advance the sensitivity (also called gain) until you get a good bottom reading (20 feet). Then, crank it up a bit more, until a second echo appears at 40 feet. This indicates that the sound wave is going to the bottom and bouncing back to the surface twice. Now you know you have adequate sensitivity to show bottom contour and any objects (hopefully fish) that might exist between your boat and the bottom.

A transducer (arrow), which sends a sound signal to the bottom and picks it up again, is mounted on the transom slightly below the bottom of the boat for high-speed sonar readings.

The second echo bothers some folks. If you are one of them, simply back off the gain slightly until it disappears. Keep in mind, however, that it must be respectively reduced or increased when you survey shallower or deeper waters.

If the new unit is an LCR, it will be in the automatic mode when you turn it on, and you won't need to bother with setting the sensitivity or seeking a second echo.

Regardless of the type of unit, you should by now be thumbing through the pages of the instruction manual. While the boat drifts, follow it step-by-step. Push the buttons or turn the knobs exactly as the manual tells you. If you need to start the motor and run at speed or troll for a step or two, do it. Then return to the quiet spot and continue.

Some features—such as the use of noise discrimination or suppression functions (common to all) to eliminate electrical or cavitational interference—may have to wait to be established if you are the only boat, with the only unit, in the area. However, you will encounter situations later that will require their use to prevent interference from electronic equipment being used on nearby boats.

Interpreting signals is the key to finding fish with any of the four types of units. While similar, each offers a different learning experience. Each type deserves special attention, since they possess different features.

Flashers

In addition to finding fish, the flasher is excellent for navigation and safety, capable of telling true depth even at high boat speeds and warning users of abrupt changes in bottom contours.

They show a constant bottom reading with proper sensitivity setting, but it may have to be increased when deeper water or soft bottom structure is encountered and decreased for shallow water or hard bottom.

Some of the sound waves emitted will be absorbed by the various things they strike—fish, bottom, brush or trees, rock and other objects. By initially setting the sensitivity to a bottom echo width that pleases you, you can determine whether you're over a soft or hard bottom contour.

Hard bottoms—which smallmouth prefer—composed of rock, gravel or sand, will reflect a great amount of sound, producing a wider signal. Soft bottoms (silt, mud, weeds and loose debris) will absorb sound, reflect less and result in a thinner signal.

The bottom and zero signals on a flasher will generally be quite wide. Thus, you should always read the bottom blip on its shallow edge. For instance, if a constant signal from 20 to 24 feet is shown, the true bottom is 20 feet, not 22 or 24.

Schools of forage or baitfish will be indicated by tiny, thin light lines. A tightly packed school will return a solid blip. Larger fish will provide larger and wider blips.

Quality flasher units can show fish, such as smallmouths, near the bottom. They will appear as "dancing" blips. If more than one fish is present several blips will be seen, all dancing at the same time.

The resolution (ability to separate targets from the bottom or

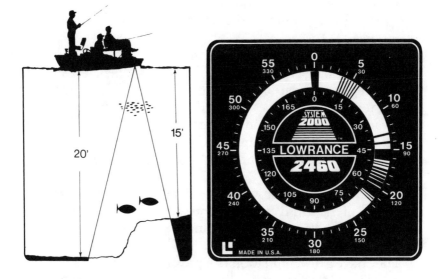

Set properly, a flasher reads everything between the surface and the bottom, but it is up to the angler to interpret the signals. Here baitfish, gamefish and drop-off are visible.

other fish) of a quality flasher is about six inches. Any fish closer than six inches to the bottom may not show as a separate signal, unless the bottom is extremely flat and hard.

There are two sources of interference on any sonar—electrical (from another boat's motor, bilge pump, aerator or similar appliance), and cavitational, from air bubbles under the transducer, which slow the speed of the sound signals. The bubbles can come from many sources—keels, strakes, ribs, rivets under the boat, backwash of a propeller or an improper transducer installation.

Electrical interference causes blips to travel around and around the flasher dial in a clockwise fashion. Cavitational blips are stationary. Some can be knocked out by suppression, but not always.

Paper Graphs Give The Best Picture

Offering the best resolution of all sonar units, the chart or paper recorder's biggest selling advantages are infinite detail and provision of a permanent record (chart) of the underwater world. It can be stopped and scribbled upon, studied, clipped, photographed, stored and compared with past and future recordings.

State-of-the-art charts offer dozens of other features, too, giving the finest detail of fish, structure, bottom contours and other objects.

While still popular, there are a number of objections to chart recorders. The paper they require is sometimes expensive, and it is hard to replace if you are riding rough waters. They have no alarms, temperature gauges or speedometers, like those featured on advanced LCR units, and they are somewhat bulky. Some say their keyboards are too complicated.

Many veterans swear by them, however, terming them ideal for smallmouth fishing.

They can pick up fish virtually on the bottom, through manipulation of the width of their sound waves, zoom capability and more. Some can be set to measure any one-foot segment of water desired, which no other unit offers.

They have a discrimination (suppression of noise) system that is second to none. Top-of-the-line charts and some popular LCR units boast a grayline feature that is a near-perfect interpretation tool.

The grayline, set properly, will separate all other objects below the boat from bottom signals, including fish, rocks, trees and brush piles, and tell the operator at a glance if a hard or soft bottom is encountered.

With its ability to show even the smallest object in black dots on white paper, it will picture individual fish as an inverted "V" or thumbnail, and schools of small fish in a ball.

Chart experts can often distinguish "schools" of smallmouths because they tend to scatter below schools of baitfish when feeding, or "stack up" (one above another), when at rest. Only smallmouths and white bass have this characteristic, it is said.

Liquid Crystal Displays Offer Easy Operation

Called LCRs and LCGs by manufacturers, liquid crystal displays are today's most popular sonar units. The first, actually quite crude by today's standards, were introduced to anglers in 1984.

Fishermen like their ease of operation, small size, "automatic" functions and low cost. Most will give accurate depth readings and show suspended objects, including fish, simply by pressing the "on" button.

Like paper graphs, they are fully computerized and "paint a

Take the time to learn how to use equipment properly to get the most out of it. Here a fisherman studies his graph and flasher to compare their use while he trains his "underwater eyes."

picture" of the underwater world on a screen, through a series of dots called "pixels." The more vertical pixels on a screen and the more features offered, the higher the cost.

LCRs have no moving parts, and they make no permanent records. However, some have the ability to "freeze" several screens of information, which can be recalled later.

Most can be used in automatic modes or manipulated manually for finer detail and greater fishfinding capabilities. Most also have zoom (range) setting capability, fish and anchor alarms, and suppression buttons. In manual mode, many have "command menus," offering dozens of other features too numerous to list. Some of these features include battery tests, temperature gauges, speedometers, odometers, and even Loran-C navigational capabilities.

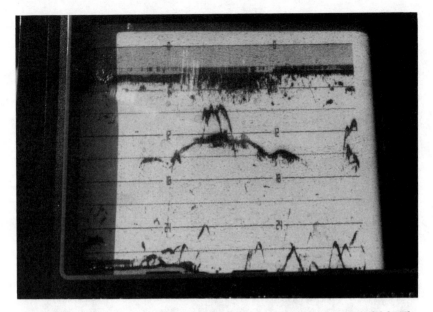

Paper graph recorders give the most accurate readings of underwater structure and fish. The large inverted "V's" on this chart are gamefish. The long mark is a school of baitfish.

The latest, high-quality, higher-priced units have a resolution that is nearing that of the best chart recorders. Some offer fish symbols instead of inverted "V's" for fish, and grayline to determine whether you are over a hard or soft bottom. They also offer excellent zoom and range capabilities and alarms galore.

Liquid crystal units are proof-positive that sonar has gained greatly with the "Computer Age."

Video Displays Best Suited To Largest Boats

Because many anglers perceive the number of negatives to outweigh the positives, video units, boasting television-like cathode ray tubes, have gained little popularity with bass anglers.

Generally speaking, they are confined to larger fishing boats that feature overhead coverings and large consoles, such as those which ply the waters of the Great Lakes and oceans.

On the positive side, most top-end models display targets (fish), bottom and other structure in seven different colors, ranging from light blue for the weakest signals to red for the strongest when set properly. Large schools of fish usually display three or four colors, for instance, with a red core. Small schools have fewer,

Liquid crystal displays are preferred by many fishermen for their ease of operation. They can be inexpensive, but unless you decide to spend more, you may get a unit that gives a crude picture.

When you begin to use sonar properly, you can match the depth of your lure to the depth of the fish. For catching smallmouths, this is especially important around deep structure.

weaker colors. Other positives, on both color and monocolor (two-color, lower-priced units) are zoom controls, ranges to as little as 15 feet, excellent resolution, alarms and automatic settings, if desired.

Negatives of video units include the fact that they are big and heavy, requiring considerable space for installation. They cannot be read well in sunlight and the tubes are somewhat fragile and not waterproof.

A Final Test To Gain Confidence

With the instruction manual steps now completed, it's time to take rod and reel in hand, with a heavy lure (jig or casting spoon) attached, and proceed through one more exercise.

Slowly lower the lure directly below a transducer and follow its progress to the bottom. On a flasher, the bait will show as a blip progressing deeper and deeper. On a chart recorder or video screen, it will be a line, slightly diagonal because of the drift and the paper movement through the unit. On the LCR, it will show as a dotted line, also diagonally, as the boat moves and the scrolling on the screen moves from right to left.

Move the lure up and down, and watch it on the dial, chart or screen. It is a fascinating experience and will lend proof to the stories your friends have told about "dropping a lure on the fish's head."

About now you will suddenly realize that you made a brilliant choice when selecting your sonar unit. At your fingertips, awaiting your commands, you have a well-constructed, yet delicate piece of equipment that is going to serve you well and be your number one fishing partner for many years.

You will marvel that such a tiny instrument can unravel so many of the secrets of the smallmouth's world.

If you do not break your arm patting yourself on the back, it is time to go fishing! If you are a novice, however, your education has only started. Sonar, regardless of how well you have mastered it, can only help you find fish. It cannot catch them for you!

10

Wading Gear

Smallmouths like current and rocks. That makes them an ideal river fish, and wading is an ideal way to fish for them. For waters that are impossible to wade, float tubes are an important adjunct.

Many shallow smallmouth rivers are so skinny that using a boat is just about impossible, or would create so much noise, water turbulence and mud that getting to the right spot would scare any fish you might be after. Some areas are so shallow that even poles and paddles are out. In shallow-water areas, a few locals use air boats with large airplane-type blades on the back. Even with such boats, getting out to wade is the way to fish.

In some cases, good spots on a river might be boulder-clogged or rife with riffles or waterfalls. These areas are also perfect for wading.

Getting Acquainted With The Basics

Wading is a natural extension of shoreline fishing. While shoreline fishing does take smallmouths, it implies being unable to reach any farther than your longest cast. Wading solves this.

How you wade will depend upon personal preference as well as local conditions, weather and season. Wet wading is perhaps the easiest and least expensive. On its simplest level it does not require any gear other than a pair of old sneakers.

Hip boots are good for small stream wading when the water is cold and fairly shallow. For wading in deeper rivers, chest-high

Wading may be one of the best ways to catch smallmouths in rivers and streams. With the proper equipment some of the toughest smallmouth terrain can be negotiated with confidence.

Wading Gear

waders are a must. In colder climes and during the spring and fall, insulated neoprene waders are best.

Float tubes, often called belly boats, can be used when fishing waters that are too deep to wade. They also extend your range on a variety of still and flowing waters.

Using The Right Wet-Wading Gear

Wet-wading is best in midsummer or at least after the water warms up enough to make such fishing comfortable. Wet-wading gear is simplicity itself. Wear a lightweight, long-sleeved shirt for protection from the sun and long pants of rapid-drying chino or poplin fabric. A cloth belt is preferable to leather because it will not stiffen up and crack after a few trips.

Footwear should include heavy socks that will cushion feet from the strain of pushing through water and against the occasional bits of gravel and rock that might be picked up through your shoes. Wool/nylon blend socks are best since they resist shrinkage when laundered.

Any old sneakers will work, but "high-tops" are best because they pick up less gravel and provide protection from sharp rocks and ankle-turning. Avoid sneakers with holes or rips that will allow sand and gravel to invade the shoes and irritate feet. Shoes designed for stocking-foot waders are also available. Be careful about size, however, as these shoes are made to wear with waders and an inner and outer pair of socks.

Be sure to bring a complete change of clothing for the drive home.

Choosing Wading Shoes, Hip Boots Or Waders

The alternative to wet-wading is to wear some sort of hip or chest boots. Hip boots are two separate boots that reach thigh height and are held in place with belt attachment straps. Waders, or chest waders come up to the armpits. They have built-in or added suspenders to hold them up. Both hip boots and chest waders can have either boot or stocking feet.

Boot-foot waders are just what they sound like—built as a boot and worn over socks. Put these on and you are ready to fish. They are heavier and more bulky than the stocking-foot style (something to consider when traveling), but more convenient.

Boot-foot waders take many forms. You will have to choose

A well-equipped angler wearing chest waders works a river run for smallmouths. The line running across his shoulder is a keeper for a wading staff used to negotiate the rough bottom.

between fabric boots (either rubber or nylon coated) and neoprene boots. Neoprene boots can be either thin-wall (usually 3mm) or thick-wall (5mm). Thick-wall neoprene boots are more durable and better suited for cold waters and inclement weather.

Stocking-foot waders require separate wading shoes, innerliner socks and an outer sock or guard to protect the wader from being chafed and torn by the boot.

Stocking-foot wading shoes are made of fabric or leather, often with special cleated soles to grip rock. The inner socks are usually standard wool or wool-blend. The outer socks are now a special neoprene or foam slipper that is wrapped around the foot for protection and comfort. Some even have ankle protectors that fold down over the top of the shoe to prevent intrusion of sand or gravel. Standard wool or wool-blend socks can be used for the

Hip waders or wading shoes can be fixed with felt soles to improve traction on slippery bottoms of streams and rivers. Commercial wading shoes with felt soles are also available.

same purpose if you do not wish to go to the extra expense.

Other accessories for wading include suspenders, separate hook-and-loop cuffs to hold pants down while putting waders on and special soles for both boot and stocking-foot styles. Sole accessories include single or combination strap-on chains, cleats and felt soles for increased gripping. In addition, some felt soles are designed to be glued in place on the boot as an add-on or replacement for worn-out soles.

Safety Gear And Wading Aids For Smallmouth Fishing

Safety gear worn fishing does not have to be bulky anymore! Modern personal flotation devices (PFDs or lifejackets) have become lightweight, almost fashionable items today. Often, type III PFDs can be used in place of a fishing vest since these usually have four or more pockets to hold spare tackle and lure boxes. In addition, they are lightweight, comfortable and have flotation foam spread evenly around the vest. This means nothing bulky or awkward in front of or alongside you that might interfere with handling tackle or landing fish.

If this is still too bulky for your tastes, consider one of the CO_2

A life vest designed for fishing should always be worn when wading in fast current or deep water. The best, like these from Stearns, offer pockets for equipment. Some are available with pressurized cartridges for instant inflation.

flotation devices. These are simple, flat vests with pockets that can be instantly inflated by pulling a rip cord to release a CO_2 cartridge. A slower method of inflation uses your own breath to inflate the pockets through a valve-controlled tube. One company makes these in a suspender style for ease in wearing with chest-high waders. None of these, however, are Coast Guard-approved at this time. If using a boat to get to a wading spot, you will still need a standard Coast Guard-approved PFD of the type required for your vessel.

Wading belts for those using chest-high waders are also important. Made from fabric with a quick-release buckle, they are designed to go high on the outside of waders and thus reduce the amount of water entering in the event of a spill or fall. While waders or boots will not pull an angler "down," (water inside waders weighs exactly the same as water outside), belts do help to reduce the amount of water shipped. Belts are especially important on rubberized fabric waders because these are larger and looser than the more form-fitting neoprene style.

A wading staff is useful in providing additional support while wading. It can be used wet-wading or with any style of boot or wader. Although it is possible to improvise by picking up a stout branch along the shore, most branches that are easy to break to length are also easy to break in the water and thus are of marginal help. Commercially available wading staffs of wood, steel, aluminum and telescoping materials are best. Most wading staffs have a rubberized or pointed metal tip. A combination foam grip, wrist strap and lanyard is also standard. This allows the staff to float in the water yet remain tethered to the vest when not in use. Telescoping staffs are especially handy since they can be placed in the back of a vest when not needed.

Tubing Your Way To The "Big One"

Float tubes have evolved dramatically since the first ones came onto the market 30 years ago. Today, float tubes are made from truck-style inner tubes for high flotation with quick release buckles in the seat, skirts to hold fly line when fly fishing, inflated back rests, side and rear pockets for fly and lure boxes, D-rings for stringer and net attachment, suspenders to hold the tube while out of the water and handles to carry the tube from the car to the water.

In addition to a float tube, you will need fins or flippers. Try to find the type that clamp onto your feet or ankles and allow forward movement. (The skin-diver type works better going backward than forward.)

Always be safety-conscious—use a PFD or inflatable vest whenever tube-fishing.

Choosing The Right Vest, Tackle Belt And Shoulder Packs

Unlike shore or boat fishing where you have plenty of room to store all you need, wading requires carrying everything with you. This is where the fishing vest, tackle belt or shoulder pack come in. There is an endless variety to choose from.

Before buying a vest, consider the size of your lure boxes. Make sure that the lure or fly boxes you use can fit into the pockets of the chosen vest. Take one when you shop for the other, or buy both at once. Make sure that any other accessories that you wish to use will fit in or on the vest.

Accessories may include fishing pliers, clippers, line spools, tippet wallets or cases, sinker or split shot containers, thermometer, stringer, hemostats, fishing knife, rain top or parka, insect repellent, sun block, sun glasses, fishing knife and so on.

Some vests have a zip-off bottom while others are made in one

A good vest and chest waders give this angler the confidence to stalk a deep pool. Many fishermen who use chest waders use a belt outside their waders to prevent them filling with water in a spill.

Wading Gear

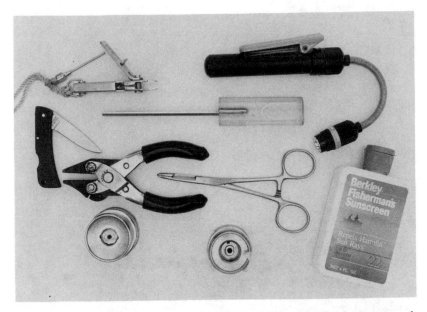

Wading aids (clockwise from top left): clippers (Walton's Thumb) with tube for tying nail knots, pocket light, hook sharpener, sunscreen, hemostat, spare spools, pliers, pocket knife.

of two lengths: a waist-length model usually used by hip-booted anglers or an elbow-length model for wearing with chest-high waders. Make sure that any chosen vest has quality construction including strong stitching, bellows pockets and a full-length zipper.

Belt-style tackle packs are like a streamlined version of the old army belt with attachments. Some tackle belts have sewn-on pockets while others allow additions or changes. Most consist of a series of several pockets around the waist with a quick-release buckle in front.

Belt-style packs ride on the waist so they are not as handy as the higher-riding vest or shoulder pack because you will often be in waist-deep water.

In the opinion of many experts, shoulder packs are ideal for smallmouth wading. They look like two book bags, and each pack is subdivided into several smaller compartments and connected with shoulder straps. The rear compartment is usually larger and meant for rain gear, lunch and spare reels or line. A front bag contains multiple compartments to hold lure and fly boxes. It is easy to reverse the front and rear bags by flipping the shoulder pack.

Most also have D-rings for stringer and wading staff attachment, and fleece patches to keep flies conveniently within reach.

Choosing The Accessories You Need

Since you must take it all with you when wading for smallmouths, wise decisions in accessory selection are crucial.

Fishing pliers, preferably the kind with parallel-acting, compound jaws, are a must for fishing. Though they sometimes get wet, many anglers carry them in a sheath on their belt.

Line clippers are another "must-have" item for changing lures and removing abraded line. Keep them on a small pin-on lanyard reel on your vest.

Sometimes added weight is necessary to get a fly down to the fish, or to cast a tiny lure with light spinning gear. Keep a small assortment of split-shot, rubber-core or pinch-on sinkers handy.

Although you seldom lose the entire leader on a fly line, you still need to keep tippet material on hand. Be sure to carry a spool of each needed size. (Suggested sizes include 2-, 4-, 6- and 8-pound test.)

Sharp hooks are imperative. Always carry a small hook sharpener with you, preferably a diamond-coated one for fast honing.

If you plan to be on the water early, or stay late, carry a flashlight. Clip-on head lamp or flexible-stem styles are best because the beam of light can be aimed where you wish for changing lures and tying knots.

If you plan to bring fish home, remember your stringer. Fish on a stringer are a nuisance, though, so consider this before carrying one afield.

Bring a wader top or parka if rain seems possible. Both short and long styles are available.

There are few wading trips where sunblock and insect repellent do not come in handy. Keep both away from fly lines because they will harm the PVC coating.

11

Smallmouth Lures

When choosing a smallmouth lure, take environmental and biological factors into consideration. Smallmouth habitat tends to consist of rocky, open areas rather than the weedy or dense, woody cover preferred by largemouths. As a result, food staples also vary.

Crayfish and large insects are staples of river smallmouths although small catfish, stone cats, dace and similar river minnows are also eaten with relish. In lakes, smallmouths feed on crayfish, minnows and insects. The smaller size of the smallmouth dictates that anglers use slightly smaller lures than would be used for large-mouths. It is not that a smallmouth cannot or will not strike a large lure, but you will catch more fish on lures in the $^1/_4$- to $^1/_2$-ounce range.

Catching Smallmouths With Topwater Lures

Topwater lures are excellent for catching smallmouths when fishing in shallow rivers, around rocks, along the shoreline or any time the fish may be close to the surface. Stickbait lures are also good when fishing big water impoundments, canyon reservoirs and open-water structure.

Typical topwater smallmouth lures are no different from large-mouth lures apart from size. They can include small stickbaits that look like plain cigars, those with fore- and aft- or rear-props, those that are chuggers with a squared, popping face, and those with plates or designs that allow a surface-wobbling, side-to-side ac-

Topwater baits (from top left/right): Rip Shad, Horse Fly, Ole Ben's Cry Baby, Crippled Killer, Poe's Jackpot 1300 and 1400, Zara Spook, Zara Puppy, Hellraiser, Smithwick Dancer.

Smallmouth Lures

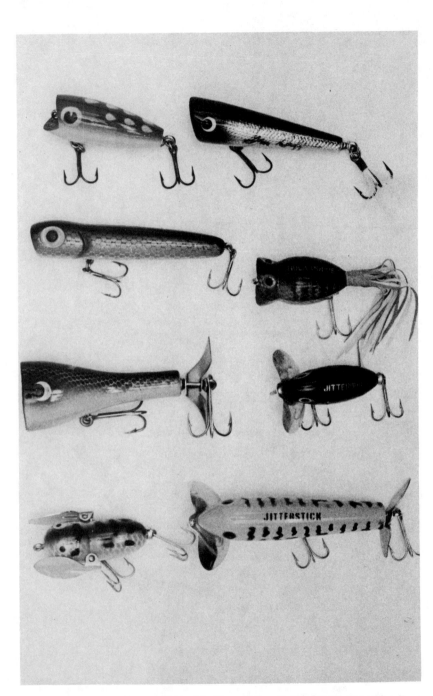

Chuggers and crawlers (from top left/right): Blurpee, Sam Griffen Wobble Pop, Chug Bug, Hula Popper, Ozark Mountain Woodchopper, Jitterbug, Crazy Crawler, Jitterstik.

tion when retrieved slowly across the surface.

Like largemouth bass, smallmouths can be "called" to the surface to strike a topwater plug, even from depths of 10 feet. Sometimes fish suspended over very deep water will rise to topwaters. The action that results from these kinds of strikes is nothing less than spectacular. While most surface lures come in a wide variety of colors, most have only three belly colors—white, yellow and black. Choose white or yellow belly plugs for daylight fishing and solid black plugs for night. (The black will show up far better against the night sky than will other colors.)

Catching Smallmouths With Crankbaits

Crankbaits, once called plugs, comprise a wide range of plastic and wood lures that work under the surface of the water. Many are floaters that have a lip designed to make them dive. Those with short lips placed well under the body dive only a little; those with long lips parallel to and at the end of the body go deep.

Although the entire spectrum of these lures is needed to effectively fish all smallmouth waters, some may be more important in your local waters than others. Make your choice based on the environmental factors already discussed. You will also need to choose shape and color. Crankbait shapes range from the slim minnow form of many shallow runners to the fat "pregnant minnow" shape of medium divers and stubby, big-lipped bodies of deep divers. Generally speaking, smallmouths are most attracted to the slimmer baits. Colors range from baitfish designs to solid colors and from translucent lures with colored inserts to glitter coatings or iridescent shades that change with the direction of light. Color choice should be based on the forage of the waters being fished. In most cases these will include dark colors and patterns that imitate crayfish, but on larger lakes in the South and West this might be the shiny, slab-sided baits that imitate shad, the forage of those areas.

As with topwater lures, choose small or medium crankbaits with weights of $^1/_4$- to $^1/_2$-ounce. Exceptions will depend upon the size of the fish and the water covered. In some lakes with populations of big smallmouths, big lures are a must. In shallow rivers and streams, the smallest of crankbaits, even the $^1/_8$-ounce sizes, barely longer than one inch, work well for catching the fish you normally find.

Shallow-diving crankbaits (from top left/right): Bagley Shad, Spitfire, Poe's RC 1, Hellcat, Creek Chub Darter, Rebel Fastrac Shad, Storm Shiner Minnow, Baby Ashley.

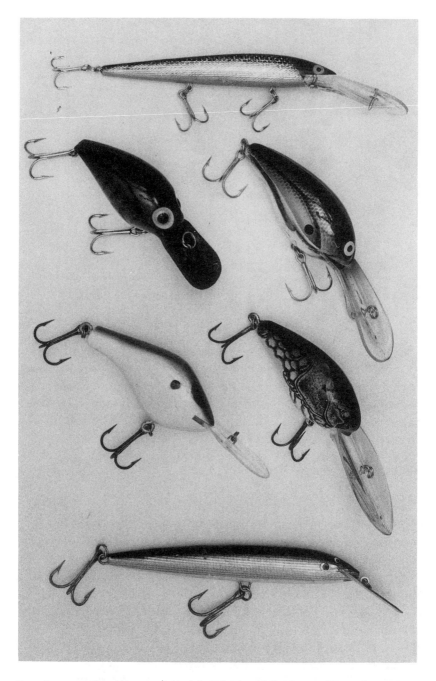

Deep-diving crankbaits (from top left/right): Rebel Spoonbill, Magnum Wart, Norman Deep Diver, Poe's Super Cedar, Bomber Magnum, Rapala Sinking Magnum.

Smallmouth Lures

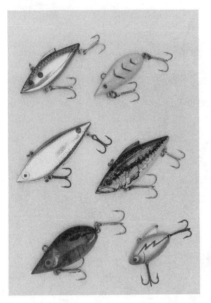

Vibrating plugs (from top left/right): Rat-L-Trap, Storm Li'l Tex, Cordell Spot, Rat-L-Trap, Storm Texas Shad, Heddon Sonic.

Using Sonic (Vibrating) Lures To Catch Smallmouth Bass

Sonic or vibrating lures are also made of wood or plastic, but with a slim, slab-sided shape and no bill. Their design is such that they will vibrate in the water on retrieve. Many have rattles creating even more noise. The smaller sizes are ideal on almost all waters while large sizes are a first choice when fishing big lakes that have a shad forage base. Since they are a great shad imitation, bright colors are best.

Fishing With Spinnerbaits

Spinnerbaits consist of a safety-pin style wire form holding one or two spinner blades and a skirted leadhead. Although primarily a largemouth lure, on certain waters and under certain conditions they work exceptionally well for catching small-mouths (see Chapter 24).

In some parts of the South, large spinnerbaits are used in impoundments. The so-called "short arm" style, named for the short length of the upper arm holding the single blade, is used in a falling pattern, letting the lure fall while the blade helicopters.

On most other smallmouth waters the $^1/_8$- and $^1/_4$-ounce sizes work best.

Spinnerbaits include (from top left/right): Strike King short arm 380, Mr. Mean, Double Chance, Whizk'N Spin, Limberneck, Stanley Vibra Shaft.

Jitterbugs are popular for both smallmouths and largemouth bass, and come in a variety of sizes. They work best at a speed that makes them pop and gurgle most.

Spinnerbaits should be fished with a reversed skirt for added fullness and sometimes with a short trailer strip of plastic or pork.

Surface Fishing With Buzzbaits

These great river lures are similar to spinnerbaits but are designed to work on the surface with a large churning propeller blade. Like spinnerbaits, they have a leadhead and plastic or rubber skirt. Buzzbaits are effective when smallmouths are on or near the surface or are taking lures or baits from the surface. Use smaller sizes of about $^1/_8$- to $^1/_4$-ounce around rocks and structure in flowing current.

Catching Smallmouths With Jigs

Jigs, also known as "hair flies," "hair jigs" or "bucktails," are one of the all-time top smallmouth producers. They are painted leadhead lures, molded on a special bent shank hook and finished with a tie-on skirt of fur or feathers, or a slip-on skirt of rubber or plastic. Often combinations of fur and rubber are used for maximum attractiveness.

Choose jig color based on the color of the water and the type of water fished. Choose size based on current or depth.

Jigs can be purchased either in plain or "weedless" styles. Weedless jigs are not meant to be fished in heavy weeds, but they do prevent hang-ups when the lures are being maneuvered around light weed cover and rocks. Hook guards on jigs are made of wire, plastic or nylon brush. The brush style can be spread to protect the hook from snags.

Experienced smallmouth anglers often like to fish jigs with a tail or trailer such as a pork chunk, pork strip, grub tail or a short, 4-inch floating worm. The floating worm is preferred since it will float high and attract fish while the jig is sitting on the bottom.

Using Grubs To Fish Smallmouths

Grubs are nothing more than jig heads with soft plastic tails. Grub heads can be either painted or unpainted (in most fishing this seems to make little difference), and round or shaped like the head of a fish. When these "fish-heads" are mated with a soft tail, they make convincing, fish-shaped lures. Like jigs, grubs can come with or without a hook guard (weed guard). Weed guards can be wire, plastic "Y" guards or brush-style.

Using a short length of plastic worm with a jig and pig or fly and rind prevents the pork trailer from sliding up the hook shank where it might interfere with hooking a fish.

Tails for grubs (they are incomplete without them) include straight, soft, plastic tails, curly tails, fish-like tails, fish tails with a tail flap that causes them to "swim" on retrieve, crayfish-like tails and multiple-leg tails.

Deep Fishing With Tube Lures

Soft plastic tube lures look like vinyl versions of the fingers from a glove. The open end is split into tails and the lure is fished on a specialized jig head or in combination with other lures. Originally designed for fishing deep water on light lines in the West, they are now popular in many areas of the country for both largemouth and smallmouth bass. Most are available in the same colors as plastic worms. Clear, smoke, pumpkinseed and glitter are the most popular. They are ideal for fishing deep canyons, impoundments and flowage reservoirs; but the smaller-sized lures can also be used effectively on rivers and streams. Since they are usually sold unrigged, they are used on a jig head. Some rigs include a worm on the jig with the tube lure threaded over the head of the worm.

Catching Smallmouth Bass With Worms

Although worms are primarily a largemouth bait, short, 4- to 6-inch worms work well for catching smallmouths. Deep-water, clear lakes such as canyon reservoirs and rocky impoundments are good places to try these. Short 3- or 4-inch worms can also work in rivers.

Worms are available with either straight or curly tails. Use curly-tailed worms in flowing water and straight-tailed worms when still-water smallmouth fishing.

Worm colors that are commonly used for catching smallmouths include motor oil, smoke, glitter colors, pumpkinseed, grey, black, dark blue and purple. As with most lures, the light colors are best in clear water, darker colors in stained or dirty water.

One ideal worm is the pre-rigged, do-nothing style that has one to three molded-in hooks. This style should be fished with a slow, even retrieve. Other worms are sold unrigged, have jig heads or are rigged in various popular worm styles. Short worms are also good for adding to other rigs, such as spinnerbaits, buzzbaits, tube lures or jig heads.

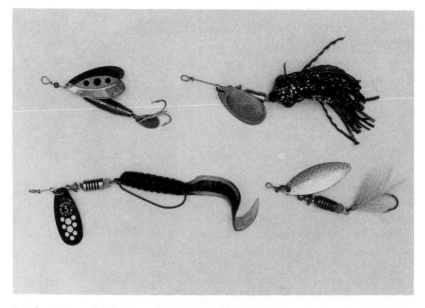

Popular spinners include (from top left/right): Mepps Black Fury Combo, Les Davis Bolo, Mepps Aglia Long #2, Bass Buster Weed Invader.

Fishing In Current With Spinners

Some spinners are line twisters, but all are great for smallmouths. They are particularly suited for fishing fast, running water where a cross-stream cast will keep the lure shallow and spinning so that it can be raked through the best riffles and pools. In these shallow waters, chrome- or nickel-plated spinners are too bright. Plain brass is the best overall color.

Deep-Water Fishing With Jigging Spoons

Structure spoons, or jigging spoons, are flat, heavy and slab-sided. They usually have a free-swinging single or treble hook. When practicing deep, vertical jigging for smallmouths in deep water, these are ideal. When coupled with light line, they are a top-rated lure for deep-water, clear canyons, rock faces in impoundments and deep holes in large river pools.

Since these lures are fished deep, select a bright finish. Styles to choose from include thick spoons, which can be jigged vertically in one spot, or flatter, thinner spoons, which will fall with a fluttering action, thus covering a wider band of water.

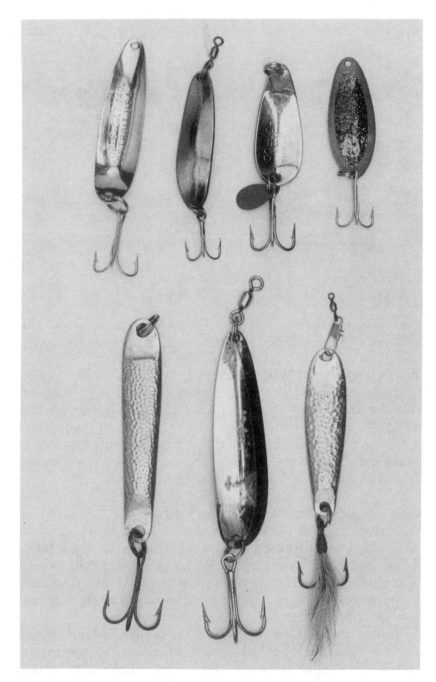

Structure or jigging spoons (from top, left to right): Dardevle Cop-E-Cat, Luhr-Jensen Krocodile, Davis HotRod, DevleDog, Hopkins No Eql, Jensen Krocodile, Hopkins Shorty.

Lures And Flies For The Fly Rod

Fly tackle is ideal for smallmouth fishing in shallow or running water. A number of excellent flies and bugs can be used in this kind of fishing.

Popping bugs are small cork or hard-foam-bodied surface bugs with flat faces that pop or gurgle when jerked on retrieve. Painted and finished with a fur or hackle skirt and tail, they are the fly rodder's equivalent of the topwater chugger. For smallmouth fishing, choose either small bass bugs or large panfish bugs with hooks in sizes 2 through 6. Good colors are red and white, yellow, black, green and yellow or green and orange.

Slider bugs are popping bugs built in reverse. Thus, the front of the bug is rounded and tapered rather than flat. Like poppers, they have fur or feather tails. Unlike poppers, they will not make a noise or throw water when worked and are designed to be skittered slowly on the surface.

Keel flies are tied on special hooks that have a bent shank. When tied and fished correctly, they will ride with the point up, protecting the hook from snags. They are excellent for fishing in weeds, structure and brush or around rocks and logs. Any pattern can be modified for tying on this style hook. Keel fly designs are especially good for weighted flies since by nature they are almost snag-free.

On the other hand, weighted flies can be tied on any style of hook. Most are long, minnow-like imitations tied in a streamer or bucktail pattern. Tying weighted flies in nymph or wet fly patterns is an alternative that is popular with many anglers.

Flies are weighted by including a lead wire body under standard fly body materials and/or by using lead dumbbell eyes. The heaviness of these weights determines sink rate. Because weighted flies may be fished around deep cover that could cause snags, they are best when tied in weedless style with hook guards.

Streamers most often resemble the baitfish of lakes and rivers. These long patterns are tied with a long wing of fur or feathers. Many alternative streamer patterns are available.

Nymphs resemble the nymphal or immature stage of aquatic insects. These buggy-looking, often weighted flies are fished under the surface in the runs where smallmouths feed.

Special fly patterns that imitate crayfish, tadpoles, large river nymphs, leeches and hellgrammites are also available to the

Sliders used for fly fishing have sloping faces that do not pop or gurgle in the water, but instead slide along noiselessly. Face shapes vary but all are pointed in the front.

smallmouth angler. These special patterns can be purchased, or tied at home.

Choosing Lures To Fit The Conditions

When choosing a smallmouth lure, you should take these eight factors into consideration: water conditions, water clarity, water depth, forage base, smallmouth size, fish aggressiveness, feeding habits and tackle used.

Deep-diving crankbaits are often difficult to retrieve in extremely fast current and will hang up almost immediately in shallow water, making fishing difficult. Rough waves and surface action preclude the use of surface lures (a light chop is okay) and also make worm fishing difficult because of the difficulty of seeing line changes or detecting and feeling light pickups. Fishing with light jigs under the same conditions can be equally difficult. Water filled with rocks, wood, brush or other hook hangers can be fished most effectively with lures that resist snagging, such as weedless jigs, Texas-rigged worms, spinnerbaits, buzzbaits and weedless tube lures.

One of the most important factors in lure selection is a knowledge of the forage base in the water fished. Thus, in southern and western lakes with large shad populations, light-colored or shiny shad imitations are good choices. The slim minnows of other lakes dictate long, slim lures. In rocky areas and rivers, crayfish are usually abundant, and brown or black jigs, crayfish-colored crankbaits and grubs are good bets, particularly when fished in short hops that simulate the crayfish swimming pattern.

If you know the average size of the smallmouths in the waters you are fishing, you will be able to determine whether to tie on a tiny $1/8$-ounce crankbait or $1/16$-ounce jig, or to go with a larger $3/8$-ounce plug or $1/4$-ounce jig. While large smallmouths will take small lures, they often prefer good-sized meals. Smaller fish cannot get a big lure in their mouths, resulting in missed strikes.

Smallmouths are, by nature, more aggressive than largemouths, but the way they strike lures in a given situation will vary with some of the conditions mentioned earlier. Clear or shallow water will often make smallmouths very cautious. If they typically feed in shallow water, they may completely ignore a nearby boat or a wading fisherman in the frenzy of looking for the next crippled minnow or floating mayfly.

Tackle should always be chosen to match the lure. You obviously cannot throw a $5/8$-ounce plug with a fly rod or a $1/8$-ounce lure with a heavy casting outfit. Choose the lure first, based on the above conditions, and then choose the rod, reel and line best suited to the circumstances.

12

Live Bait For Smallmouth Bass

A rtificial lures, no matter how realistic, will never match live bait exactly. The color, movement and scent of live bait have been imitated for decades by lure manufacturers, attesting to the deadly attraction live bait has to a feeding predator.

Live bait does have disadvantages, however. First, it must be fished slowly, so covering a lot of water quickly is impossible. Secondly, smallmouths tend to take live bait deeper into their gullet. This often results in injury to the fish that could threaten survival if it is released.

Live bait fishing requires only a few hooks, a float or two and some specialized sinkers—a whole season's accessories can be bought for the cost of only a few lures. Although bait can sometimes be expensive if you purchase it, it is easily collected from local fields and streams with homemade or inexpensive equipment.

Live bait can be effective at any time of year, but it is particularly effective for cold weather fishing when fish metabolisms are low and they are apt to feed less aggressively.

Acquiring The Proper Bait Containers

When smallmouth fishing with bait, it is important to keep it alive and healthy for as long as possible. This entails the use of a proper bait container.

Bait buckets are necessary for bank fishing with live minnows, shiners or shad. (Be sure to change the water frequently, especially

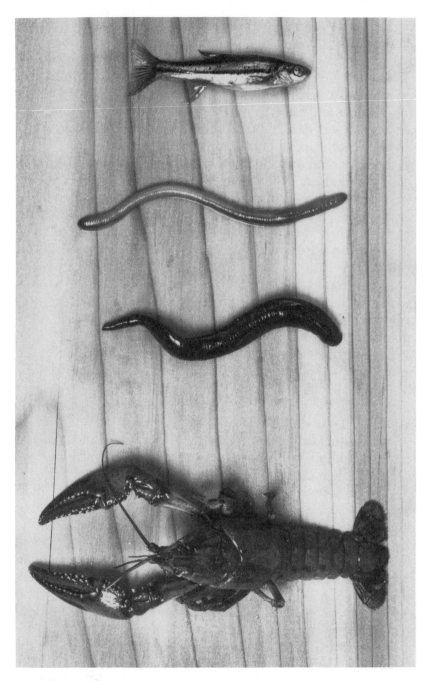

It is difficult to argue with the effectiveness of live bait, especially during periods when smallmouths are inactive and hard to entice into striking an artificial lure.

Live Bait For Smallmouth Bass

for shad and shiners.) There are many varieties of these metal or plastic buckets. Some float, others have a perforated inner liner that comes out of the bucket and can be used when boat fishing. These liners tie to the boat, allowing a constant flow-through of water to keep the bait fresh. Bait buckets are also good for carrying frogs, leeches and hellgrammites. Leeches and hellgrammites can be placed in water; frogs should be able to get out of the water onto small rocks or wood chunks.

Belt-mounted containers to hold worms for bank fishing or shallow wading are available in plastic or metal. Small boxes designed for holding worm bedding are also available for carrying in boats. Because worms tend to go to the bottom of these containers, the best of them will have lids on both ends. This makes it easy to flip the container and get to the worms that have moved to the bottom.

Cricket and grasshopper boxes are equipped with a small perch on which just one insect can sit. A little door gives access to only that one insect. This prevents the rest of your bait from escaping.

Lacking the above, a good container for worms or insects can be made from a coffee can. Cut out both ends and cover with flexible, plastic lids.

Attaching Your Bait To The Hook

Just having the proper baits will not catch smallmouths. You must attach them to the hook in a way that presents an attractive meal to a reluctant smallmouth.

All fish baits can be hooked in a variety of ways. The most popular way to hook baitfish is through the lips, making sure that the hook penetrates both lips completely. This keeps the bait secure and lively for the longest period of time.

Another good method is to hook a baitfish through the skin along the back, being careful to avoid the spinal cord since this would paralyze the fish and prevent it from swimming. This method is best for bobber fishing when the bait is suspended above the bottom.

Baitfish can also be hooked through the tail, or you can run the hook and leader through the mouth, out the gills and into the tail.

Common fish baits include shad, a typical forage on large lakes; chubs, popular in rivers; mad toms and small bullheads, es-

Redtail chubs (or hornyhead chubs) and creek chubs are stream minnows commonly found east of the Rocky Mountains. They make an excellent bait for smallmouths.

pecially good for river fishing; and shiners, which are good in all waters, particularly lakes. Mad toms are very hardy; shiners and shad are very delicate and difficult to keep.

Crayfish in small sizes are good for both lake and river smallmouths. They can be fished whole or in parts, such as tails alone. When hooking live, whole crayfish, insert the hook so that it passes completely through the meaty part of the tail or through the hard exoskeleton just forward of the tail. If the bait has large claws, crush or damage them to make the bait less intimidating to a smallmouth. Whole, live crayfish can also be hooked through the body, or better still, held on a hook with a rubber band around the middle.

Fishing with leeches has always been common in midwestern and north-central states, but is gaining in popularity across the rest of the country. Leeches are fished live and hooked so they can still swim in their typical undulating fashion. Hook them once through the head (the wider end) or once through the sucker located on the tail.

Hellgrammites are the large aquatic larvae of the dobsonfly that are found in most smallmouth rivers and streams. They are so

Live Bait For Smallmouth Bass   135

There is little doubt that smallmouths devour leeches. Ribbon leeches, sold commercially as bait, can be easily kept under refrigeration and make a sturdy bait on the hook.

popular that excessive harvesting in some areas has reduced their numbers. Hook them through the forward collar just behind the head and run the hook from aft to forward.

There are dozens of varieties of worms, all good for fishing smallmouths. Worms are better for stillfishing in quiet water than for drifting in current, but can be used for all smallmouth fishing. Ways of hooking them include setting a single hook through the end or belly, threading the worm onto a long shank hook, using several small worms on one hook or hooking with the multiple hooks of a bait harness.

Any type of land insects are attractive to smallmouths, particularly in mid- to late summer when such insects abound along stream and riverbanks. Use them live, threaded through the body with a light-wire, long-shank hook. Better still, use light-wire or small rubber bands (those for dental braces are ideal) to hold the insect on the hook without piercing it. The insect will last longer, kick more and take more fish this way. Fish in or just under the surface film to keep the insect lively.

Small frogs can be used anywhere since they are common to rivers, streams and lakes. They should be hooked through the leg or lips and cast, then drifted or retrieved like a lure.

Waterdogs, the larvae of tiger salamanders, and woodland, or lungless, salamanders common in the Appalachians, are both used as bait for smallmouth bass. Salamanders can be found along most lakes, rivers and streams and can be fished effectively hooked through the mouth or leg. Smaller, 3- to 5-inch sizes work best.

Rigging Your Bait

Bait can be drifted, stillfished, suspended at a specified depth, or, in the case of minnows and baitfish, allowed to swim freely. Each method requires a different rigging.

The slip-sinker rig is a freshwater version of the surf angler's fish-finder rig. It is good for still fishing, fishing a deep river hole, or drift fishing. To rig, place a slip-sinker such as an egg or bait-walker on the line. Attach a small barrel swivel and tie in a two- to three-foot leader with a hook at the end. The swivel prevents the sinker from sliding down to the bait, while the sliding sinker allows a smallmouth to take the bait and run without dragging the sinker.

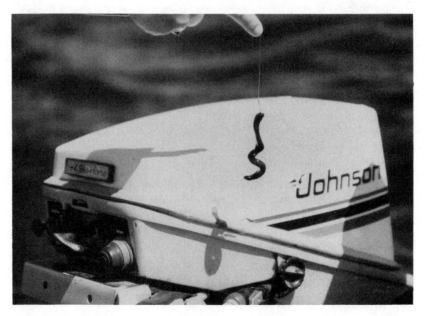

Hook a leech with a small, short-shanked hook once through the head (the narrow end of the body) to simulate its natural swimming action. Use a light bait rig to present the leech.

When drift fishing, stillfishing or casting and slow retrieving, use a split-shot rig. This is nothing more than a line with the hook at the end weighted with split shot. Use enough split shot weights to get the bait down, but not enough to impede any natural drift. To prevent this rig from snagging on rocky bottoms, spread the split shot out with several inches of line between each weight. For variation, make up flexible sinkers of lead-core line, each tied with a nail knot loop at the end attached to the line and a leader. The lead-core line promotes an even distribution of the weight with less snagging. Because of the light weight of these rigs, they are primarily used for ultra-light fishing in shallow rivers.

To hold a bait off the bottom or at a suspended depth, tie a hook to the end of the line, add a rubber core and a pinch-on split shot or other sinker to the line at a distance of 12 to 18 inches from the hook. Clip a float to the line at the distance you want to suspend the bait. This rig can be difficult to cast if the float is more than a few feet up the line. For casting, use a slip-bobber rig.

The slip-bobber rig is just like the bobber rig with one notable change—the float is adjusted so that the line can slip through the small eye, and a bobber stop is rigged on the line where you wish the bobber to rest. The easiest way to do this is to attach a small piece of yarn, mono, string or tape to the line at the point at which you want the bobber to stop. Use a nail knot or overhand knot to tie the stop. Then thread a small bead onto the line, followed by the bobber. Finally, tie the hook to the terminal end of the line and add split shot about 12 inches up the line to balance the float. The yarn or tape will slide through the guides and onto a casting or spinning reel with no (or very few) casting problems. When the rig is cast, the bobber and bead will slide up the line from the sinker weight to the yarn stop. The result is an easily cast rig that will allow you to fish any depth. To change depths merely slide the yarn or tape stopper along the line. You can purchase pre-tied stop knots and beads.

Setting Up A Lure/Bait Combination

The best lures for combining with live bait are jigs, tube lures, spinners, small spoons and flies.

Jigs and single-hook spoons work well when tipped with a lip-hooked minnow, mad tom or small bullhead, leech or worm hooked through the head, or a crayfish tail.

Best Live Bait Rigs

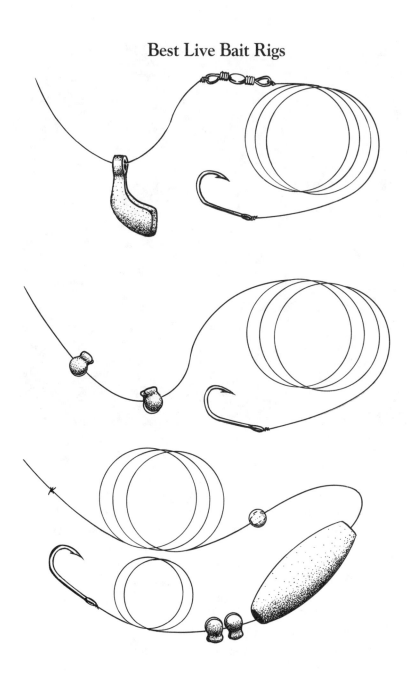

Three popular and effective live bait rigs for smallmouth include trolling rig (top) with bottom-bouncing sinker, straight-line rig (center) and slip bobber rig (bottom) with adjustable stop knot.

One of the most versatile live-bait rigs is the jig tipped with bait. Use a minnow, leech, worm, crayfish or any cut portion of these live baits to add scent and attraction to your jig.

Spinners with treble hooks, and spoons with treble hooks work best with small minnows, leeches and mad toms. A small section of worm on the end of a spinner or spoon also helps draw strikes.

Bait that is too large will tend to impede the action of a spinner or spoon. A jig or tube lure, however, has no inherent action so bait size is not as important a consideration. Nevertheless, match jig weight with bait size to gain maximum control of the lure.

Tube lures on single hooks (almost like a jig hook) work well with streamlined baits such as minnows, small thin strips of cut bait, worms or leeches.

When using jigs or tube lures, try hooking a minnow upside down so that when the lure hangs right the minnow will be inverted. This causes the minnow to constantly try to right itself, causing a struggling motion that results in more action and strikes.

Casting Tips When Using Bait

If you cast a bait with the typical back-forward snap used for lures, the fast change of direction will snap off all but the toughest baits. As a result, casting with bait requires a slightly modified technique. For best results, bring the rod back slowly to an angled position, making sure that any dropper loops stay clear. Bring the rod forward in a slower, wider arc to cast the bait. The brief pause at the end of the backcast and the slower, wider arc stress the bait less and lower the likelihood of throwing it off the hook.

Baitfishing also requires that a longer length of line hangs down from the rodtip when casting. Take care to keep the line and dropper straight, untangled and away from people and potential snags.

Finding
Smallmouths

13

Streams

Smallmouth bass streams seldom contain the violent waters favored by trout, salmon and grayling. Rather, they often consist of a more gradual flowage with alternating pools, riffles and runs, some small waterfalls and an occasional area of rapids.

Locating smallmouths in streams is easier than locating them in lakes and larger rivers. These small waters allow anglers to switch from shallow areas to deep pools quickly. Once the fish are located, concentrate your efforts in similar areas of depth and current.

A common characteristic of smallmouths found in small streams is that they are often smaller than their brethren in large, expansive rivers. Stream smallmouths sometimes travel more than smallmouths in rivers, because in winter they must seek out a deep hole in which to hold until spring.

Locating Stream Smallmouths In Spring

Spring finds stream smallmouths abandoning the serenity of deeper pools and gradually moving toward the shallows to spawn. This does not mean that the fish will be found in the shallows, but only that there is movement back and forth as they work their way toward spawning areas.

Much of this movement is affected by photoperiods—the length of daylight—as the season progresses into summer and the longest days of the year. Movement is also affected by tempera-

Streams offer some of the most idyllic smallmouth fishing to be found anywhere. A variety of habitat can be found within a short stretch of stream water, challenging the angler's savvy.

Streams

ture. During days of high temperatures and clear weather, smallmouths will move into shallow water. During dark, cold periods the fish temporarily settle back into deeper water.

Just how shallow smallmouths will locate depends upon the individual stream and conditions. Smallmouths prefer a gravel or sand substrate for spawning and generally spawn in water from four to nine feet deep. If this habitat is not available, however, they may be found nesting in shallower water.

Once the fish spawn, the females head for deeper portions of the stream while the males guard the nests. After spawning and nesting is completed the males will join the females in deeper pools or new structure.

To find smallmouths in streams in the spring, an angler must pay attention to stream temperatures. Smallmouth feeding increases when water temperatures warm to 50 degrees, and they are most active once water warms to 60 degrees. They feed less when water temperatures climb above 78 degrees.

Locating Stream Smallmouths In Summer

During the summer, smallmouths scatter widely in small streams, choosing the best pools, runs and deep cut banks as their warm-weather homes. Unlike lakes, reservoirs and larger rivers, the colder waters and constant oxygenation (through rapids and riffles) of most streams allow smallmouths to spread out and select positions based on cover and available food. Smallmouths may be anywhere at any time. Stream smallmouths tend to roam and cruise less than those in larger shallow river systems do. While known as a fish favoring cooler water, smallmouth are seldom deterred by warmer water if food, cover and flow of oxygenated water are available.

Still, the best places to find smallmouths in small streams during the summer are the deeper pools and substantial riffles that can hold both good-sized fish and good populations of smallmouths for an indefinite period. Anglers should look first in deeper holes for the most and biggest fish, and only after exhausting these places try riffles, backwater eddies, slick glides and similar water.

Locating Stream Smallmouths In Fall

In the fall, smallmouths begin to reverse the cycle begun in the

An angler takes a nice smallmouth while wading. Note the riffle between the large rock on the right and the angler. A small pool is visible in the flat water below the riffle.

spring, searching out the shallower water and food they instinctively know they will find there. During this period, smallmouths become increasingly aggressive in their quest for food and will readily attack lures.

As the weather and water become colder, the fish again begin to migrate to deeper pools and holes, perhaps even moving upstream or downstream (usually downstream) through several pools until they find one to their liking. At this time, they also will form schools and in the process become particularly susceptible to your presentations. The right lure, presented from an appropriate distance, can often take fish after fish when they are schooled this way. Unlike rivers, where the same conditions often occur, the schools in stream pools are smaller in number and contain smaller fish. But trophy fish do exist.

Taking smallmouths from streams requires proper lure selection and presentation. The best stream anglers choose their casts from a distance as they study the water ahead.

Stream fish become increasingly less active as winter approaches and water temperatures fall below 50 degrees.

Finding Smallmouth Bass In Stream Habitats

In streams, smallmouths tend to hold tight to any structure that will provide protection from the continual current, yet keep them close to that current where they can pounce on a potential meal as it moves by. Streams might have protective boulders that are only the size of a bread box, but these thin buffers blocking the current will often attract fish. To keep from fighting the current, smallmouths will hold in these buffer areas in front, along or behind the rock.

Smallmouths also like to linger just below a riffle where the water spreads out into the slower current of a pool. Here, water

Fly rods are an excellent choice for streams because they can cast a very light lure with distance and accuracy. They also provide a natural-looking drift for the lure.

Sometimes you just have to get your feet wet to catch nice stream smallies. Once you catch a few of these tough battlers on light tackle, it may be you that is hooked.

will rush through slots in the rocks at the upper end of the pool, creating fast reaches that are bordered by quieter water. Small-mouths rest and wait for food along these current lanes.

Runs that consist of a long glide with a lot of small rocks on the bottom are also ideal places to find smallmouths. The rocks break up the current, provide a buffer of protected water and allow smallmouths to rest in relative comfort while the water and food rush by overhead.

Long runs, or glides, of fast, smooth water that lack any rubble, ridges or rocks to break the current make relatively poor smallmouth habitat. There is little in the way of rest areas in these runs and they are usually open, making smallmouths susceptible to predation from eagles and ospreys.

Islands are rare in streams, at least rarer than on rivers. But when the island breaks the flow of the stream into two courses that rejoin at the tail of the island, these merging current edges are ideal spots to find smallmouths, provided the bottom is not too shallow or silted.

Depending upon the geology of the area, some small streams have small ridges along the bottom that run parallel or at right an-gles to the current. These ridges are sharp, ankle-turners for the wading angler, but the deep water between and downstream of them will hold smallmouths.

Small waterfalls can occur along the course of a smallmouth stream. They are good places to try as they break the current flow and oxygenate the water. The pools below waterfalls are often deep and generally hold smallmouths.

Logjams are not uncommon in streams, and while not the classic rock or gravel favored by smallmouths, they do provide protection from the current and thus offer the buffer area provided by rocks, boulders and steep banks. Because they are often on or near the water surface, they can be difficult to fish effectively without snagging.

Some streams will have rocky bluffs or cliffs along an outside bend, forming a deep, protected pool or eddy. A current buffer close to the edge of the bank or bluff is an ideal place to fish for smallies.

Though streams are small, they are still fed by smaller creeks, tributaries, feeder springs and streams. If these feeders enter the main stream at a spot that can be reached by smallmouths, they are often ideal fishing locations because they provide smallmouths with two important things: cool water and a constant supply of food.

This food supply becomes even better after a heavy rain when terrestrial insects and small fish are washed into the stream when the current becomes too strong for them. This disgorging of food during a heavy rain makes these ideal locations to try. Naturally, under such conditions, catch-and-release should be encouraged to prevent large catches that will reduce and ultimately ruin such fine, small water stream fishing.

= 14 =

Big-River Smallmouths

Rivers have all the same characteristics as streams but on a larger scale. There is more water, more variety of current, deeper pools and more and larger small-mouths. Beyond that, smallmouth rivers can vary widely, from those that are wide and shallow with lots of cover and structure, to those that are deep and strong, to those that are influenced by tides. The size of rivers also results in more man-made structures that affect fish. Bridge pilings, locks and dams, wing dams, docks, loading piers, boat docks, mid-water structures and channel markers all hold meaning to the smallmouth angler.

Often, rivers have large enough pools and riffles to afford smallmouths the opportunity to spend their whole lives in one pool or pool area. River smallmouths tend to be homebodies. They don't migrate like trout, salmon, shad or striped bass. The result is that a good stretch of water will usually continue to be a good producer, be it a pool, long riffle or run.

River Examples
Examples of good smallmouth rivers vary widely. The mighty St. Lawrence River, which empties into Lake Ontario, is an example of a strong, deep-flowing river. Peppered with rocky bluffs and islands, the Thousand Islands area is filled not only with smallmouths, but also largemouths, pike, muskies and perch.

The French River of Ontario, which flows into James Bay, is another smallmouth river with a good mixture of species, but one

River waters may be wide and deep, or shallow and fast. Where you find smallmouths will depend on time of year, current and food. River smallmouths do not move far during the year.

Big-River Smallmouths   153

that is totally different from the St. Lawrence. It alternates between open bays and narrow gorges, fast water and slick pools, with rocky boulders and islands everywhere.

The Hudson River is more like the St. Lawrence, but on a smaller scale. Around Catskill and other areas in New York there is good fishing for both largemouths and smallmouths. Here, grass beds and "lighthouses" (the local name for the small, but lighthouse-like channel markers) affect the bass populations and movements. Even in Catskill, 100 miles north of New York City, the tide affects both the river and the daily movement of smallmouths.

Some rivers fall into the flowage category (See Chapter 15) in that they have dams and locks that slow and vary the current at different times. Examples include the upper Mississippi as well as some TVA waters and the Alabama River in the Montgomery area.

In distinct contrast are rivers such as the Pennsylvania portion of the Susquehanna River, the Juniata (a tributary of the Susquehanna), the James and Shenandoah of Virginia, and the Potomac bordering Maryland and Virginia.

Because these are so shallow, they are commonly fished by wading or drifting.

Finding River Smallmouths In Spring

As with smallmouths anywhere, river smallmouths winter in deep water. In rivers this means deep pools or channels. As in streams (see Chapter 13) smallmouths come out of these deep holes in late winter and early spring and gradually scatter as they work their way to shallower gravel bars, sandbars and rocky shorelines.

River smallmouths often spawn in waters as deep as 15 feet. They must be out of the main current, but are usually located in areas where there is some water movement. During the spawning, the fish will select their beds over a wide area, each finding the best possible site. Like the largemouths and smallmouths in lakes, many smallmouth pairs may be found in a given ideal area. After the spawn the females are almost impossible to find. Usually they are back in deep water, probably recovering from the strain of spawning. The males can be caught at this period as they hover over their beds protecting the eggs. Give the fish a chance to com-

Begin your river search for smallmouth by keying likely locations through repetition. When you find fish, keep trying to locate the same conditions in other portions of the river.

plete their spawning before fishing them. Once this period is over the males will abandon the nest and begin to move into their summer hangouts.

Finding River Smallmouths In Summer

During the summer, smallmouths can be found almost anywhere in rivers. Current often dictates location. In the strong current caused by rains or water released through dams, smallmouths may be forced into areas that will protect them from the strong flow, while still allowing them access to food.

In early summer, smallmouths are just as readily found in riffles, long glides, boulder-strewn runs, pools and around structures or the downstream side of islands.

As summer progesses, they may gravitate to deeper pools and

Current breaks are not the only places to find smallmouths on rivers. Often wide, slow stretches of river offer excellent fishing, especially if the channel runs deep.

venture out only at dawn or dusk. At this time they will cruise riffles and shallow pool waters to take insects from the surface, much like a feeding trout.

Finding River Smallmouths In Fall

Fall fishing finds smallmouths moving gradually out of the shallows back into deep pools. They will also become more aggressive and are easily caught on deep jigs or lures once they are located.

Late fall and early winter can be a time of severe storms and heavy rains, which flood smallmouth rivers, often forcing smallmouths and forage fish into steep or undercut banks where they can be found holding in small eddies. Often these eddies occur along small indentations in the bank, just large enough to

Some river hotspots for catching smallmouths just seem too obvious. It can be that easy—sometimes. At other times, locating smallmouths in rivers may seem to require some sort of magic.

give shelter to smallmouths. The high waters and strong flow at this time mandate caution and extreme safety in boating, but such spots often pinpoint the fish for easy casting.

Current And Buffer Zones—Keys To River Smallmouths

Understanding how seasonal changes and current affect fish and the way current reacts around structure are the real keys to successful river smallmouth fishing. Just as high waters in late fall or early spring force smallmouths and their prey into the banks, a knowledge of current and river hydraulics is the key to locating fish.

Water does not flow evenly and at the same speed through a river. Even a concrete channel to funnel water will have the slowest flow of water along the sides and bottom and the fastest flow in a core that would be in the center and slightly below the surface.

Anything added to this concrete channel would block the flow of water and create a buffer zone of almost still—or certainly quieter—water around the obstruction. Thus, a rock, log, piling, series of boulders, small wing dam, bridge abutment or even a thick grass bed will tend to slow the flow and create a protected area. Imagine that the current is not within a concrete channel, but within a living river, and the same factors apply. The quieter waters at the side of the river or around structure provide a good place for a smallmouth to live without constantly exerting energy to fight the main current.

While riverbanks will often slow the water, they may also be silty, muddy and extremely shallow—certainly not favorable conditions for smallmouths. First, smallmouths want a fast current nearby to provide food. In addition, the proximity of the bank presents dangers from raccoons, skunks and other predators. Best spots for smallmouths are the mid-river structures that break the water, provide access to food in the adjacent fast current, and provide protection from predators such as ospreys, eagles or larger fish such as pike or muskies.

All the structures that break current in streams are likely spots to find smallmouths in rivers. Rocks, riffles, boulders, shelves, bottom ridges, waterfalls, current edges, log or debris jams, islands, creek mouths and sharp, rocky bluffs (see Chapter 13) are all good bets. Larger rivers also offer the angler additional structures that may hold smallmouths.

River Bridges

Most bridges that cross rivers have pilings extending into the water. These pilings can be constructed of concrete, rock, timber (or timber protected) or steel girders. Even bridges that lack central pilings usually have a rock or concrete abutment on each shore to support the bridge. In deep water, these provide good habitat for smallmouths as well. Often, pilings cause the current to scour out the area immediately around them, making extremely deep holes, which attract big smallmouths.

River Dams

As water is released through the turbines and gates of large river dams, violent currents may be produced immediately downstream. When the gates are closed and the water flow drops, you can try out the main channel. Look for smallmouths in the eddies on either side of the main flow.

Wing Dams
Built of concrete, rubble or rock that is deposited to make a low wall in the river, wing dams can offer good smallmouth fishing. Some are built below water level, while some extend above. The best wing dams are those constructed of rock or broken substrate, since they will provide more cover and draw small fish, crayfish and other smallmouth food.

Gravel Bars
Large rivers often have large, expansive gravel bars that offer good smallmouth fishing throughout the season, from mid-spring through fall. These might be located at a point, on the inside curve of a river bend or found randomly along the sides of pools and riffles. In all cases, gravel bars provide cover for crayfish, hellgrammites, insect nymphs, stone cats, dace, minnows and tadpoles and are thus excellent locations to find and fish smallmouths. Since they are known to provide a good food base, smallmouths in the area are often looking for food and are thus receptive to both lures and live bait.

Grass Beds
Grass beds line the banks of many smallmouth rivers, bordering some islands, rock shelves and bars. Grass beds also hold food for smallmouths, including frogs, crayfish, tadpoles, insects and insect larvae, salamanders and some terrestrial insects and animals. As such they are ideal places to find smallmouths, particularly in the morning and evening when fish are actively moving and looking for food.

=15=

Flowage Reservoirs

Perhaps the most challenging smallmouth river fishing exists in what are known as run reservoirs, that is, those with current. Although current is desirable, especially to feeding fish, it can make it difficult for the beginning angler to locate active fish.

River-run reservoirs, in one form or another, are prevalent throughout the country and provide ideal smallmouth habitat. There is, however, a vast difference between a river where the current is constant and a river-run reservoir whose current is largely controlled by a dam that adjusts the current speed and water level on a sometimes irregular basis. Here, smallmouths may favor a particular area for the short-term benefits provided by forage or temperature.

Because most river-run reservoirs are used for navigation, a steady water level is normally maintained. In some river-run reservoirs, however, current and water levels fluctuate routinely, and for this reason it is imperative that the fisherman understand how this affects the fish.

As with other bodies of water, anglers will find that smallmouths associate closely with deep water in river-run reservoirs. In addition, their movement will be heavily influenced by the water temperature, water level and current strength. Smallmouth bass will never allow themselves to be caught "high and dry." They avoid areas where low water levels may trap them in shallow pools. You, too, should avoid these locations.

Complete Angler's Library

Flowage reservoir smallmouths have both current and rising and falling water to contend with So do smallmouth anglers who ply these waters in search of their favorite fish.

Flowage Reservoirs 161

How Current Affects Smallmouths In Flowage Reservoirs

Current plays a major role in the life of river-run reservoir smallmouths. It usually prevents formation of a thermocline, allowing smallmouths to roam the water column at will. The fish, however, will never be far from deep water.

Forming a fish-catching pattern in river-run reservoirs depends on two things: your knowledge of how smallmouths use current to feed and where they hold when not feeding.

Smallmouth bass do not live in direct current. In order to find them, you must look for a current break such as rocks or a stump; or the down-current side of a point, a bridge abutment or any other objects. Smallmouths will not exist in areas free of such breaks.

When fishing a river-run reservoir, anglers must condition themselves to think of depth as a relative term. "Deep water" in a river-run reservoir may mean 10 feet. Even during the hottest months you often find fish at this depth. Occasionally they will be in a foot of water or less!

River-run reservoirs are unique in that they are constantly being altered by man. Navigable reservoirs, for example, are often dredged or graded to deepen or widen their channels. Timber cutting also occurs around many of these lakes. Debris created by these alterations makes excellent habitat for smallmouth bass.

Adapt Fishing Tactics To Time Of Year

Even though flowage reservoirs are completely different from other kinds of lakes and impoundments, they still go through seasonal changes. The fisherman must adjust tactics and techniques accordingly.

While spring is traditionally the best time to find and catch smallmouth bass on nearly every other form of water, it is not necessarily the best time to fish on river-run reservoirs. The prime time for trophy fish is between January and March (depending on the severity of the weather) particularly in the South. The big fish are on the move and away from their deep-water haunts. They stay in shallow water to feed on baitfish, crayfish and aquatic insects as the time for spawning approaches.

This movement begins when water temperatures reach 47 to 50 degrees. Though these smallmouths are staging fish, their locations are different from what you would find in natural lakes or im-

Creek arms become meccas for smallmouths when it comes time to spawn. Look for smallmouths in arms with a deep, central channel and a firm bottom of rock or gravel.

Flowage Reservoirs

poundments without a current. In impoundments or natural lakes, solitary females often hold along the top of a drop-off.

In a river-run reservoir 10 to 20 similarly sized fish may occupy the same location. In fact, while they are on the drop-offs, it is not unusual to take several fish from the same area. These fish will not be hovering in a random fashion, however. You can be sure they will be using the existing cover and structure to break the current's flow. The drop-off itself may be only six or eight feet deep and may be shallower, depending on the depth of the lake you are fishing.

During the winter, baitfish will probably be schooled up and are likely to be found in one of two places, either along the edge of the river channel or in the main channel. Smallmouth bass often follow these schools of baitfish or position themselves to intercept these schools as they swim by. It is important to work any current break because it could be home to a big smallmouth bass.

As winter turns to spring and the water temperatures rise into the 58- to 65-degree range, smallmouth bass move up from the drop-offs looking for places to bed. During this period, smallmouths are farther from current areas than at any other time of the year. Flats, as we mentioned earlier, may have some spawning smallmouths, but so will other areas away from the current where the bottom makeup is conducive to nesting. Spawning smallmouths often move to shallower spots in river-run lakes and can be located just about anywhere if the conditions are right. It is important that deep water is nearby and that the bottom is composed of gravel or hard mud. Large rocks, stumps and other current breaks are also essential.

Search For Rockpiles In Early Summer

When the spawning season comes to an end, smallmouth bass will move off flats and rock rows and begin seeking out rock piles. Rock piles will be the most productive structure throughout the remainder of the year, especially in late spring and early summer. During the early summer, these rock piles will provide an abundance of action, especially at night.

In addition to rock piles, drop-offs on the main river channel and the intersections of creek and river channels also become important habitats for smallmouths. It is at this time that smallmouths use deep water most, going shallow only when necessary.

Main points along the current-washed main channel of the reservoir will draw smallmouths during midsummer. The best points should have habitat to support crayfish and baitfish.

There is normally an abundance of creeks merging with the main river channel in river-run reservoirs. These are key locations to catch bass, but it is essential to understand that the bass will not actually hold in the direct current. They hide behind current breaks rather than hovering in the current itself. Take, for example, a fish caught at the intersection of a creek and river channel. This fish has undoubtedly dashed into the current to feed or was lured into the current by the angler himself. In either case, the fish will not stay in the current for long. In fact, bass spend the majority of their time waiting behind a piece of structure for a meal to pass rather than actively seeking a meal in the current.

Structure And Temperature Dictate Summer Locations
During the summer months, the key places to look for

Although many flowage reservoirs in the United States are too warm or too fertile to support smallmouth bass, a number in the mid-section of the country offer excellent fishing.

smallmouths will be river channel drop-offs, creek and river channel intersections, stump rows, rock rows and other man-made structures and open-water structures.

Humps, islands and other structures are especially important places to fish if you are interested in big smallmouth bass. The big fish use these places for the protection it affords them from the current and because the water temperatures are more to their liking.

Smallmouths will occasionally venture into shallower water to feed, depending on the location, but for the most part these areas will be home throughout the summer and on into the winter. The ideal hump or island will have a plentiful supply of stumps or rocks, and the fish will be found on the down-current side of these structures.

By late summer and early fall, smallmouth bass generally follow the baitfish into shallow water. Do not assume, however, that these fish move very far. Look for fish in the backs of creeks, in current pockets and near man-made structures, as opposed to the intersections of creek and river channels where you found them staging earlier.

Deep Patterns Prevail In Winter

During the coldest months, smallmouths in river-run reservoirs return to deep-water structure, and their feeding activity slows down considerably. All of the open-water structure mentioned earlier will hold fish, especially in the deepest parts of the reservoirs. Seldom will you find smallmouths in the shallows during the coldest months. If you do, keep in mind that this is a situation that will last only briefly, and a pattern formed on these fish will probably not hold for more than a few hours.

Current in river-run reservoirs is what prompts smallmouths to eat. If the current is stopped (by dam manipulations) in these reservoirs, fishermen will find the fishing extremely difficult. When this happens, these fish will move back into cover and simply not feed until the current resumes. Baitfish, on the other hand, will move away from structure and cover to avoid hovering bass. When the current returns, baitfish move away from the current and smallmouths will pursue them.

River-run reservoir smallmouths are always challenging to fish. To be successful, fishermen must analyze how the fish relate to the current and plan their fishing presentations accordingly.

16

Impoundments

During the last 30 years, reservoirs have sprouted up all over the United States. Though the primary purpose of these reservoirs was to control flooding and in many instances to generate electricity, they have evolved into some of our country's finest fisheries.

Impoundments are formed by man-made dams and most range in size from 3,000 acres to 100,000 acres or more. Needless to say, finding fish in the midst of these vast bodies of water tests the skills of even the most experienced fishermen, but once found they can produce some memorable action.

Non-current reservoirs (still bodies of water that may be fed by streams, but do not have a definable current) may or may not be used to generate electricity, and in the majority of non-current impoundments, there are no means of locking through the dam to the river below, as is customary with river-run reservoirs. For example, Kentucky Lake on the Kentucky-Tennessee border, is a navigable river-run impoundment capable of locking-through boats, whereas Dale Hollow, in Tennessee, is an impoundment where boaters have no such option. A boater putting in at the Kentucky Lake Dam could, by passing through a series of locks, travel all the way to the Gulf of Mexico.

Every impoundment seems to develop its own personality, but what they all have in common is the fact that they are capable of holding smallmouth bass.

Seasonal patterns on impoundments are greatly influenced by

Fishermen who ply the waters of impoundments must cope with high and low water at various times of the year. Flats with access to deep water can be prime smallmouth spots here.

Impoundments

both weather and water temperature. Water levels, which are highly variable, are affected by rain, and fish must adjust to these high and low water situations as they do in other bodies of water.

Flats Offer Prime Fishing In Impoundments

An angler looking for the ideal structure and cover combination in a non-current impoundment can pretty much plan to fish the same general vicinity all year, especially when fishing for smallmouth bass. For example, an ideal location would be a flat with access to deep-water drop-offs.

During the spring, smallmouths will use the flat to spawn and then move to the drop-off leading into deep water after the spawn and remain there into summer. If there is a creek or river channel near these drop-offs, it is likely the fish will retreat to these areas during the hottest weather and again during the winter. By forming fish-catching patterns appropriate to the season, it is possible to move from pattern to pattern and season to season without ever leaving the same general area.

Smallmouth bass living in impoundments are extremely sensitive to the weather. If the barometric pressure suddenly changes from low to high, the fish that were shallow move into deeper water. If there are a few warm, sunny days in mid-winter, the fish will move from deep water into the shallows until the next change in the weather. All of these reactions to weather, however, still center on some form of cover or structure. Therefore, to thoroughly understand how to fish an impoundment, it is essential that you understand how the fish use the cover and structure that are found in them.

Primary Structure Types Hold Smallmouths

There are six primary types of structure that exist in impoundments: flats, drop-offs, humps, steep banks (45-degree banks), roadbeds and other man-made structures, creek beds and river channels. Cover includes stumps, some forms of brush, rock and grass.

As a general rule, any time you can find any of the above mentioned structure in conjunction with one or more of the four types of cover, you have the proper ingredients for a good smallmouth spot. If you can find these ingredients in association with access to deep water, you have hit upon ideal smallmouth habitat.

Smallmouths in impoundments seem to react quickly to weather changes. Low barometric pressure may bring fish up shallow, while the reverse may send them deep in a hurry.

Finding Smallmouths In Impoundments Through The Seasons

Most impoundments have three very distinct fishing seasons: the spring season, which includes the spawn; summer and early fall; late fall and winter. Late fall is the transitional period when the fish begin to move back into deep water.

Smallmouths stay deep, for the most part, throughout the winter. What is meant by "deep" depends entirely on the body of water you are fishing. In some reservoirs it is not unusual to find smallmouth bass in waters 40 feet deep. During this period, the fish are generally inactive, but they will feed occasionally when the food is within easy reach. Winter is also the time when large schools of bass bunch up on the end of a bluff or along the bottom of a deep drop-off. They will seldom venture into shallow water because of the low surface temperatures, often less than 40 degrees. Deep water serves as both structure and cover, although they will hover near stumps if they exist. River and creek channel intersections will also hold smallmouth bass, if there is sufficient depth.

Late fall and winter are undoubtedly the most difficult times to find and catch fish, although the patient angler will discover that these seasons can produce some of the biggest fish.

In contrast to winter, spring is the easiest season to both find and catch smallmouth bass in reservoirs. To consistently catch them, however, it is essential that you follow a spring pattern from the beginning of the season to the end.

Follow Fish To Spawning Flats In Spring

With the onset of spring, the water begins to warm, and as smallmouths become more active they move out of the deep water in preparation for the spawn. The spawning period actually takes place in three stages.

The first stage finds smallmouths moving from deep water to a position closer to a spawning flat, though they remain in deep water. During the second stage, smallmouths move from the drop-off onto the spawning flat. After the spawn (stage three), they retreat back to the drop-off where they remain until summer.

These three distinct movements, or stages, should dictate where to look for fish. For instance, in stage one, you should concentrate your fishing efforts along the edge of the river channel, near the ends of bluffs, long points and drop-offs that are near the spawning flats themselves to maximize your chances of success. When fishing here, look for areas of suitable cover.

During stage two, big females become loners, seeking out beds the males have prepared for them. Typical locations they explore include flats with a combination of gravel, hard mud and some form of scattered rock or wood cover. This is also the type of structure the fisherman should be seeking. The depth in which smallmouths bed varies, but normally falls into the range of six to 12 feet. Flats that gradually extend into deep water will often hold more than one bedding smallmouth bass, depending on the size of the flat.

While bedding, females do not actively go out and seek food, but will aggressively go after any bait that crosses their nest. This makes them easy to catch. Accordingly, this is also the time of year when the species, as a whole, is most vulnerable. A female taken from a nest and killed means that not only will spawning efforts be extinguished, but she will not be around the following year to reproduce. Therefore, serious smallmouth anglers advocate releasing fish during the spawn. If you do fish, it is especially important to practice catch and release.

Studying an impoundment during times of low water can insure you outstanding fishing once the water returns to more normal levels. Take the time to map out specific structure and cover.

When the spawn ends, smallmouths retreat to the deep-water drop-offs, moving into shallow water only at night to feed. Anglers have found that during the course of a night smallmouths can be found at depths ranging from one foot to 20 feet. And, for a short period of time after the spawn, it is not unusual to find them in the exact same area in which they spawned and sometimes even shallower.

The movement from deep to shallow water gradually begins in the late afternoon and early evening. The most productive hours to fish are after dark. Night fishing is excellent at this time of year, and fish can be found at every possible depth.

Fish Deeper, Or At Night, During The Summer Period

As the summer wears on, and the water temperatures increase, there may still be a few fish on the flats, but generally in the deeper portions. Since smallmouths are extremely sensitive to water temperature, the warmer the water, the deeper the fish go. They will, however, leave the cooler depths to move into warmer water at night when the baitfish and crayfish become more active (see Chapter 24).

During the summer months, fishing drop-offs is also a good choice, provided the drop-offs are associated with creeks or river channels. Smallmouths will move up and down drop-offs, holding at the depth that offers the most suitable temperature. Locating fish on these drops is usually not difficult, but to consistently catch them it is important to pay close attention to the depth your first catch comes from, and adjust your technique accordingly.

Obviously, not all smallmouth bass living in impoundments are found on drop-offs, but most of them will be associated with deep water.

As the summer progresses, two other deep-water structures—45-degree banks and open water humps—come into play. Fish move up and down steep banks and humps in the same way they do on drop-offs, and these structures are likely to hold fish throughout the summer and into the fall. Because water temperatures are normally cooler on the deeper side of these structures, smallmouth bass tend to hold on the deeper side. If either of these places are in close proximity to deep water, such as a creek or river channel, the fish will probably continue to use this structure throughout the summer, fall and to some extent, the winter.

Impoundments are not always large reservoirs. Some are smaller, man-made waters such as flooded mine pits. A portable boat may be necessary to reach these prime smallmouth waters.

Impoundments

Learning to read the water, and what is under it, is the key to fishing impoundments. The best flats, banks and offshore structures hold some kind of cover, and, if you are lucky, fish like this.

Look For Cover On Deep-Water Humps

Humps, more than any other form of structure, must have cover in order to be productive. An assortment of wood, preferably stumps, rock or even brush is necessary to hold fish. Most humps found in impoundments will, in fact, have stumps (the timber has been cut to facilitate boat traffic). Smallmouths will normally inhabit the side of the hump with the most cover. Generally speaking, any time you catch a smallmouth from this structure, it is likely to yield more.

While smallmouths can and will live on humps throughout the winter, the best time to catch them on this type of structure is during the warmest months of the year. The same holds true for steep banks.

Late fall, like spring, is a transitional month for smallmouth bass. As water temperatures drop, smallmouths begin making a gradual descent back into deep water. As the water gets cooler, the smallmouths move from their deep-water haunts to follow the baitfish. During this period, the baitfish form large schools and the bass follow, taking full advantage of the last easy meals before winter sets in. In fact, it is not unusual to find smallmouth bass chasing shad along with stripers and white bass.

The key to locating smallmouth bass in the late fall and early winter, unlike the other seasons, is to follow the baitfish. This is not, however, a long-term proposition, for as soon as the water temperature dips into the 40-degree range, bass retreat into deep-water, winter homes. They will remain there until water temperatures begin to rise and the urge to spawn starts the cycle over again.

While impoundment fishing offers you ample opportunity to hone your skills, it will also test your patience. A good topo map of the impoundment you are fishing is of utmost importance in eliminating unproductive water. As is the case with most other bodies of water, 10 percent of the water will hold 90 percent of the fish. This is especially true in the case of smallmouth bass.

17

Highland Reservoirs

W hen you think of giant smallmouth bass—fish exceeding 6 or 7 pounds—the image of a deep, clear, rocky reservoir comes to mind. The classic smallmouth reservoirs of the Southeastern United States, including Center Hill in Tennessee, Cumberland in Kentucky and Dale Hollow straddling the borders of these states, have traditionally been the proving grounds for dedicated anglers intent on catching the smallmouth of a lifetime. Fishing is not easy in highland reservoirs. Many competent fishermen throw down their rods in disgust after days of going strikeless in these super-deep reservoirs. Put simply, to consistently catch smallmouth bass from a highland reservoir you must virtually relearn the sport of bass fishing.

Highland Characteristics

No matter where you find them, highland reservoirs share certain characteristics that, when combined, can buffalo even the most skilled bass fisherman. Here is what you will find when you fish them:

Depths of several hundred feet are not uncommon near the dam in these reservoirs. A look at the countryside surrounding highland reservoirs tells you why. The term "highland" comes from the fact that these lakes are found in hilly or mountainous terrain. These lakes, when formed by damming a river in this type of terrain, fill up the valleys and hollows.

Highland reservoir smallmouths are never easy to catch, but the rewards can be great once you have mastered these beautiful lakes. Some of the world's largest smallmouths grow here!

Highland Reservoirs   179

Notice when driving into a marina or launching ramp near the lower end of a highland reservoir that you usually must drive down a steep road to get there. By paying attention to the way the hillsides near the lake drop and taper, you can get a reasonably good idea of what is beneath the water at the lower end.

Midsections Abound With Structure

As you move up away from the dam in highland reservoirs, you will likely notice that the surrounding hills begin to become lower, and the banks entering the reservoir become less steep. Here you are likely to begin seeing islands, points with an extremely long and gradual taper and banks of mixed rock and clay or mud composition. A glance at your depthfinder will reveal that the bottom contours rise and fall much more frequently and dramatically than in the lower end, where your depth indicator may barely move out of the 100-foot zone. These fluctuations are evidence of "humps" beneath the surface. When you move into the narrow river channel of the upper reaches, the channel is likely to be anywhere from 40 to 65 feet deep. The channel will bend and twist through the hillside in serpentine fashion, intersecting numerous points, flats and tributaries along its path.

There is often very little cover in these reservoirs. Bass fishermen are trained to look for shallow humps, brush or weeds. But in a typical highland reservoir, there often is a near-complete lack of cover.

These lakes are often quite old, many dating back to the days when hydroelectric dams were viewed as saviors for poverty-stricken, remote areas. Most were clear-cut of timber before being inundated. Any flooded brush or weed growth that existed in the shallow areas eventually rotted away, leaving many highland reservoirs "as slick as a baby's backside," as one angler described them. Where cover is available, it tends to concentrate many species of fish in the lake.

Water is typically very clear in these lakes. "Gin-clear," as outdoor writers are prone to say. These lakes are usually highly infertile because farming opportunities in the hilly, rocky terrain are limited at best (runoff from agricultural areas tends to greatly increase plankton growth, turning some lakes a milky green color).

Clear water means that bass are often deep, but it also means that visibility is vastly improved so that fish are capable of seeing a

As you move into the midsection of a highland reservoir, banks lose their height and shorelines begin to taper more. Underwater cover, however, is conspicuously absent.

lure, especially one presented above them, at long distances.

These lakes are typically very rocky with different types and sizes of rock occurring in different areas of the reservoir. Limestone is very common. Shale, a flaky, black rock, is found in some of the best smallmouth-producing reservoirs.

Rock size is very important to note when fishing these lakes. Anglers speak of catching smallmouths on "fist-sized" or "softball-sized" rocky banks, or on gravel, or around boulders. Pay careful attention to the size and type of rocks you encounter along a bank. The interface of two or more different sizes or types is often an excellent place to find smallmouths.

Food Sources Target Smallmouths

The primary forage species in highland reservoirs are usually

Watch the bank to detect changes in rock or substrate type. The place where different sizes or types of rocks meet can be a hotspot for smallmouths in highland reservoirs.

shad and crayfish. Threadfin or gizzard shad thrive in large schools in highland reservoirs and are a primary food source for smallmouth bass. Shad are plankton-eating baitfish.

While highland reservoirs are not nearly as fertile as flatland reservoirs, plankton does exist in limited quantities. Schools of shad will follow drifting plankton blooms driven by currents or the wind and will gang up on offshore structures, especially long points.

Crayfish are typically nocturnal and tend to hide under rocks and bottom debris during daylight hours. They will emerge after dark or on cloudy days and crawl around seeking organic matter trapped in rocky crevices. This helps explain why highland reservoir smallmouths often come to the banks after dark or on stormy days, when crayfish are most active, and seemingly most abundant.

Springs And Points Play A Major Role

Springs are especially prevalent in highland reservoirs when limestone is abundant. Springs are important because they can make the area immediately surrounding them warmer in winter and cooler in summer. Look for water dripping from the face of a rocky bank or bluff as an indication of a nearby spring. Or, on windy days, watch for a glass-smooth patch of water; thermal variations here reveal the spring's presence beneath the surface.

Points assume great importance to the chain of life in highland reservoirs. Because much of the life in the reservoir is driven offshore, points tend to gather and concentrate both forage fish and predatory species such as smallmouth bass. Scuba divers who frequent these clear lakes report being able to see points clearly beneath the surface. Expert anglers view these as reference markers by which fish orient themselves in these coverless, often featureless lakes.

Throughout much of the year, points will be among the most important places you can fish for smallmouths in highland reservoirs. When evaluating a point, pay attention to how quickly the structure falls off into deep water. Bass may station themselves on deep, fast-tapering points at certain times and on shallow, slow-tapering points at other times. Once you have begun to learn a body of water, you should know plenty of places to fish when you find one of these "patterns."

Locating Suspended Fish

Smallmouths often suspend in these reservoirs, especially when they are inactive, making them tough to find and catch. During hot weather, look for suspended fish near the thermocline, usually where it intersects the old river channel or an adjacent food shelf. In cold weather, look for suspended fish in the "hollows" or small "V"-shaped indentations so abundant in these reservoirs.

If the above factors make you think highland reservoirs are tough cookies to crack, you are exactly right. But once you understand what makes them tick—once you realize that smallmouths are not likely to be hugging the banks in shallow water—you can score big. As a Dale Hollow guide once remarked, "Smallmouths ain't largemouths!" This quip goes a long way toward explaining why smallmouth bass can thrive, even reach record size, in waters that look barren to the largemouth fisherman.

Highland Smallmouths Are Homebodies

The quickest way to gain proficiency on a highland reservoir is to fish one often, and note the movements of the fish from one season to another. The smallmouth bass is a notorious homebody, as fisheries biologists can attest.

Transmitter studies have shown time and again that smallmouths tend to stick close to an area that will provide all of their needs, rather than roam widely as stripers or walleyes do. Therefore, prior to fishing, scan a topographic map of the lake for areas that meet a smallmouth's requirements.

Spawning Sites

Smallmouths in highland reservoirs tend to spawn on expansive flats composed of gravel, clay, mud or a combination of all three. Unlike largemouth flats, which are typically loaded with submerged brush, weeds or stumps, a smallmouth flat may be practically barren. Smallmouths will bed anywhere from 8 to 15 feet deep on these flats, and you will not see their beds as easily as you can those of largemouth bass, which spawn shallower.

During the spring, smallmouths can also be found spawning on submerged roadbeds or points with a very slow taper. Use a good topographic map to identify these areas before arriving at the lake. This time-saving tactic will improve your results.

Points concentrate baitfish and their predators, including smallmouth bass. The taper, or steepness, of the point impacts how smallmouths relate to it during different seasons.

Feeding Sites

As we have seen, points tend to concentrate baitfish, and bass, in highland reservoirs, so look for an area with plenty of points. This will not be hard to find, because the numerous tributaries and bank indentations found on these lakes make points a common structure. Also look for a deep channel drop-off, especially when the water is warm. These drop-offs should be composed of chunk rock or shale capable of holding large numbers of crayfish.

While the largemouth conceals itself in brush, stumps or weeds, the highland reservoir smallmouth may not have any of these forms of cover. Instead, the smallmouth conceals itself in deep water. The reptilian markings of smallmouth bass denote it as a fish of rocky areas.

Deep water with rocks provides all the cover these fish need. Indeed, one of the keys to catching smallies from these lakes is to always have deep water within a cast or two of wherever you are fishing!

If you can find one, two or a dozen places that offer all of the above in a relatively small area, fish these thoroughly and you *will* catch smallmouths!

Highland Reservoirs
185

Spring Patterns In Highland Reservoirs

Most people fish highland reservoirs during the spring of the year. Spring is not necessarily the best time to fish them, but that is when most people will be testing their skills.

The majority of these fishermen will go away with an empty livewell. Many will confuse highland reservoirs with the cover-filled lakes they are used to fishing and use the wrong tackle or lures or fish too shallow. Others will do the right things, but have a cold front foil their attempts.

With some basic understanding of what makes smallmouths tick in highland reservoirs, and some cooperation from Mother Nature, you can connect with trophy-class bronzebacks in the spring.

Spring is one time when the water of highland reservoirs is likely to be murky. Heavy spring rains are common in the Southeast, where some of the best smallmouth reservoirs are located. The right amount of rain can turn the water a light milky color, which can push big smallmouths to the banks. Too much rain can turn the water muddy, particularly in the upper end, which will push smallmouths deeper.

Because "spring" is an amorphous concept at best, we should talk in terms of water surface temperatures instead of the calendar. Most Southeastern highland reservoir fishermen begin a serious quest for a big smallmouth when the water temperature hits 50 degrees. This normally occurs sometime in March in this region, but can occur as early as February when an unseasonably warm rain falls. Now is the time to think ahead.

Smallmouths normally spawn in water from 62 to 68 degrees on flats, shallow points and roadbeds. The biggest smallmouths tend to spawn first, moving up shallow at the earliest possible time to claim the best spawning spots. Begin fishing in the spring close to these areas, but in deeper water than you might fish after the spawn actually takes place. An excellent example is on a large mud flat in Dale Hollow Reservoir that extends more than half-way across the lake at a very slow taper.

When this flat reaches 18 feet, it drops sharply into a 60-foot channel. In early March, good fish can be caught at the end of this flat, at or close to the drop-off. Some days fish will be on the flat in 15 to 18 feet of water. Other days, they will be hanging 25 feet deep along the drop-off. Rapidly changing weather conditions move the bass up and down like a seesaw.

If you have two or three days of stable weather, look for the fish to move up shallower. If the weather has changed recently, look deeper for them. But always stay close to deep water at the end of a big spawning flat.

When fish are "staging," or gathering and holding prior to making a serious move to spawn in shallower water, the channel drop-off at the end of a flat is a perfect place to find them holding as they prey on schools of baitfish that roam the channel. There are not many lures you can successfully fish in this zone, for it is likely to be deep. Leadhead grubs and hair jigs dressed with pork rind are two standbys in the early spring. The water is still cold and these lures present a small mass to a rather lethargic fish. Sinking metal lures also make excellent choices. These lures can be cast long distances, even in the wind, and they sink quickly. When fished close to the bottom or the drop-off, they look much like a baitfish.

When the water reaches the upper 50s, begin moving to shallower water on these flats and be prepared for a vicious strike from what may be the biggest smallmouth you have ever tied into!

While highland reservoir experts often proclaim the winter as the best time to catch a giant smallmouth, spring fish will be fat

Two hair jigs with weedguards (top) lined up with a couple of excellent smallmouth-producing metal lures for deep fish: Spinrite by Uncle Josh and Silver Buddy (bottom).

In the spring, move well off the bank when fishing a flat. This angler, fishing more than 100 yards from shore, has hooked a nice smallmouth on a grub in 15 feet of water.

with spawn and in an aggressive mood prior to bedding. The biggest mistake you can make now is fishing too close to the bank. Pounding the shoreline may net you a largemouth or two, but if it is brown fish you are after, move away from the banks! Putting your boat in the 15-foot zone and working shallower in three-foot increments is a good plan at this time. The fish are often more active, and located shallower, on overcast days when a chop breaks the water.

If these conditions prevail, try faster-moving lures first (driving crankbaits or spinnerbaits). If it is sunny and calm, fish slow-moving baits, especially leadhead grubs and hair jigs. You should rarely fish in water shallower than eight feet deep during this period!

Focus On Mid-Depths As Water Warms

Once the spawn is underway, with surface temperatures in the 60s, you should concentrate heavily in the 6- to 15-foot zone. Wear polarized sunglasses and look for the occasional stump or weedy patch you might encounter. Concentrate your casts near these structures, which can serve as reference points for spawning smallies. Smallmouths tend to spawn close to, but not tight against, this scattered cover, and always where the sun can reach

In the spring, look for off-colored water, and fish flats with a gradual taper. Many of these will be in tributaries, but an equal number will be on the main lake.

the eggs through the clear water. The leadhead grub is by far the best lure now. (If you fish during the spawn, practice catch-and-release fishing.)

During the late spring, some of the fastest action takes place either in the extreme shallow areas of the flats or out at the deepest part of these structures—depending on a couple of factors. If the lake is high enough to have flooded shoreline bushes, break out your heavy artillery and cast spinnerbaits close to cover. If the water level is low and the bushes are not flooded, fish the area close to the drop-off with topwater lures such as floating minnow imitations.

In the spring, good fishing can be found both on the main lake and in the tributaries. The extreme upper end of the reservoir is likely to have the warmest water in early spring, but can quickly become unfishable after a heavy rain. The lower end may lack enough large flats to provide good spawning opportunities. The best bet for consistent fishing will probably be the middle of the reservoir, which has a deep channel plus plenty of flats. Catches of giant smallmouths would bear this out. In March of 1986, an angler landed a 10-pound, 8-ounce smallmouth, one of the biggest ever caught, in the midsection of Dale Hollow Reservoir.

Summer Days (And Nights)

Although it is possible to catch a big smallmouth bass from a highland reservoir during the day in hot weather, few fisherman have ever tried it! Hot, humid weather can make fishing conditions unbearable (with water surface temperatures in the low 90s). Still, smallmouths will bite—if you can find them.

By far the best daytime fishing method during this period is trolling. Once the thermocline sets up, smallmouths will move out to the submerged river channel and suspend, usually just above the thermocline. If you use a paper graph, you can easily see this level of temperature change as a dotted, diffuse band.

Often everything—baitfish and gamefish alike—will suspend at close to the same level during this period. For example, on the southeastern highland reservoirs, it is common to see a band of fish from 40- to 46-feet deep during July and August. These fish will suspend in very deep water and move from the channel to adjacent structure, but often at the same depth. They may be 45 feet deep over the old river channel one hour, then hold 45 feet deep at the end of a nearby point when they are ready to feed. Downrigger trolling, so common in the Great Lakes, has been experimented with very little on the classic smallmouth reservoirs, but it can pay big dividends.

By far the most popular and pleasant way to fish a highland reservoir during the summer is at night (see Chapter 24). Insects are usually not a big problem on most of these waters, and balmy air temperatures prevail. Plus, the hordes of water skiers and houseboaters are bedded down for the night, leaving the lake to the fishermen.

Begin fishing shallow areas (no deeper than 15 feet) close to the spawning flats. Sometimes these places have weed growth on them. If so, by all means fish these areas thoroughly, because when available, weedy cover can outdraw any structure during this time

If you can find weed growth, it can outdraw all other cover in a highland reservoir during hot weather. Troll a deep-running crankbait to find weeds during the day, and return after dark.

of year! Begin fishing weedy or shallower areas close to flats when the surface temperatures are in the low 80s, and stay with these until the action slows. Then it is time to move deeper.

Target Submerged Islands At Night

In midsummer, most night fishermen agree that the submerged island or hump is the best bet for a bone-jarring strike. These high spots may be far from shore.

During daylight hours, cruise the lake with your depthfinder running and watch for the depth to rise and fall. Note the areas on your map and return after dark. Use marker buoys (lighted ones are available) to delineate the hump. The best humps have a few stumps or weeds peppered on them. Look for humps that rise to about 12 feet on top and as much as 60 feet on the deep side or end.

In the summer, fish may be very deep, even after dark, and may be tough to catch. Fish deep channel banks with heavy jigs down to 35 feet or so. These banks often have rock slides along their course, which will place large boulders or chunks of rubble in deep water—excellent places for big smallmouths to be found.

Points are good almost any time after dark. As the summer

progresses, you will find fish moving deeper, and you, accordingly, will have to fish slower. Fish shallow points early in the season and deep points as summer progresses.

Fall Fishing

When the leaves begin to change, many fishermen hang up their rods and stay glued to the football games on television. This season is often the best for large numbers of smallmouths, however, so give it a try.

By now you are probably growing more accustomed to paying attention to the slope of the banks surrounding the lakes. Look for banks that slice into the water at a 45-degree angle during fall months (see Chapter 30). This type of bank is usually composed of some form of rock. The best ones tend to have shale on them. Shale is loose and flaky and provides great habitat for crayfish, which can burrow easily into it. But do not make the mistake of casting your lures right up onto the bank in the fall, for the fish will probably still be deep.

These lakes cool down more slowly than do shallower bodies of water, and the water is likely to be warm at 40 feet as late as October! The best lure when the surface temperature reaches back down into the 60s is probably a sinking metal bait, one that can be dropped quickly to deep water. If you spot breaking fish, by all means try a topwater lure. Smallmouths will move in and out, suspending off these banks at varying distances. A big topwater plug can draw explosive strikes when fished off the banks in this season.

When the water temperature drops down into the 50s, continue to fish the 45-degree banks, in both tributaries and main lakes. Often the tributaries provide more relief from the wind and can be more easily fished on rough days. But, as you will quickly see, fish will be very scattered along these sloping banks.

Instead of painstakingly casting to every inch of bank, try a faster approach: With your trolling motor at a fast speed, move down the bank until you spot "something different"—a change in bank composition, a place where a gully slices through the hillside, a fallen tree in the water. Any such change is likely to attract fish. By concentrating on these "transitions," as many anglers call them, you will catch more fish and cover more good water. Fish are likely to be shallower and more active when the water dips into the 50s and may be taken on crankbaits, leadhead grubs, even topwater plugs.

The points close to deep water in the tributaries and main lake will provide perhaps the most consistent fall fishing. But do not fish too shallow, especially during the period when the leaves are still on the trees!

Watch your depthfinder and move very slowly and quietly to the extreme end of the point where it falls off into the old channel. Look for suspended fish close to this drop-off and vertical-jig them with spoons. Even during late fall, big smallmouths are rarely shallower than 12 or 15 feet on deep points.

Dead Of Winter

How serious are you about finding and catching a trophy smallmouth? If you are very serious, you will fish highland reservoirs in the winter months, when frigid temperatures keep all but the hardiest anglers at home.

By far the best winter structures are deep points, usually those in the major tributaries. The lower end of the lake often has the greatest majority of these. The "hollows" or indentations between two points will hold fish when they are not holding tight to the points themselves. Fish in hollows are usually inactive, but can be

Clear water means smallmouths are susceptible to striking a topwater lure, even when the fish are suspended.

In winter, choose sunny days for your smallmouth fishing. Experts agree that bass bite best when light penetrates the depths. Concentrate on deep points.

caught by vertical jigging or presenting live bait. Large, live creek minnows are the best bait. Drift these with the wind or slow-troll them using your electric motor along depths at which fish are marked on your depthfinder.

Live bait can also be fished on deep points. Many anglers still-fish minnows from an anchored boat. If you drift bait or move it via your trolling motor, be sure to hold along the depth contour all around the point.

If you are catching fish on the sides of the points in 18 feet of water, for example, and want to try the end of the point, do not cut across the point on your drift. Instead, follow the 18-foot contour all the way out and fish it around to the other side of the point. This may put you halfway across the creek, but you will be fishing the proper depth zone. Move deeper in 5-foot increments until fish are located.

Fish are likely to be deep and sluggish during the winter, but they will strike live bait hard. Expert smallmouth anglers have found better bait fishing to be had on calm, sunny days, when light penetrates farthest into the depths. As in all live-bait fishing, a slow presentation works best.

Highland Fling!

For classic smallmouth bass angling at its finest, try fishing a deep, clear, rocky highland lake! Using the seasonal guidelines presented here, you will have a good shot at a big fish. Just remember to approach these beautiful lakes differently than you would a shallow, cover-filled reservoir. They are tough...but not impossible.

=18=

Canyon Reservoirs

Whenever you travel to a new lake, either within your home state or to one nearby, you are apt to discover that the fishing conditions are more similar than different. If you travel from any of the eastern, southern or northern states to a western canyon lake, however, you will discover that everything changes.

First of all, within most of their range, smallmouth bass associate with rock, hard clay, grass or wood. In fact, the ideal flat, point or drop-off, where bass are likely to live, usually contains at least two or three of these elements. It is different in the West. There, hard mud bottoms, grass and wood are usually nonexistent, and it is easy to quickly become lost. However, with the right methods, smallmouths in these waters can be taken, though you may be thrown for a loop your first time out.

Like smallmouth bass in other parts of the country, those living in canyon reservoirs also associate with drop-offs, steep banks, flats and of course, deep water. But these elements of structure are nearly always barren of woody cover. Normally, stumps are ideal homes for smallmouth bass if they are located in or near deep water. But when stumps are not present, as in canyon reservoirs, a slight depression or large rocks takes their place.

Smallmouths in canyon reservoirs often relate to deep water. In fact, it is not unusual to find a school of them hovering near baitfish at depths of 50 feet or more. Even experienced anglers are surprised to learn how deep these fish may be found.

Canyon reservoirs may be the most unique smallmouth bass environment found anywhere.
Their steep sides, extremely deep water and lack of cover make them a challenge to fish.

Canyon Reservoirs

The Unique Face Of Desert Impoundments

Canyon reservoirs in the West are like no other body of water. If they could be compared to any other type of lake in any other part of the country, they come closest to resembling the highland reservoirs of the South. Like their southern counterparts, canyon reservoirs are characterized by steep banks and deep water, but unlike most other lakes, they can experience dramatic changes in water level over very short periods of time.

With little or no grass or wood on their banks, runoff from a hard rain can raise a canyon lake 20 feet or more seemingly overnight. In the same vein, these man-made impoundments can be emptied just as quickly. It is not unusual to witness a 20- or 30-foot fall in water level in a matter of a few days.

In addition, a canyon reservoir can go from muddy to clear in only a day's time.

It is evident that with the potential for rapidly changing conditions, an angler hoping to master western canyon smallmouths must be adaptable.

A solid understanding of structure and cover as they relate to smallmouth bass, along with a working knowledge of deep-water fishing, is a must to successfully fish these impoundments. In the western part of the country temperatures can soar higher than 100 degrees and stay there, driving smallmouths deep. That is where you must fish.

Flats Are Important

Nearly all canyon lakes will have flats that are easily recognized. During the months prior to and after the spawn, which occurs between the months of February and April, these flats are reliable producers, provided the flat is located near deep water or near a runoff. Runoff areas are created by rain, which forms a trench or ditch into the lake. These areas provide a channel for both smallmouths and baitfish to move in and out of deep water. Smallmouth bass will create their nests near rocks, preferring to rest on a sandy bottom.

Flats will produce fish throughout the year, but as spring turns into summer, they are good at night or very early or late in the day when the fish move to the flats to feed. During the summer, the best part of the flat is the area closest to the deep-water drop-off. As fall approaches and the water begins to cool, smallmouth bass

It is not unusual for water to rise or fall more than 20 feet in a canyon reservoir during a short period of time. Notice the water line visible on the rock wall.

will move farther up the flat to feed at various times of the day, but never with the same frequency as they do in the spring.

Humps Are Fish Magnets

It is not unusual to be running over 200 feet of water in a canyon lake and suddenly find yourself in five feet of water. The humps that exist in most canyon lakes are underwater rock formations, and year-round homes for smallmouth bass. The structure is suitable, the movement of baitfish around the humps is frequent, and the deep water needed by the fish is always present. On one day you may find fish on top of the hump in five feet of water, and the next day they will be hovering 30 feet down one side or other of the hump. Smallmouths on humps are extremely unpredictable, often making it difficult to catch these fish. One thing you can count on is the fact that the fish are there.

Humps in canyon reservoirs can be quite steep, and for one reason or another, one side of the hump will hold more fish than others. During the spawn few fish will be found on open-water humps, but when the spawn is over and water temperatures begin to rise, humps are the type of structure they seek.

Canyon Reservoirs

199

Exposed humps today may be covered by water tomorrow. Knowing the exact location of these underwater humps is essential if you want to catch bass.

Reefs: What You Need To Know

The term reef is one many anglers associate with saltwater, and in canyon lakes its meaning is similar in that it denotes a long, underwater protrusion of rock. These reefs, while they can be of any length, will usually be no more than 10 to 20 feet across. Another interesting fact about canyon reefs is that they remain close to the same depth along their entire lengths. If you find fish on these reefs, it is easy to use the same lure to cover that same depth along the whole reef.

Like humps, these structures give fish access to deep water, allowing them to move up and down, or on and off the reef, as needed. Both weather and the location of schools of baitfish dictate the depth and distance from shore smallmouths will choose along the reef. Horizontal movement along the top of the reef is determined by the location of forage; vertical movement by weather.

While reefs can produce at any time of the year, they are most likely to hold fish immediately after the spawn. Smallmouths will be staging then, providing night anglers with an excellent opportunity for good catches.

Points Draw And Hold Smallmouths

Points in canyon lakes are completely different from reefs, but are often mistaken for them. The only similarity lies in the fact that they both consist of rock. While points begin at zero feet and drop gradually into deep water, reefs maintain nearly the same depth for their entire length. Most canyon points consist primarily of rock, sand, gravel and occasionally some form of desert flora that was present when the lake was created (this small amount of wood cover, however, plays a very minor role in the overall makeup of the point).

Points that end in deep water, like their counterparts in other parts of the country, hold fish nearly year-round. If there is such a thing as "prime time" for points, it would have to be during the winter, spring and fall months. Some fish will hold on the points in summer, but these smallmouths associate more with the deep-water drop at the end of the point, than the point itself.

Steep Banks

Canyon lakes, as you might guess, have an abundance of steep banks (meaning 45 degrees or steeper). To the first-timer, most of

Points and pockets in the shoreline account for a majority of the good smallmouth bass fishing locations in canyon lakes. Seek these areas when you first launch onto the lake.

these banks will look alike. You read earlier the adage stating that 90 percent of the fish in a given lake live in 10 percent of the water. When referring to the fish that live on the steep banks in a canyon lake, this adage especially holds true. Needless to say, trying to cover all of the banks in these waters would be a waste of time. The secret to finding the most productive smallmouth bass spots is to look for an irregular feature, such as a small cut on the bank, a protrusion or maybe a rock slide. Bass will gravitate to these areas first.

Steep bank areas are usually the last choice for the experienced canyon fisherman. While they can and will produce fish, fishing along banks is generally time-consuming unless you have fished the same lake over a long period of time and know where to go. Any steep bank angler will tell you to fish only a specific portion of a 45-degree bank.

The fall and winter months are the best times to fish steep banks. During the winter, fish use these banks as they begin their movement into shallower water prior to the spawn. When they locate a suitable place, irregular feature, cut or rock slide on the bank they will stage, or hold, in that particular area.

Rounds And Pockets Are Good Places To Try

Rounds and pockets are the only two types of structure you can lump together because they are almost always physically connected. Rounds are gently curved areas of banks, either steep or shallow, that have a pocket formed on the inside of the round. The pocket may be no more than 10 feet deep, or may go back as far as 40 yards or more. The pocket will be deep in the center and then rapidly become shallower as you move toward the back. If there is an obvious run-off area in the back of the pocket, the spot will be all the more productive.

Smallmouth bass will move from the round to the shallow areas of the pocket to feed and then move back to the round. If you are able to locate these fish in a feeding mode in the back of the pockets, count on some very fast action. If the action suddenly slows, move quickly to another location, such as the round associated with the pocket.

Cover on rounds, for the most part, will be sparse or nonexistent. If rock is present, it is likely to range from small stones to huge boulders.

Complete Angler's Library

Small pockets adjacent to rounds are prime places to find smallmouths. Notice all the growth around the banks. This vegetation plays a very small role in patterning smallmouths.

Pockets and rounds are prime locations as the water begins to warm in the early spring. During the hotter months the fish move to open-water structure in deep water, but when it cools down in the fall, the fish return to the pockets and rounds.

Drop-Offs

In no other part of the country does the word "drop-off" mean what it does in canyon reservoirs in the West. If you have ever driven through the canyons, you know what this means. The drop-offs in canyon reservoirs are steep and deep. As with the humps, western bass will move shallow and then deep and back to shallow for any number of reasons, but they will nearly always associate with a drop-off of some kind.

Drop-offs are the most likely places to find large numbers of fish at any one time. The angler who finds them and presents an effective bait or lure can quickly catch a limit of smallmouth bass. If the action slows down, reposition your boat or change to a bait that will work at a different depth, or do both. On drop-offs, the fish have probably not actually left, but instead have repositioned themselves on the same piece of structure. This change could represent a 5- to 30-foot difference so the angler must be ready to adapt by using both boat and baits to facilitate the change.

Drop-offs produce fish in canyon reservoirs all year-round. Proper boat positioning and choice of baits are of the utmost importance in these areas.

Canyon Walls

Canyon walls are certainly the most breathtaking part of a canyon lake, but are also the least productive areas for catching bass. While some smallmouths will occasionally roam freely, they normally must have some piece of structure to associate with. Baitfish are the same in this respect. If there is no place for them to hide, they will not stay in a particular area.

Although canyon walls are not prime locations for bass, the

Rock formations that extend into the water are perfect locations for smallmouth bass. These areas serve as both cover and the source of a food supply.

Isolated brush may be a good place to find smallmouths in southern impoundments, but it plays only a minor role in canyon smallmouth bass fishing.

ends of the walls or irregular features that are associated with these walls can hold fish (the ends of the walls being the better choice). In many cases, rock deterioration on the extreme ends of these walls form reefs, rock piles or dug out areas closely resembling the washes that were mentioned earlier. It is these areas that hold smallmouths.

Walls are easy to see in canyons, but fishing them is a different story. Concentrate your efforts on only those spots that are irregular to the area. These will be the places that will allow baitfish to hide and provide some cover from which smallmouths can feed. These ambush-type areas could be ledges protruding from under the water, but more often than not they will be the ends of the bluffs or canyon walls.

If there is a good time to fish canyon walls it would have to be during the late winter months when fish are still in deep water, but have started moving to the drop-off to stage prior to the spawn.

Shallow Water Is Important—Sometimes

If conditions are favorable, shallow water can produce some fast action. Naturally, these conditions require that baitfish are

Canyon Reservoirs

The rewards of fishing for smallmouth bass in canyon reservoirs include beautiful scenery and beautiful fish like the one this angler is landing.

holding or feeding close to the bank. This can occur at any time of the year, but will be confined to those banks closest to deep water and primarily during the spring, the evening hours of the summer and the early part of winter when water temperatures are still within the bass' active range.

Baits Needed For Canyon Reservoirs

The same baits you are accustomed to using back home will probably work in canyon reservoirs, but your presentations will be different. For example, the baits you use in deep, wood cover will work, although there will be no deep, wood cover to work them through. Laying off a steep bank and working your bait down the bank and back to the boat may work just fine in your area, but if the water under your boat is more than a hundred feet deep, the bait you are using will be in the strike zone for a very short period of time before it swings back to the boat and, in some cases, may never reach the level where the fish are holding.

Fishing parallel to a steep bank is the recommended method to use to reach all levels effectively. Flats can be worked in the same way you would work flats in your neck of the woods. Humps are worked almost the same way, but if the fish go deeper, use a parallel approach.

So what is the major difference between canyon reservoirs and other lakes? *The extreme depths in which the fish will hold.*

In other parts of the country, when smallmouth bass move "too deep," most anglers head for the docks. In western canyon reservoirs, the angler simply relies on his graph and keeps on going.

With the aid of a graph, locating large schools of fish in the places we mentioned is easy. Once located, vertical jigging methods often make the spoon the most effective bait in your tackle box. Jigging straight up and down at the level the fish are holding is the ticket.

For the most part, any smallmouth bass bait will work, but choice of color is especially important. Heavy rains often muddy the usually clear water of canyon reservoirs in a very short period of time. Be prepared for the change. Light line (4- to 8-pound test) is preferred by most anglers for clear water situations; heavier lines are reserved for muddy water.

Canyon reservoirs are about the only places that fishermen can use the terms "structure" and "cover," almost interchangeably, since most canyon reservoirs contain little or no wood cover. When a western angler refers to "cover" he is probably referring to a rock lying on the side of a drop-off while the drop-off itself is considered the structure.

Canyon reservoir fishing is an experience no smallmouth angler should pass up, but your success will depend on the extent of your deep-water fishing knowledge and an understanding of how to fish the kinds of structure you will encounter.

19

Canadian Shield Lakes

T he term "Canadian Shield lakes" describes lakes in a broad geologic region in Canada and parts of the northern United States containing exposed bedrock. "Canadian Shield" land is characterized by scant soil and high amounts of rock, much of it exposed slabs of granite caused by relatively recent glacial scouring. Hence, the lakes in the Canadian Shield region generally have a rugged, rocky look and seem like prime smallmouth habitat with their miles of rocky shorelines. These lakes are often very clear and surrounded by pristine forest land, which also enhances their appearance.

However, the "fishy" appearance of these lakes is only partially correct. While it is true that many shield lakes have good populations of large smallmouths and can provide tremendous fishing, the total pounds of smallmouths in these lakes is often fairly low.

General Characteristics Of Shield Lakes

Shield lakes are generally deep, with much of the water exceeding 30 feet. This puts most of the lake off-limits to smallmouth bass. This deep water is too cold and contains too little food to be good habitat for smallmouths. Large amounts of deep water plus the northern latitude of shield lakes cause them to warm relatively slowly during the spring, thereby limiting the "growing season." The other trademark of shield lakes is that they are extremely rocky and much of the rock is large, unbroken

Complete Angler's Library

Smallmouth fishing on Canadian Shield lakes can be exceptional. These clear, oligotrophic (in-fertile) lakes produce long-lived fish, though numbers may not be high.

Canadian Shield Lakes

stone. This type of rock supports little food for smallmouths and hence few smallmouths.

These three features (deep, cold and rocky) are important for the smallmouth angler to understand. The combination of deep, cold water and unfavorable bottom composition results in lakes that support smallmouths in only a small percentage of the total lake area.

Small Habitats Support The Bulk Of Smallmouths

There are two reasons smallmouth fishing is often so good in shield lakes. One, the fish are concentrated in small areas and once you find them they can be easy to catch. Two, fish mortality is generally low.

Many shield lakes are in remote areas with limited angler use. Some shield lakes in Ontario, for example, are accessible only by air. Still others require travel by watercraft to reach, including the hundreds of lakes in Minnesota's Boundary Waters Canoe Area Wilderness. Fortunately, this has allowed many of these fragile waters to maintain a higher percentage of their larger small-mouths than in more heavily fished waters, where many of the larger bass have been cropped off. Anglers who do fish Canadian Shield lakes should practice catch and release for the larger fish, because these delicate fisheries can easily be harmed with even moderate amounts of fishing pressure.

Because only 5 or 10 percent of a shield lake may have suitable habitat for smallmouths, it is essential that you be able to accurately (and quickly) key in on these areas. While knowing how to catch fish after they are located is important in any type of water, in Canadian Shield waters the primary task is first finding the fish. The next section will examine the lake features that allow an angler to quickly find shield smallmouths.

General Features That Target Smallmouths

The basic smallmouth-producing features to look for in Canadian Shield lakes are large amounts of small rock in depths less than 18 feet. Optimally, this small rock should include significant amounts of cobblestone (fist- to head-sized rock) and also some small boulders (two to four feet in diameter). Rock of this size is the best for supporting smallmouth forage. The small boulders also serve as cover and ambush sites for smallmouths.

Shield lake smallmouths favor cobble-sized rocks like these visible beneath the clear water. Only a small portion of most shield lakes contain habitat suitable for smallmouths.

Finding Smallmouths In Spring

To find Canadian Shield smallmouths in the spring, it is best to treat this season as two periods—pre-spawn and spawn. Both of these periods are very temperature-dependent, and the fish behave differently in each.

In early spring, pre-spawn fish are always attracted to the warmest water available. This means they can be found in any areas of a shield lake that have a quick warm-up in the spring. One such warm-water area in these lakes is around rivermouths.

Incoming stream water may only be a couple of degrees warmer than the lake itself, but it often draws pre-spawn smallmouths like a powerful magnet. (Water may be considered "warm" at only 50 degrees, for example, if most of the lake is still 47 degrees.) The fish, including very large ones, can be extremely concentrated near one of these warmer-water stream inlets, with as many as two dozen large fish in an area the size of a living room.

The other spot to find early spring smallmouths is in shallow bays, especially those isolated from the main lake. These bays warm up more quickly and the fish can be highly concentrated in very small areas.

In spring, smallmouths gravitate toward streams which empty into lakes. These inlets often contain the warmest water to be found and serve as pre-spawn holding areas.

Finding Spawning Smallmouths

During the spawn, smallmouths have very specific needs and will be found in areas of the lake that fill those needs.

When water temperatures reach the upper 50s, adult smallmouths begin seeking out areas in the lake suitable for building their spawning beds. Bottoms covered with gravel and slightly larger rocks are preferred for spawning. The most favored areas in a lake will be along north shore banks, where the water is two to eight feet deep over a gravel bottom, and the very best sites will be near a log or large rock.

At this time of year, shorelines on the north side of a lake or bay receive the most sunlight and are most protected from prevailing winds. Hence, they warm up the quickest. Logs or large rocks on the bottom offer the nest-guarding male and the fry protection and security from predators. Of course, not every fish will be able to find an optimum spawning site. Some will be forced to settle on southern shorelines, without protective cover or suitable bottom material.

To locate likely spots for spawning smallmouths prior to fishing, examine a contour map of the lake; this is the easiest way to target probable areas. Of course, the best way to find spawning fish is by actually observing smallmouth beds. Since many shield lakes

Large, unbroken rock characterizes the topography common to many shield lakes. These structures and their associated deep drop-offs do not attract and hold smallmouth bass.

are very clear, it is possible to see the lighter-colored, circular spawning beds. Bed observation is best done during calm and bright mid-day periods with the aid of polarized sunglasses. If you do fish during the spawn, please practice catch and release.

Finding Fish In Summer

Summer, like the spring season, is best dealt with as two periods. The first, early summer, is a time when spawning has been completed, the water is warming, the fish are starting to actively feed and food sources have not yet become extremely plentiful.

The fish are now dispersed into all suitable summer habitat, including small bays, island shorelines, underwater humps and rivermouths. During the bright light of midday, look for fish in the 12- to 20-foot depths around these structures. During the low light

In remote Canadian Shield waters, a canoe is often required transportation. Some anglers pack lightweight, inflatable rafts into backcountry lakes.

of early morning and evenings, you can find the fish in considerably shallower water, sometimes no deeper than three or four feet. At either of these times, smallmouths will consistently be found where there are significant amounts of gravel and rubble on the bottom.

Rivermouths and heavily stained lakes are exceptions. If an incoming waterway is large enough, it may bring enough food into the lake to attract smallmouths at all times of the day, even if the water depths or bottom type would otherwise be unsuitable. And the relatively few shield lakes that are heavily stained may have such low light penetration that the fish can be found in water less than 12 feet even during the brightest conditions.

As midsummer progresses into late summer, water temperatures, aquatic weeds and food sources rise to their annual peak.

Smallmouths in Canadian Shield lakes react to these changes in their environment in several ways. The fish spend more time in deeper water. They also eat more food, while actually spending less time looking for food, because forage is plentiful at this time of year. This all means you should look for fish in the daytime around underwater humps and in channels between islands, targeting water from 15 to 25 feet and occasionally 30 feet deep.

One situation, however, will draw late-summer smallmouths into shallow areas of a lake. If a shield lake develops significant patches of aquatic vegetation (something that does not occur in all lakes), these "weeds" can draw later-summer smallmouths. Patches of vegetation in five- to eight-foot depths often attract forage species such as yellow perch, which in turn interest predator species, including smallmouths.

The smallmouths that relate to this vegetation at this time are often quite large. This is either because smaller bass cannot easily capture the large prey that is available, or because they choose not to compete with other weed-related predator species, such as northern pike.

Finding Fish In The Fall

Fall is a time of dramatic changes in Canadian Shield lakes. Water temperatures are falling and rapid flip-flops between Indian summer and winter-like weather can occur.

The fall "turnover" also takes place, when the surface water cools and sinks, mixing with the warmer, deeper water. This short period of mixing in the lake water is usually complete by the time the surface water temperature reaches 54 degrees. All these changes in the fish's environment naturally influence the behavior and locations of fall smallmouths.

Fall fish locations and feeding activity in shield lakes are not as consistent as in the summer season. But if the fall season is understood, some of the largest smallmouths of the year can be caught. Fall is the time when the fish are at their maximum annual weight, the largest smallmouths often concentrate together and the bigger bass continue to feed later into the fall than smaller-sized fish.

In early fall (before water temperatures have fallen below 60 degrees) the fish are still in some of their summer locations. For instance, if the lake supports aquatic vegetation, smallmouths will still relate to the vegetation before it dies off. However, bad

In early fall, smallmouths may be taken around shallow weedbeds. You may want to protect your best lures at this time of year because sharp-toothed northern pike lurk in the same spots.

weather such as sudden cold spells or cold, rainy weather can quickly push the fish out of these shallow areas (or at least slow down their feeding activity).

Conversely, a few days of good weather can bring the fish back into these summer-season areas. Humps or underwater points in close proximity to deeper water are also good early-fall locations to find active smallmouths.

The late-fall period comes to the smallest lakes by mid-September and comes to the largest ones by early October. This period is characterized by low water temperatures in the shallows. Slow down your approach because the fish's metabolism has also fallen and they are not as aggressive.

Smallmouths can often be found in deeper water near places where they were found earlier in the season. These locations can be off points or humps in depths of 20 to 30 feet. Look for the fish to be clustered around some unusual (and probably small) feature in these locations.

A small depression or pile of rocks will often hold several fish. This is a good time to use your sonar to key in on any unusual bottom features and to locate the fish themselves.

Final Tips

Here are some points to remember when fishing smallmouths in Canadian Shield lakes:.

- Before fishing, carefully examine a good map to help identify incoming streams, underwater humps, gradual slopes and other fish-holding features.
- Bottom types can often be determined by examination of the nearby shoreline.
- Moving water coming into, going out of, or passing through a shield lake is often a powerful smallmouth magnet.
- Several islands (whatever their size) close together are generally good summer smallmouth habitat.
- Light conditions are very important in shield lakes. The general rule is "low light—fish shallow, bright light—fish deeper."
- Polarized sunglasses, which are helpful in nearly all types of fishing, are essential when fishing shield lakes.
- A thermometer (to measure water temperatures) is critical during the spring and fall seasons.

=20=

Mesotrophic Lakes

Southern reservoirs may grow some of the biggest smallmouths, but the mesotrophic natural lakes across the northern United States and southern Canada are tremendous smallmouth bass factories.

You will find these lakes in a northern belt running from the Atlantic to just west of the Mississippi River. Although many of these are considered marginal smallmouth waters, they offer better fishing than most anglers realize. Perhaps that is due to the smallmouth bass' character. These fish prefer quiet locations, where they live in schools with their own kind in places off the beaten path of most anglers. Although their needs are similar to those of the largemouth, they are more specific, especially in the natural lake environment.

Understanding the unique characteristics of mesotrophic lakes is important to NAFC members hoping to locate and catch smallmouth bass from them.

Generally speaking, mesotrophic lakes that contain small-mouths are middle-aged waters that are moderately fertile and moderately deep. They have large, sandy flats and shorelines with scattered gravel.

Rock may be scattered over the flats on some of the steeper breaks and mid-lake humps. Also, mesotrophic lakes have scattered patches of cabbage and coontail weeds on flats and breaks where sufficient sediment and light penetration allow them to take hold. The flats may have sand grass, while shoreline weeds

Mesotrophic smallmouth lakes are typified by the moderately fertile natural lakes of the mid-northern, eastern half of the United States, including parts of the Great Lakes.

Mesotrophic Lakes

typically consist of reeds. The lakes' tapering bottoms drop to 40 to 60 feet at their deepest points.

Most mesotrophic lakes offer ideal habitat for smallmouth bass. They are warm-water environments that are young enough to have firm bottoms (little sediment) and large flats with scattered weeds, gravel and rock. Smallmouths prefer scattered and isolated patches of cover in association with cleaner, harder bottoms. The lake must be fertile enough to support substantial shallow-water prey like crayfish, one of the smallmouth bass' favorite forage. However, smallmouths are opportunists and will feed heavily on the easiest to catch and most available food.

When considering smallmouth locations in mesotrophic lakes, keep a few factors in mind. First, smallmouths are homebodies, unlikely to range very far. Bigger fish, however, will utilize a broader area. As in all fishing, there are exceptions, especially when environment forces them to move to meet their needs.

Typically, smallmouths will be found in areas that provide them with adequate spawning habitat, food, cover and depth within a radius of a few hundred yards.

The ideal spawning area would include a flat about the size of two football fields with isolated and scattered patches of weeds, rocks, gravel and wood. The bottom would be irregular and the breakline would have many points and turns that drop into 30 feet of water or more.

In reality, most natural lakes offer variations of those conditions. Younger, less fertile mesotrophic lakes contain more rock and gravel, and fewer weeds. In older, more fertile lakes, bigger rocks and rubble on the flats might be missing, but sand, gravel, mud or muck and scattered weeds replace these.

The way smallmouths use specific areas throughout the year will differ between younger mesotrophic lakes and older mesotrophic lakes. On any given day, specific locations can be dictated by day length, bottom type, weather conditions and available forage. However, here are some general seasonal movements and locations that can be used as guidelines to find smallmouths at any given time:

Cold Water (Ice-Out To 45 Degrees)
At ice-out on younger, clearer mesotrophic lakes, smallmouths are predictable; the fish can be found in large schools

As in most smallmouth fishing, temperature can be a critical element affecting a smallmouth angler's success. Check water temperatures, especially during the transition seasons of spring and fall.

feeding aggressively. They gather on the ends of points or flats that extend farthest into the lake and drop sharply into deep water, and hold at the depth where the bottom changes from hard to soft. This change could be rock to marl (sand or silt) or from clay to muck, and typically occurs at 20- to 40-foot depths. Smallmouths also will locate on humps adjacent to these flats and transition areas.

On the rivermouth lakes of eastern Lake Michigan, there are man-made conditions that strongly affect cold-water locations of smallmouths. In the heydays of western Michigan's logging industry, sawmills lined the shores. Tons of slab wood fell from freighters en route to Lake Michigan, creating underwater humps and long points of wood slabs. The fish use these underwater humps, piers and points of wood much like they do the natural structures. In cold water, smallmouth schools will hold on the deeper man-made structures that extend into the lake.

On older, more fertile mesotrophic lakes, cold-water locations are less predictable. There is less deep-water structure and the bottoms generally are no deeper than 15 to 20 feet. The fertile flats attract more forage early in the year; so do the breaklines of flats and points that have relatively harder bottoms.

It is important to note that smallmouths will move very shal-

Smallmouths may move very shallow during sunny, warming periods of early spring. Shoreward winds that pile warm surface water into the shallows can account for excellent fishing.

low during the early season. You may find them hundreds of yards from deep water. These longer-distance migrations normally occur during sunny, warming trends even though surface water temperatures may only be in the 30s. Look for perch in the shallows and you can expect to find smallmouths nearby. Areas receiving warm, shoreward winds are also good spots to find smallmouths in the early spring.

The famous Lake Erie smallmouth fishing sees activity similar to that on young, mesotrophic lakes. Lake St. Clair, near Detroit, best resembles an older mesotrophic lake where cold-water smallmouth movement is concerned. There will be less pronounced early shallow-water movements on St. Clair early in the season.

In all cases, activity levels and daily movements in early spring are influenced strongly by weather. Basically, the warmer and sunnier the weather, the stronger and longer the movements. Again, water temperature and depth do not seem to affect the fish as much as the air temperature and sun. During cold, cloudy days, the general activity of smallmouths will be minimal.

Pre-Spawn (46-55 Degrees)

When the water temperature rises into the upper 40s, smallmouths begin to vacate deep-water staging areas. On young mesotrophic waters, they move both horizontally and vertically. There is a pronounced horizontal movement from the offshore breaklines of points and flats to the inshore breaks and inside turns on those breaks. During stable, warming weather, fish will be very active and make journeys into shallow water.

By this time, the big schools of smallmouths located in deep water have divided into smaller, scattered groups. These groups roam the drop-offs and gather on breaks at the inside corners of points and flats. This allows the fish the quickest access to spawning areas as well as deeper water.

During shallow-water movements, smallmouths will cruise the sandy flats. As the water reaches the lower 50s, active fish may disperse across an area that offers scattered rocks, reed patches or submerged logs. When the fish are very active, each rock, isolated reed patch or piece of wood in the area can attract an aggressive fish.

As the water warms into the mid-50s on older mesotrophic lakes, active smallmouths scatter over the flats while neutral fish roam the five- to 10-foot breakline. Again, inside turns on flats and points will be the focal points of shallow-water movements.

After the fish move shallow they might be anywhere. If bait-fish are using clean sand flats in three feet of water or less, you can expect smallies to be nearby using small pieces of cover as ambush points. These features might include a small rock, tiny clump of grass or a dark spot on the bottom.

When smallmouths move shallow, they use isolated differences in the bottom for cover, and later, as locations for spawning beds. These pieces of cover may be sandy cuts between small weed patches, dark patches of dead weeds on a sandy flat, a few boulders in the middle of nowhere, a log, or a series of tiny weed patches— and those objects may be visible to you in the clear, shallow water. Fishermen often ignore these areas because they cannot see fish, yet smallmouths often reside there, lying in camouflage against the bottom.

In the rivermouth lakes of western Michigan, smallmouths use the inside corners of sunken wood piles, pilings and piers as spawning sites. Rocky shorelines that spread into a flat with nearby drop-offs also will concentrate smallmouths.

Shallow-water locations during pre-spawn are dictated by weather, but as water temperatures approach the mid-50s, activity intensifies around spawning areas. In the early stage, female and male smallmouths share the same areas, but as the spawn approaches, females move slightly deeper than males.

Spawn (55-65 Degrees)

As the water temperature rises into the mid-50s, males begin fanning beds. Bigger males often prepare beds in deeper water than smaller males will. The bigger males often are the first to begin this annual ritual.

The depth at which the fish will spawn depends upon water clarity, availability of suitable spawning areas, and size of fish. On young, clear mesotrophic lakes, the bigger fish may spawn as deep as 12 feet or more. In older, more fertile mesotrophic lakes with turbid water, smallmouths may spawn quite shallow. This is due to a lack of harder, more suitable bottom at deeper locations, a situation that can force smallmouths shallow in clear lakes as well.

Once you have pinpointed an area with all the necessary spawning ingredients, look for isolated objects and structures. On a sand and gravel flat, there may be one small area that offers scattered rock piles or a few bigger, isolated rocks.

If the lake has a good smallmouth population, there may be a nest beside each rock. Scattered logs on a suitable flat might have a nest at each end of a log. Small patches of emerging cabbage in shallow water may have a nest in a point or cut in the patch. Look for isolated reed patches that are deeper or away from the main reed bed and you will find spawning smallmouths. Do not overlook man-made objects, like a tire, a piling or a lost anchor; they attract nesting bass. On natural lakes controlled by a levy or dam at an outlet, isolated stumps will hold spawners.

Transition lines, where sand changes to gravel or rock, also attract bedding smallmouths. Choose an area offering the most pronounced change or one where the depth changes faster at the transition of bottom types. But remember: contrary to popular belief, too much of any one thing may not appeal to spawning fish.

Bigger fish will claim the best spots closest to deep water. For example, if smallmouths spawn in 3 feet of water on a given lake, the bigger fish will usually be located on the exceptional area that is in 5 feet of water and has immediate access to deep water.

Bedding smallmouths may concentrate in an area, but the bigger fish will typically be nearby in more solitary sites. During the

Shallow bays with a firm bottom and scattered weeds will harbor spawning smallmouths in mesotrophic lakes. Look for nests around isolated objects of cover on the lake bottom.

day, females will be noticeably absent from the beds, staging in deeper water on adjacent flats or inside turns of breaklines.

If spawning areas are in two feet of water and significantly deeper water is not available, look for females in the deeper water of the flat. A small hole on a flat can hold big fish if it is near the spawning area, with nearby inside turns offering the prime spots. Also, sand slots that run from deep-to-shallow water between weedbeds can be excellent.

Post-Spawn (65-70 Degrees)

The post-spawn period is the transition that sets the stage for summer. Most smallmouths are recuperating from spawning and are not aggressive. The males will scatter from the spawning flats and eventually locate on the nearest breaks. The females recuperate in the same staging areas, only deeper. As fish recuperate, summer patterns begin to form. Female smallmouths begin feeding heavily again at the end of this transition period so it is a good time to expend some energy smallmouth fishing.

Summer

Summer smallmouth locations are as varied as the number of lakes they inhabit. On any given lake, environmental conditions

Mesotrophic Lakes

As smallmouths recuperate from spawning, they move into summer locations. Check the breaks where spawning flats fall off to deeper water to find actively feeding fish.

will dictate the general location and abundance of smallmouth prey, and the bass will move accordingly. On one lake, for example, the dominant forage may be alewives and crayfish. Thus, there may be two groups of smallmouths, one that remains somewhat shallow, keying on the crayfish, and another that chases alewives in deep water.

Another factor that makes summer smallmouths difficult to pattern is their tendency to make short, aggressive forays in search of food. If you are not present at that particular time, you miss out. Most of these movements are during low light conditions or after dark.

If lake conditions and weather patterns remain stable, smallmouths can be predictable. If you can catch them from a specific area at a specific time of day, chances are good that you can do so the next day, providing weather conditions remain the same. Also, as late summer approaches, the schools will grow and their forages will become more predictable. At times, in late summer, you can set your watch by these movements.

Unfortunately, summer weather patterns and environmental conditions are not stable enough to always make it that easy to locate smallmouths, so you should begin your search near a drop-off on a large flat, mid-lake hump or bar. Points and inside turns will be key locations to find active fish. Movements often take place during changing light conditions or low light conditions, and the migration to shallow water will be brief, yet intense.

It is important to note that smallmouths can sometimes be found very shallow and a long way from deep water. Indeed, that goes against most theories, but in natural lakes it happens. When they make that move, they will relate to isolated objects or structure the way they do in spring or fall.

When smallmouths are found on deep structure in summer, they usually are scattered. A couple of fish may be on top, another on an inside turn, and yet another on the deeper breaking side.

Early Fall (60-70 Degrees)

Locating smallmouths becomes a more predictable task as early fall approaches. The schools get bigger as the fish converge on main lake breaks once water temperatures begin to drop.

On some bodies of water, such as Lake Erie, the schooling will occur in much deeper water. Instead of main lake breaks, schools gather near deeper structure, and by late August and early September, those schools can be huge.

This may be the best time to fish for smallmouths. When active, the school will feed aggressively and for long periods of time. If the school is relating on a break next to shallow water, dawn is the premier time to be there, and fishing can be incredible. Other peak periods are late afternoon and midday on overcast days. Deep-water schools are most active from mid-morning to early afternoon.

During warm, overcast, early fall days, fish using the main lake drop-offs will scatter over the flats and are very catchable along isolated objects and subtle pieces of structure. It is not unusual to catch the same fish more than once in the same day at this time of year, which emphasizes the smallmouth's vulnerability. Fishermen who consistently keep fish during this period can significantly damage smallmouth bass populations.

Fall Turnover (50-60 Degrees)

During the fall turnover, fishing success can be extremely limited. Ideally, you should choose a lake that has not yet begun to turn over or has turned over and the water temperature has dropped to 50 degrees. If you do not have a choice, concentrate on the steeper breaklines. Some fish will scatter on flats. As the water stabilizes after turnover, smallmouths will locate off main lake breaks and secondary deep flats. Inside turns and points again become key areas to take fish, although smallmouths may disperse over deep flats and along breaklines leading from shallow to deep water.

Early fall fishing can be exceptional as fish move back onto the deep edges of flats. Best fishing hours are early morning for shallower fish, midday for deep schools.

Complete Angler's Library

When the surface water temperature drops to 50 degrees or less, fishing can be incredible in both quantity and quality of smallmouths. As long as weather is stable and water temperature does not drop quickly, big fish will hold on shoreline breaks. The areas where big schools concentrated before the turnover are key areas.

Precise presentations become more critical now, because the majority of the active fish may use a very specific spot when moving on a main lake break. Typically, they will hold on a specific feature such as a point or inside turn. Look for smallmouths on the end of weed points, a finger of rocks extending off a breakline, a small notch on a break, or in a lane of sandy bottom extending from deep to shallow water, between patches of weeds.

During warm, stable weather in late fall, smallmouths will move onto flats. On older, more fertile mesotrophic lakes, shallow-water fishing can be superb and last all day, especially when weather conditions change from pleasant to cold. The fish may be roaming anywhere, as shallow as two feet or less and as far as 100 yards from deep water.

As the weather gets colder, the fish on young mesotrophic lakes migrate back to the transition areas in deep water—such as points far out in the main lake. On older mesotrophic lakes, smallmouths scatter on the breaks and inside turns of large, main lake flats where they become less active.

Catching
Smallmouths

21

Current

Current adds another dimension to smallmouth fishing. Factors that apply to fishing for smallmouths in most waters still apply, but the addition of current adds new concerns. Anglers can make current work for them in a number of ways to get more and bigger smallmouth bass. Current direction and speed do have to be constantly considered, however, with adjustments in tackle and fishing tactics made accordingly.

Fishing In Riffles

The fast, shallow water broken by rocks and boulders and commonly known as a riffle can be a good place to take smallmouths. The key to fishing riffles is to fish the edges, around exposed rocks, using lures or flies that can be controlled in the fast current. The best lures, flies and baits include spinners, spoons, jigs, streamers and, occasionally, surface plugs and bugs. Crankbaits are less effective in riffles because the lip on the baits makes them difficult to control in fast current.

Best casts in riffles cross or quarter downstream areas allowing the lure or fly to completely cover a feeding lane or section of the riffle. For best results, repeat this with successively shorter or longer casts to completely blanket the exposed water with the lure before changing lures or moving on.

Since riffle water is generally shallow, shallow-running lures are a must. Always keep the rod at a high angle during the retrieve

Riffles, fast runs, pools—you will find smallmouths in all of these riverine zones. Fishing in moving water requires an understanding of the right lures and presentations.

Current

to keep the lure or fly from hanging up. Riffles will not usually hold fish as large as those found in pools and rock cover, but these areas are always worth fishing.

Fishing In Pools

Deep pools, by their very nature, lack the current found in shallower water. As a result, the full range of casts—from upcurrent to downriver—are possible, using the full range of available lures. Medium- to deep-diving crankbaits are ideal. Other good lures include tube lures, weighted plastic worms, spinners, spoons, jigs, streamer flies and weighted streamers.

Because the current does not have to be fought in deep pools, slow retrieves are best. Cast in patterns to completely cover the pools from the headwaters to the downstream ends. Lures that will get to the bottom work best most of the time, but there are times when smallmouths will cruise just under the surface to pick up food. At these times, small topwater lures, fly rod bugs and very shallow-running minnow lures are ideal. Cast well above and beyond a feeding fish and retrieve in front of it.

Fishing Around Rocks In Current

Smallmouths prefer rocks in current because big rocks—exposed or submerged—provide cover. This fact makes both exposed and submerged rocks ideal locations to fish for smallmouths. River hydraulics are such that large rocks provide an area of quiet water in the fastest current. This "buffer zone" along the front and sides of the rock extends almost like the tail of a comet on the down-current side. This quiet water allows smallmouths to rest easily yet be immediately adjacent to a feeding lane where they can dart into the current for a quick meal.

River or stream rocks are ideal spots to use fore- and aft-bracketing casts, and cast to each side, to cover the entire area with a lure. To bracket your casts, make several casts above the rock, so that the lure is brought right across the face of the rock. Do the same thing behind the rock, making repeated casts to cover the extended "tail" of quiet water.

Next, make a cast to the near side of the rock, letting the lure drift along the side, and making small jerks to give the lure some action without removing it from this quiet water path. If the rock is low, finish by casting over it to present the lure the same way on

Smallmouths often use rocks as cover in rivers and streams, but not all rocks are as obvious as this. Look for current boils on the surface to locate submerged rocks that hold bass.

the opposite side of the rock. If casting over rocks repeatedly, check your line for abrasion.

An alternate method is to cast from upstream or downstream of the rock, bracketing the rock the same way, working the lure repeatedly through the quiet water before moving on.

If the water is deep alongside the rock, cast first with shallow-running lures and then follow up with deep-running lures such as crankbaits, jigs or spoons.

Spinning And Spincast Casting In Current

Spinning, spincast and casting tackle differ from fly fishing in that in all three the weight of the lure "loads" (bends) the rod and allows the rod to make the cast. Each cast must be designed for the potential target.

Use a long spinning rod when fishing in current to minimize water drag on the line during retrieve. Choose a position to cover your target with a quartering downstream cast.

Often the best casting position for the angler is upstream and to one side of the potential target area. That way, a quartering downstream cast can swing the lure sideways through the target area, pulled by the current. This is better than a straight cross-stream cast, which can be immediately caught by the current, the line bellied and the lure swept downstream at an unnatural, and usually unproductive, speed. Quartering downstream casts are best when using live minnows, worms, small jigs, spinners, crankbaits and tube lures.

Straight cross-stream casts do well in slow current or where eddies cause less belly in the line than current would. They are ideal as a first, exploratory cast prior to the quartering downstream cast.

One key to minimizing line bellying is to use a long rod and to hold the rod high during the retrieve. The high rod position holds the line up to prevent it being caught by the water current. Jigs are ideal here, along with crankbaits and live minnows. Quartering upstream casts are also good, but it is important to use a fast retrieve reel to be able to retrieve line at least as fast as the current. Failure to do so results in snagged and lost lures.

Fast retrieve reels are also necessary for straight upstream casts. When executed properly these casts are extremely effective because they allow sinking lures to get extra deep to scour areas favored by big smallmouths.

The key to upstream casting is to aim slightly beyond the target point, closing the bail (spinning reels) or stopping the spool (casting reels) to start the retrieve as soon as, or even before, the lure lands. This quick action allows you to retrieve the lure slightly faster than the river current to get the bait extra deep. Not doing this makes it difficult to catch up to the current and get the lure down deep. Since the movement is just barely faster than the current, it also presents any lure or bait in a more natural way.

A sensitive graphite rod is important for upstream casting because you want to retrieve the line barely faster than the current to feel the lure working. It takes a delicate touch and some practice to eliminate slack and to keep the lure just above the bottom. You want it wobbling or moving naturally just above the bottom to prevent snags. Avoid retrieving so fast that the lure planes up high, negating the effectiveness of this deep-fishing method.

This technique works especially well with crankbaits, jigs, big-blade spinners that can be slow rolled in the current, small spoons and weighted plastic worms.

Fly Fishing In Current

The same upstream, quartering upstream, cross-stream and quartering down-current casts performed with spinning or bait-casting gear can be done with a fly rod, with some differences. One disadvantage is that some anglers cannot reach quite as far with a fly rod as with spinning, spincast or casting gear. Thus, a closer approach, whether by wading or boat fishing, is required when fly fishing.

An advantage can be gained from the line weight used in fly fishing (the fly just goes along for the ride). Fly fishing makes it possible to make a cast in which the fly will drift naturally instead of being swept downstream by the line belly. To do this, make a regular fly cast, then at the end of the cast (as the line is flowing out and loop almost turned over), shake the tip sideways back and forth to create side-to-side waves in the line. The result is a "lazy-S" cast that will lay out snake-like instead of the straight line normal cast. This means that the fast current between the angler and the fly will wash out these curves first, not affecting the drift

Many fishermen avoid a fly rod because they feel it cannot attain long-distance casts. But with practice and the proper weight rod and line, you can cover a lot of water with a fly rod.

or float of the fly or bug. This is ideal for cross or quartering down-stream casts.

These casts can be done with the upstream casts also, but in truth, the fly rod is less adaptable than other tackle for these approaches in fast water. Hand-stripping in fly line during the retrieve is difficult in a fast current drift. Also, any slack, when a hit occurs, will usually result in a lost fish. You just cannot keep the line coming evenly and smoothly and strike when required in fast current. This will, however, work in current two miles per hour or less.

Fly tackle is excellent when smallmouths are rising on the sur-face or taking nymphs just under the surface. In these situations, realize that the current will show a rise or boil below where the fish is actually located. Thus, cast three to 10 feet upcurrent of where you think the fish is located and allow the fly to drift into the feed-ing lane used by the fish.

If smallmouths are moving around, as they often do on late summer evenings on shallow rivers, the fly rod is ideal because you do not have to retrieve all of the line before making another cast. With practice, you can make a quick pickup and one backcast and

Complete Angler's Library

Fly rod fishing saves time between casts. You can pick the lure up and drop it to another target quickly, giving you a better chance to catch fish like this.

Current

Drift fishing streams and rivers is one of the best ways to cover a lot of good smallmouth water in a day. Plan ahead for upstream transportation if your craft is not motorized.

then lay the fly down in front of a moving fish anywhere within 30 degrees of the original cast. It takes some practice, but is worth it all when that subsequent cast immediately connects with a surprised, surging smallmouth.

If wading when fly fishing, try to use as long a rod as possible to get the added reach necessary to hold false casts above the water. Also, if working from a boat, try to clear a deck area for the line to lie on without getting caught on tackle boxes and boat cleats. If you have this problem, get a four- to five-foot square of fine netting, rim the edge with pinch-on sinkers to keep it from blowing around and lay it over everything. You can still see your depthfinder and operate your electric motor's foot control, but the net will cover all potential line tanglers and allow line to come up off the deck on the forward cast of a double haul or when fighting a big smallmouth.

Drifting And Anchoring In Current

Boats as fishing platforms can be used in many ways for river fishing. They are ideal for randomly hitting all the hotspots along a prime stretch of river. Fishing on slow current rivers is not unlike fishing a lake where the trolling motor provides positioning after reaching a favored spot. The current is usually not so strong that modern bow-mount electric motors cannot hold a bass boat against it.

On shallower rivers, one of the best ways to fish is to drift the river, since each cast on smaller waters can place the lure into a new hotspot, be it riffle, deep pool, rock eddy or alongside a log-jam. If planning a drift in which you return to the launch spot, plan to cover as much of the river as can be comfortably fished in one day, yet leave time to return to the dock or launch ramp in daylight. On some rivers, this might be only a mile or two, on others it might be 10, depending upon the quality of the smallmouth water.

Another way to drift fish is to put in at one spot and drift to a second using two boats. This leaves more time for fishing, because you do not have to navigate back upriver. Two vehicles are a must for this (thus best for two boats or four anglers). To do this, both cars are driven to the launch ramp to drop off both boats and all tackle. At least one member of the party stays with the boats while both cars are driven to the pick-up point, one car parked and both drivers return in one car to the launch spot. At the end of the day, the procedure is reversed to take two drivers back up river to get the other car and return to load the boats. A variation of this for two anglers, one car and one boat is to float to the take-out area and have an arranged ride back to the car while the second angler stays with the tackle and boat.

In drift fishing, set a course that will take you through selected areas of the river (these areas might change, of course) allowing the boat to drift while both anglers fish. A drift anchor is helpful here (see chapter 8).

When drifting shallow waters, it is important to minimize boat noise. You can yell your head off, but a scraped tackle box might scare fish. Carpeting in the bottom of river boats helps, as do rubber-soled shoes and foam feet on tackle boxes.

22

Smallmouths On Flats

hen most anglers think of smallmouth bass, they conjure up images of steep, rocky bluffs and deep drop-offs. But during the spring of the year, smallmouths often relate to flats. Because flats that hold big smallmouths tend not to look "fishy," however, many smallmouth bass fishermen overlook them.

Fishing the flats is probably the simplest way for most fishermen to catch a trophy-sized smallmouth bass, a fish of 4 pounds or better. Some say it is a method that may be *too* simple. Once you understand how smallmouths relate to flats, and what you have to do to catch them, you will begin to see why most fishermen overcomplicate things.

What Is A Flat?

For purposes of this discussion, let us call a flat any bank that enters the water at a very gradual slope. You know from past fishing experiences that bluffs are virtually 90-degree banks—straight up and down. You also know that many sloping banks enter the water at a 45-degree angle. A flat, on the other hand, projects into the water at a much lower angle. The terrain near the shoreline will give you a good indication of what to expect underwater. If it is low and flat, you can expect the flat to enter the lake and taper off into deep water gradually. If it is hilly, you can expect the bank to drop off rather steeply.

Experienced smallmouth fishermen sometimes refer to flats as

Leadhead jigs and spring smallmouth fishing on flats are made for each other. When scouting flats that might hold big smallmouths, look for those with deep water nearby.

Smallmouths on Flats

"nothing-looking banks." While other types of banks look bassy for one reason or another, a good smallmouth flat does not look fishy at all. There may be little or no cover on it. The bank may be composed of small material (pea gravel, for example), clay or mud. That big flat on the other side of the lake—the one where your buddy caught that lunker largemouth last year—probably has brush stickups, fallen trees, weeds or stumps on it. But a good smallmouth flat needs none of these. All it needs is to be flat...and close to deep water.

Deep-Water Access Is Extremely Important

Those who consistently fish for big smallmouths—dedicated amateurs and professional guides—know that *while a big smallmouth may be caught shallow, there is usually deep water close by*. A good rule of thumb to go by when picking a site for smallmouth fishing is to make sure there is deep water—15, 20, 60, 100 feet or more—not more than two long casts away. While this might sound absurd to the experienced largemouth angler, it is a statement that will cause successful smallmouth fishermen to nod their heads in agreement. Smallmouths use deep water the same way largemouths use weeds, stumps and brush: for security and feeding.

When you spot a place on the lake that looks like it has the potential to be a good smallmouth flat, do not just examine the shoreline and shallows. Move out, way out on the flat, and watch your depthfinder to see how deep the water is once it begins to drop off. The best flats drop off into a deep creek or river channel, often several hundred yards away from the nearest bank! This helps explain why flats remain mysterious to many fishermen. Bass fishermen are a hard-headed breed. They insist on casting their lures right against the bank. But the successful smallmouth angler knows that this behavior will catch precious few bronzebacks, and usually no big fish, when the bass are using the flats. Still, it is a hard sell. For some reason, bass fishermen need a visible target at which to cast. That is okay. Let the masses keep plugging the banks. In the meantime you can learn how to really catch the big boys when they are on the flats!

What is a good smallmouth flat? Main components include a "slick" flat, one without a lot of cover on it, or, a big flat, one encompassing a broad area, and one that runs way out into the

Anatomy Of A Smallmouth Flat

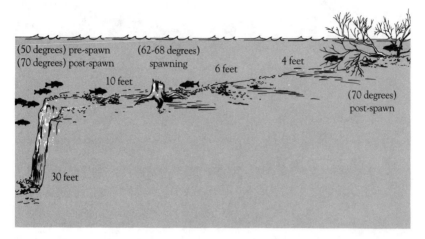

Good smallmouth flats are broad with clean bottoms. Spawning fish will use the main body of the flat, while pre- and post-spawn smallmouths utilize deep drops and shallow cover.

lake—maybe a couple of hundred yards—before getting deep.

The Contour Approach

It is a fact that even when big smallmouths are actively spawning, they are often in water eight feet deep or more, especially in a clear highland reservoir. This seems awfully deep to the bank-chunker, but it explains why you have seen smallmouth guides patiently working an area in the middle of the lake, even in the spring! On a good flat, eight feet of water may not occur until you are several hundred feet from the bank, so gradual is the slope. This means that to cast *into* water eight feet deep you may have to put your boat in 10, 12 or even 15 feet of water. Get a feel for the area by quietly running your trolling motor at a slow speed so your boat heads toward the bank. Watch your depthfinder and note how slow or fast the flat tapers. Then use this input to help you gauge how far away from your target you need to be when you begin casting.

Know this: *Most of the time, most fishermen will be fishing too shallow on these flats to catch a big smallmouth bass. By following the deeper contours, you will be a giant step ahead of the pack.*

If you are properly fishing a flat, you will most likely be fishing far from the shoreline, as this successful angler knows. Cast away from the shoreline, rather than toward it.

Seasonal Savvy

Once you are onto a flat with good smallmouth potential, learn what parts of the flat will be most important during different phases of the spring. This is vital information, for some flats are very large, and you will waste a lot of time by fishing in places where smallmouths are not that likely to be.

In the early spring, start getting serious about flats when the water temperature reaches about 50 degrees. But do not fish shallow! Move to the first deep drop-off and concentrate your casts in this zone. The biggest females tend to "stage" during this period and hold along these drops close to spawning flats. This is never easy or fast fishing. You might cast all day for one strike, but experience has shown that when that strike comes, it is often a trophy fish. Some of the biggest smallmouths of the year are caught during the staging period—fish fat with roe and itching to spawn. These fish are super-moody; sometimes the least little change in conditions will turn them on or shut them off. Most fishermen give lip service to this deep fishing, only to give up quickly when a strike does not jerk the rod from their hands. Remember what the environment of the bass is like during these early days of spring.

The water is likely to be cold, sometimes muddy from spring rains. The fish have just moved up from their deep-water winter lairs. They are moving slowly and so should your lures! Never "burn" a crankbait or fast-hop a jig during this period! The best early-spring smallmouth anglers succeed most consistently with slow-moving lures and a painstaking approach.

Choose a lure that has some action to it even when fished with the slowest possible retrieve. Your first casts onto the flats in spring must be deep and your retrieves very slow.

When the water temperature reaches 60 degrees, fish shallower, up on the flat most of the time. Be warned, however, that once smallmouths make the commitment to move shallower, it takes little to make them drop back deeper again. Boat traffic is a common culprit during the spring. On one Southeastern reservoir known for big smallmouths, you cannot even begin to catch fish on the flats during the weekend. Zip-zapping bass boats churn the water to a froth, sending waves washing over the flats and sending smallmouths down deep. On some lakes, it is hard to get away from boat traffic even during the week. The solution usually requires heading up into tributaries and leaving the main lake to the

A selection of leadhead jigs includes hair-bodied models with weedguards (top), tube body (center), Mr. Twister twister tail (lower left) and Mann's Sting Ray paddletail.

hot-rodders. Or—how is this for an exciting idea?—fishing the flats at night. Very few smallmouth fishermen get into night fishing until summer. But some of the best smallmouth anglers report good catches of big fish on shallow flats after dark, particularly in the days prior to the new and full moon.

Smallmouths typically begin to spawn in earnest when the surface temperature is about 62 degrees and are usually done spawning when it reaches the upper 60s. But avoid pounding the banks! Smallmouths like to spawn in fairly deep water. Start by fishing the eight- to 10-foot zone, maybe even deeper if you are not catching quality fish. Smallmouth guides agree that the biggest smallmouths often spawn deepest, sometimes 15 feet down. Usually a slow approach is necessary during this period, using subtle, quiet lures like leadhead grubs. Of course, practice catch-and-release when fishing during the spawn.

One of the best times to fish the flats is after the spawn—when the surface temperature has climbed to about 60 degrees, and when daytime temperatures call for shorts and a T-shirt. In the Southeast, this usually occurs around the first of May; in the North, about a month later. This is a time when you can catch a real jewel of a smallmouth. The fish that have spawned and had a short period to recover are at their most aggressive. They are hungry and they are likely to be found in some of the shallowest water you will find them in all year. Here is one time when you can toss out the rulebook about staying off the banks for big smallmouths. The key to catching the big ones lies in finding them visiting the shallows.

Reservoirs, as you probably realize, are used as storage vats to hold or release water. After heavy spring rains, the level of reservoirs usually rises to inundate small bushes and brush along the banks. Baitfish will hang tight around these bushes. It is common to see clouds of small "pin minnows" (immature baitfish) hovering close to this cover. It is also common to see a big smallmouth burst into this school, sending a silvery cloud of bait into the air! You can catch these fish on a number of lures, but one of the best is a big spinnerbait fished on a stout baitcasting reel, but with fairly light line (10-pound test works well). The light line lets your lure swim much more naturally and is less visible in the super-clear water of late spring. By bumping the bushes with this bait, you are liable to catch your biggest smallie of the year.

Swimming A Lure

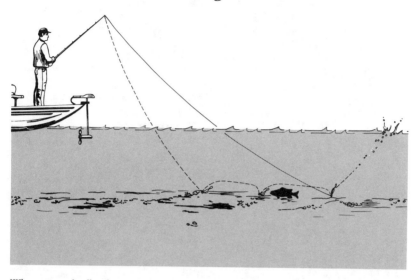

When using a leadhead jig or spinnerbait on a flat, swim the lure along the bottom in a slow, steady motion. If you feel the lure is too high, stop reeling and let the lure touch bottom again.

When the surface temperature reaches 70 to 75 degrees, if you can no longer catch fish up in the shallows, try a different approach: move back out to the drop-off, the place where you began fishing back in the early spring. Only now, instead of casting a slow-moving, sinking lure, try a topwater bait. Cast this lure out over the drop-off, even in water *as deep as 100 feet.* During this late-spring/early-summer period, the fish will suspend, often at a depth of 15 to 30 feet and will rise up to nail the lure. The best lure choices are floating minnow imitations (when the water is in the low 70s) and then, as the water reaches the mid- to upper 70s, a larger, noisier topwater lure works best.

You have fished the flats from, perhaps, early spring through early summer. If you have fished the right places, you have probably caught good smallmouths. By fine-tuning your approach with the right lures, you will stand an excellent chance of landing that trophy of a lifetime.

The Right Lures And Tackle

We have mentioned some of the lures you will need to properly fish the flats, but let us look at them more closely:

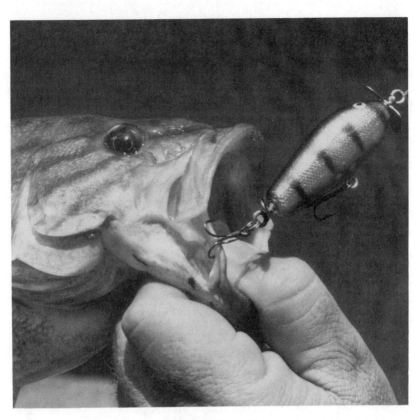

Topwater baits like this propeller model called an A.C. Shiner work great on the deep edges of flats when the water temperature climbs past the 70-degree mark.

•**Leadhead Grubs,** or jigs from three to five inches in length with soft rubber bodies and $^1/_8$- to $^1/_4$-ounce leadheads. Ask the best smallmouth anglers which bait they would choose if they could use only one, and 90 percent will pick a grub! Choose a grub you can cast a good distance on a spinning rod, even on windy days (common in the spring). As a general rule of thumb, use a $^1/_8$-ounce leadhead until conditions (depth, wind) begin to cause you to lose touch with the lure during the retrieve, then go to a $^1/_4$-ounce leadhead. On the toughest days, when the fish just are not biting and the water is still cold, fish a small grub no more than three inches in length. In the midst of the spawn, and after it, try a big grub—many fishermen report bigger catches on a 5-inch lure in waters where large smallmouths reside. Rig the grub with the tail down most of the time (on a twist-tail grub) and the hook exposed (there is little cover for the lure to snag on). Stick with light colors that you can see through. The time-honored favorites include chartreuse, green, smoke and pumpkin pepper. Metalflake lures will also work well on smallmouths. Keep leadheads sorted by size in small peanut butter jars (this way they will not fall down into the depths of your tackle box) and consider buying a jig mold to pour your own leadheads (you will lose a million of them if you are a good smallmouth angler!)

•**Hair Jig And Pork Rind** or "fly 'n rind" is a little-known lure outside of the Southeast. Most bass fishermen know about big, rubber-legged jigs for largemouth bass. But for the smallmouths, the fly 'n rind is better. It produces a more compact, slimmer profile that smallmouths prefer. Again, choose a $1/8$-ounce hair jig when conditions let you fish it; $1/4$-ounce when the wind comes up or the smallmouths are deep. Dress the jig with a small pork frog. The best smallmouth fishermen pay strict attention to color with these lures. When fishing a black jig, they use a trailer that will provide some contrast, but still present a dark pattern to the fish— like brown. In murky water, they fish a jig with a "hot" color like chartreuse or orange mixed in with brown or black hair, and a

A fly 'n rind is nothing more than a leadhead hair jig, like this $1/8$-ounce model, with Uncle Josh U-2 Twin Tail pork rind attached—simple, but deadly.

Three of the most productive lures for taking smallmouths that hold in deep water on the edges of flats: (top to bottom) Gay Blade, Silver Buddy, Spinrite.

trailer that is either dark (if the water is moderately stained) or chartreuse (if the water is downright muddy). The fly 'n rind is best fished in the early spring, when the water temperature is still in the 50s and the fish are lethargic.

•**Spinnerbaits** may work well for a long time after the spawn, when the fish are concentrated around shallow cover. Often this pattern lasts only a few days and then the fish return to deep water. If you try night fishing on the flats (see Chapter 24), be sure to try a spinnerbait, but fish it with heavier line than you would during the daytime. A heavy spinnerbait (at least a $^3/_8$-ounce) is recommended, so that you can reach the shoreline without moving your boat in too shallow. Try a willow-leaf blade here because this mimics the flash and profile of a small baitfish.

•**Crankbaits** work well at times, especially during the early stages of the spawn when the water temperature hovers between about 58 and 62 degrees. A $^1/_4$-ounce deep-diving lure such as the Bomber Model A or Bandit, in chartreuse, red or crayfish patterns work well at this time. If you don't get bit fairly soon after starting to fish a crankbait, switch over to a slower-moving, single-hooked lure, especially a grub. Be cautious when fishing crankbaits in big-fish territory—these lures are easily thrown by a tough-jawed lunker smallmouth!

•**Sinking Metal Baits** are ideal when you first begin fishing the flats, when those big smallies are staging in the channel. Fish them on a stiff baitcasting outfit with 10-pound line. Smallmouth ace Billy Westmorland once caught a 10-pounder on a tailspin! Slowly reeling the lure right over the bottom will make the tiny spinner blade flash and spin. The lure matches the thin profile and slow speed that fish are looking for at this time. Metal vibrating lures also work great when the water is in the 50-degree range. Cast these baits out and drop them on a tight line, using a medium-action baitcasting outfit and 10- to 12-pound line.

•**Topwaters** are tons of fun to fish in the post-spawn. The thrill of seeing a big smallmouth rise up and strike a minnow lure or big stickbait is unbelievable! The extreme upward visibility present in some of the best smallmouth waters makes these lures big-fish producers even when the bass are suspending in deep water. As already mentioned, fish them at the deep edges of the flats after the spawn. On a rainy or very dark day, try a noisier lure, especially a floating propeller.

The Swimming Technique

Smallmouth fishermen often speak of "swimming" a lure. This is such a simple technique that it is easily misunderstood by anglers wishing to make it more complicated than it need be! The most common lures employed with this technique are leadhead baits—grubs and jigs. Spinnerbaits can also be retrieved in this manner. The object is to keep the lure "swimming" or gliding just over the bottom. If you feel you are too shallow, stop reeling and let the lure touch bottom again, then resume reeling. Repeat this all the way back to the boat. A strike will often feel as though the lure has hung on a leaf. Immediately set the hook hard as soon as any resistance is felt!

Flats Are Fantastic!

Do not let the drab look of a smallmouth flat fool you! They are absolutely the best places you can fish in the springtime. Just use the approaches and lures mentioned and you will hang more big smallmouths than you ever dreamed possible!

23

Spawning Fish

W hen fishing during the spawning period, it is important to understand what smallmouths are looking for—and be prepared to release your catch. As the term states, spawning fish are doing just that—spawning. Their primary interest (and ours) is successful reproduction. They are seeking the most favorable water temperature and the best depths, bottom materials and current protection (if in a river or stream). And during this time, the fish consume little or no food. These points apply to spawning smallmouths no matter what type of water they inhabit, from small streams to large lakes and reservoirs.

Favorable Spawning Temperatures

Water temperatures most conducive to spawning vary only a few degrees across the smallmouth's range. Smallmouths everywhere start relating to their spawning areas when temperatures rise into the mid to upper 50s, and actual egg laying normally begins after the water reaches 60 degrees or higher. Since spawning is dependent on water temperature, it takes place from as early as April in the warmest waters, to as late as early July in the coldest.

Bottom and Depth Requirements

Smallmouths require nest-building sites composed of hard bottom material. Gravel (pea and pebble-sized rock) is preferred, but other hard materials such as coarse sand or slab rock is occa-

Spawning smallmouths are seldom looking for food. But with the right enticement, you can get them to strike. Expect to find some of the best fishing of the year during this period.

sionally substituted if gravel is unavailable.

Water depths for spawning can vary from as shallow as one foot to more than 10 feet, depending on the location of proper bottom substrates, clarity of the water, and even the size of the fish. In general, smallmouths spawn in shallower depths when water visibility is low, and the larger male bass spawn in slightly deeper water than smaller males (the males actually choose the sites).

In relatively shallow streams and rivers, the most common spawning depths are two to three-and-a-half feet. In lakes and deep rivers, beds are most commonly built in three to six feet of water. Because water clarity is largely the same throughout a body of water, the bass in a given lake or river often spawn at similar depths. For instance, the fish in lake "X" (which is quite clear) may spawn mostly at the five-foot depth, while those in lake "Y" (which is stained) mostly spawn at the three-foot depth.

Nest Protection

Another element that smallmouths strongly prefer to incorporate into their choice of nest sites is nearby cover or protection. Studies have shown that male fish definitely prefer to build their nest or bed next to (or under) some protection. They seek sunken logs, large rocks or the banks of the stream or lake, with logs being the most favored protection. This accords both the nest-guarding male and the newly hatched fry with a degree of protection. In rivers, large objects also act as current blocks, affording the fry with protection from current flows that would otherwise sweep them away. Even if stream or river smallmouths do not nest behind a rock or log, they still seek areas in the river where the current is slow—an eddy on the edge of a pool, or perhaps the slow water along a river bank.

In general, the larger river smallmouths occupy the best spawning sites. Recent studies have shown that choosing optimum bedding sites is a learned response among older (larger) male bass. Smaller fish, on the other hand, often cannot identify the best sites or sometimes are forced into more marginal areas by larger males. The sites chosen by larger males are generally more protected from predators and from strong currents and are in slightly deeper water than those used by the smaller bass.

Smallmouths in still water (lake and reservoir fish) do not

Whether you release spawning smallmouths or not is a personal decision, but by doing so, you will be helping to ensure the future of smallmouth angling in your favorite waters.

have currents to contend with, but do face the problem of threats from predators and cold water. Falling or slow-to-warm water temperatures are a serious threat to the reproductive success of smallmouths. In fact, falling water temperatures can significantly delay or interrupt reproduction, resulting in greatly increased mortality of eggs or fry. So the fish seek out spawning areas where the danger of cold water is minimized. For example, they may build their beds in areas where the bottom gradually slopes into deep water. This prevents upwellings of cold water from being pushed over the beds, which could happen if beds were built right next to deep (and cold) water drop-offs. Another way lake smallies try to overcome rapid temperature changes is by nesting along shorelines on the north side of the lake. A north shoreline receives the most sunlight during this time of year and is the most protected from prevailing winds. These areas warm the fastest and are least subject to rapid cooling.

These biological requirements or preferences of spawning smallmouths tell the angler several important things. First, finding where smallmouths spawn is essential for catching them during this period. Secondly, where and when they actually spawn is governed by the understandable biological factors. It is also important to understand that spawning smallmouths eat little during this period and are not interested in food. Rather, they strike out of a desire to protect their nest site from intrusion. Another key fact not understood by many anglers is that the larger spawning fish (the females) are very skittish while actually on the beds. The fish feel especially vulnerable in the shallow water and are easily spooked or put on their guard by anglers.

How To Fish Spawning Smallmouths

Fishing for spawning smallmouths can be understood best by discussing two fishing periods; the fish behave differently in each, so different techniques are needed. The first period is when the females are not actually on the beds, but are in the spawning area—a time that can be termed the *pre-bedding* period. The second period is when both the males and the females are physically on the beds—the *bedding* period.

Pre-Bedding Smallmouths

During the pre-bedding period, male smallmouths stay near the nest, but females remain nearby in deeper water. In lakes, pre-bedding female fish are often in water just a few feet deeper than the depth of the nests; probably nearby on the sloping bottom. For example, if the bed sites are three feet deep, the pre-bedding females will probably be in six to eight feet of water. If the nearby sloping bottom has some sort of structure, such as a small pile of rocks, two or three females may concentrate around it. In rivers, the females may only be several feet away from the next site. For example, if there is a pool adjacent to the beds, the fish will be lying on the edge of the pool closest to the nesting area.

Pre-bedding fish can often be caught more quickly than bedding fish, since they are in deeper water and aren't as skittish. Working crankbaits or jigs (or in shallow rivers, in-line spinners) is a good way to cover considerable amounts of water. If the fish seem particularly inactive, slow down your jigs to produce more strikes. And remember, a "concentration" is only two or three fish, so it pays to keep moving and cover plenty of water.

Bedding Smallmouths

When bedding, both sexes lie on or very near the nest and, if

A nest-guarding smallmouth looks out from its position beside a submerged log (lower left). Smallmouth nest sites are almost always located beside this type of cover if it is available.

in clear water, can sometimes actually be seen by the angler. Anglers must exercise plenty of caution when fishing during this time. If fishing from a watercraft, keep at least 35 feet away from the beds and keep noises to an absolute minimum (for instance, shut off outboard motors a considerable distance away).

Visually identifying individual beds is desirable in order to pinpoint target areas. Nests can be seen best during bright midday periods under calm water conditions using polarized sunglasses. Get as high as possible (either in a watercraft or on a bank) in order to spot nests at a distance. After spotting a distant nest from a higher vantage point, get as low as possible when actually approaching the bed to cast. If individual nests cannot be seen because of depth or lack of water clarity, work areas of *suspected* beds thoroughly.

Techniques For Bedding Smallmouths

To consistently catch bedding smallmouths your presentation must come close to the nest. If using subsurface lures, cast past the bed and slowly retrieve over the bed area. Remember, you want the lure to be in the area the fish is protecting for as long as possible. Lightweight jigs are good because they can be fished slowly. Each bedding site is worth several casts, but if no strike occurs after half a dozen casts, let the area rest and move on to another bed.

If using topwaters (often the best type of lure to use) drop them quietly right above the target. Surface lures should be left motionless for at least 10 seconds before giving them any action, and then the lure's action should be limited. The goal is to keep the lure over the bed for as long as possible. As with subsurface lures, each spot is worth several casts with a topwater lure. If there is no response from the fish, quietly move away and rest the area. Trying specific beds after letting them rest for at least 30 minutes will often elicit strikes from fish that previously ignored your offerings.

To catch shy, clear-water spawners, try fishing during low light conditions such as early morning or evenings. If waters are very clear, you may want to consider spotting the beds during

Great Lakes anglers often find spawning smallmouths in relatively deep water because of high water clarity. These waters warm more slowly than inland lakes and streams.

For best results, scout bedding areas during midday periods when the sun is high—then return in low light to cast for the fish.

bright midday hours, but fishing them later in the evening, or waiting until dawn of the following day.

Special Tips For Stream And River Angling

Fishing for spawning fish in small or shallow streams can sometimes require special sneak approaches in order to avoid spooking the fish. If the fish are spawning in shallow water along stream banks, the best way to approach them is to sneak along the bank. Get your silhouette as low as possible, both while approaching and when actually casting. Kneeling while casting is helpful, and sometimes you can use a strategically placed tree or bush on the bank as cover to approach unseen. Also be very careful not to stomp on the bank, which will send alarming vibrations into the water.

Fishing surface lures in moving water also requires a special technique. River currents often sweep surface lures away too fast. The way to keep a topwater over the fish for as long as possible is by getting into a position upstream of the fish. Locating upstream of the fish allows you to retrieve against the current, keeping the lure in almost the same spot. Sometimes, quietly working the lure in place for as long as 45 seconds will tease even difficult-to-catch fish into striking.

When fishing for smallmouths on beds, wear polarized glasses and keep a low profile. Fish on their nests are nervous and often refuse to strike after being spooked.

Lures For Catching Spawning Smallmouths

Lure choice depends on several factors, including: the depth and clarity of the water, the amount of wind, time of day and even the average size of the fish. For example, if windy conditions are causing considerable surface disturbance, surface baits cannot be used. Overall, three broad categories of lures are good for catching spawning smallmouths—topwater lures, shallow/medium runners, and "extra-slow" baits. Selections from these categories will cover just about all types of spawning situations encountered.

Topwater lures can be used whenever the water is fairly calm. Surface lures that aren't too noisy or too large are generally best for smallmouths, and the spawn period is no exception. Small propeller-equipped topwaters are good, as are lures that lightly gurgle or pop. Other types of good surface enticements include lures that make little or no noise and floating minnow imitations. Minnow imitations 3 to 4 inches long act as deadly topwater lures if fished properly. Let them lie motionless for at least 10 seconds, and then barely jiggle them in place without actually pulling them under the surface.

Good fly rod topwaters include cork-bodied poppers and

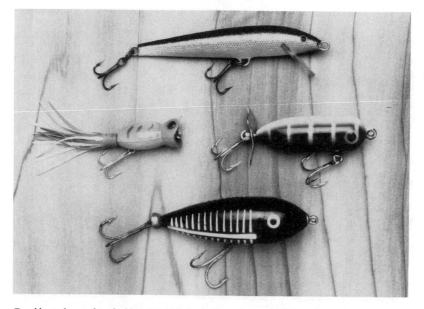

Good lures for catching bedding fish include shallow-running Rapala (top), and topwaters like the small Hula Popper and Tiny Torpedo (center) and Heddon Baby Zara (bottom).

small deer-hair bugs treated with floatation paste.

A second category of lures effective for catching spawning smallmouths includes shallow to medium runners. These are designed to be fished faster than topwater lures and are often especially effective when the females are not actually on the beds but nearby in slightly deeper water. These lures allow the angler to cover more water than the other two categories of baits do. This category of subsurface lures includes a variety of baits, including shallow- to medium-running crankbaits, thin-minnow plugs and in-line spinners. For fly fishing, various types of streamer patterns work well as shallow-running subsurface flies.

The last category of enticements to include with your spawn-period lures are the slow-retrieve lures. These baits are meant to be fished very slowly, and will elicit strikes when other baits will not. Lightweight jigs, especially those with heads no heavier than $^1/_{16}$-ounce, can be deadly. Tip the jigs with grub bodies or live minnows for best results. Other good slow-retrieve baits include slow-sinking, lightly weighted "reaper"-type plastic baits. Weight these by attaching a small amount of lead on the line ahead of the lure. Fly anglers can effectively use lightly weighted patterns such as

This 16-inch stream smallmouth was caught from its bedding area, a location in the eddy behind and to the right of the angler, then quickly released.

light-colored woolly buggers as slow retrieve lures. "Light is Right" is an appropriate slogan for spawn period tackle. Because the fish are generally shallow and skittish and the lures used are not particularly large, lighter lines and rods are best.

To Catch Or Not To Catch

The debate over catching bass on their beds has been around for many years. Some states close the season during this period; other states leave it open. Individual anglers also have mixed views on the issue. A couple of things are important for anglers to understand in order to make their own informed opinions on the matter. First, catching and releasing spawning smallmouths causes no higher mortality to the adult fish than catch-and-release fishing does any other time of year.

The other question to consider is this: What effect does catching spawning fish have on reproductive success? Studies have shown that catching and releasing spawning females has little negative effect on spawning success. Repeated catching of the nest-guarding males after the females have spawned and departed, however, can reduce spawning success. This is because each time

Complete Angler's Library

the male is removed from the nest, the eggs, or fry are exposed to predators. And, of course, actually killing a nest-guarding male means all the eggs or fry will certainly be lost.

These facts should tell us two things. First, catching the larger females during spawning or the males before actual egg laying will have little effect on the spawning success. Secondly, catching nest-guarding males in heavily-fished waters will diminish spawning success even if they are all released. In these waters, it is best to leave the males alone after the females have left the area.

Of course, to maintain good populations of valuable larger-sized smallmouths, it is essential to release most of them no matter what time of year they are caught.

24

Smallmouths At Night

Through the year's warmest months, smallmouth experts know that there are few better times to cast for their beloved brown bass than after the sun has set. Bronzebacks prefer a relatively cool environment, and as a result, they tend to haunt the cooler, deeper portions of lakes and impoundments during the summer.

The largest portion of the smallmouth's forage base, however, is located in shallower waters. In order to feed, summertime smallmouths often must move from deep-water, daytime holding areas into shallower waters. They make that move at night in order to take advantage of falling water temperatures, the security of a decreased light intensity and abundant forage. Crayfish, which are nocturnal, roam rocky areas in search of food, and smallmouths can feed most easily on these creatures by night. To bronzeback fanatics, losing a little sleep is a small price to pay for the chance to do battle with our gamest gamefish.

As discussed in other chapters, the most productive areas for smallmouths in an impoundment tend to be associated with the old river channel. The same is true when fishing at night. Prime target areas for nocturnal bronzeback forays include points dropping into the channel, channel banks and bluffs, submerged flats bordering the channel and underwater humps and islands surrounded by deep water. In essence, productive smallmouth areas should include a relatively shallow feeding ground with quick access to a nearby deep-water sanctuary.

Like most smallmouth fishing in large bodies of water, smallmouths taken at night are not far away from some deep-water sanctuary. They move shallower to feed at night.

Spinnerbaits: The Night Fisherman's Best Friend

At night, smallmouths can be taken with virtually any lure that is productive during the day. However, most bronzeback experts agree that a spinnerbait is the most versatile and usually the most productive lure for nighttime angling. These little gems can be buzzed on the surface, worked at depths where submarines fear to tread, and at every depth in between. Like a worm or a jig, spinnerbaits are superb drop baits, and like crankbaits, spinnerbaits are productive when utilized with a steady retrieve. These bladed marvels are virtually snagless too!

In most cases, a $^5/_8$-ounce, short-armed spinnerbait is your best night fishing tool because it is the most versatile. Most spinnerbaits tossed by bass anglers are long-armed baits, meaning simply that the upper blade arm extends out to the hook point, or even a bit farther. Short-armed spinnerbaits, those featuring a short upper blade arm that extends no farther than the lead head of the bait, are not produced by many tackle companies, and as a result they are quite often difficult to locate.

The shortened blade arm of this lure serves several functions. First, because the blade is positioned forward of the skirt, it allows the blade to pull upward when falling and remain unimpaired by the skirt, which also pulls upward.

Secondly, the shorter arm transmits a great deal of vibration through the line and rod so that it can be felt by the angler. This serves not only to help the fisherman keep in touch with his bait, but also as a strike indicator of sorts. When a smallmouth inhales the bait, the blade will stop turning, causing a cessation of the vibration, and thus signaling a strike.

Short-armed spinnerbaits can meet virtually every need of the angler fishing for smallmouths after dark. On steep banks, points, river ledges and drops into the old river channel, they can be used as drop baits. In this situation, fish the spinnerbait with a pump-and-drop retrieve just like you would fish a jig. Basically, all you are doing is jerking the bait off the bottom and then allowing it to flutter back down.

When falling, the blade on a short-armed spinnerbait will pull upward and spin, and they may be the only lures that exhibit any true action on the fall. Short-armed spinnerbaits are also effective when retrieved with a slow, steady retrieve over shallow flats, humps and long, sloping points.

These Stan Sloan Aggravator Spinnerbaits are designed primarily for the night fishing enthusiast. Both short-armed and long-armed models are represented here.

Smallmouths At Night

When dropping a short-armed spinnerbait, it is important to keep in contact with the bait at all times. If the lure is falling on a slack line, you will never feel a fish hit it. Sometimes, smallmouths will just inhale the bait, and your only signal of a strike is that the blade will stop turning or you might see your line jump a bit if you are using a black light.

Other times a smallmouth will smash a spinnerbait, and there is no way to miss that strike unless you have several feet of slack in your line. Another reason for maintaining a tight line is to keep the bait from rolling over. Some spinnerbaits tend to roll, and thus become ineffective, unless you keep just a bit of tension on them.

A long-armed spinnerbait is a useful tool in some nocturnal bassing situations, but they are a more specialized bait than their short-armed counterparts. Expert night fishermen use these baits in two specific situations. After dark, smallmouths will sometimes move into stump fields and relatively shallow brush. A long-armed spinnerbait works better here because they are more snag-resistant than short-armed baits.

When smallmouths are holding at depths of 20 feet or more, use heavy, 1-ounce long-armed spinnerbaits. Some anglers add additional weight to make a lure even heavier. When you are trying to work a spinnerbait at that depth, you need a heavy bait that will not only sink rapidly, but will also hold that depth upon retrieve. A lighter bait will tend to rise as it is retrieved, and you will spend all night fighting to keep the bait on the bottom. If you retrieve a 1-ounce bait slowly, as it should be fished, it will hug the bottom.

When smallmouths are found to be holding at these submarine depths, work parallel to the bank with these heavy spinnerbaits. Position the boat over the desired depth and make long casts ahead of the boat. This will keep the bait at the desired depth at all times. Use a slow, steady retrieve with frequent pauses to allow the bait to touch bottom. This is a simple technique, yet devastatingly effective for catching deep-water smallmouths.

Whereas short-armed baits may be utilized with virtually any baitcasting outfit, a long-armed spinnerbait designed for deep-water night fishing is a heavy piece of gear requiring beefy tackle. Casting these hefty chunks of lead and steel is akin to casting a brick, but long flipping rods will handle the job quite nicely. Heavy lines (fluorescent is best) in the 20- to 30-pound range are

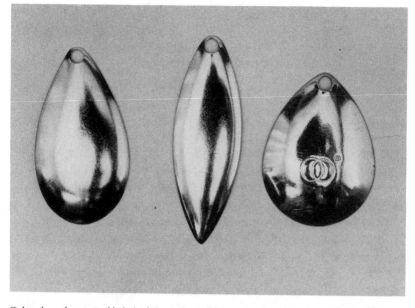

Colorado-style spinner blade (right) in sizes 4, 5 or 6 are preferred by night fishing experts because they displace more water than the Indiana (left) and willow leaf (center) styles.

required. Be sure to match lure weight with a properly adjusted casting reel to avoid backlashes.

Using The Right Blade

Most after-dark smallmouth specialists feel that a spinnerbait's blade is a key element in the lure's effectiveness. By providing vibration and water displacement, the swirling blade offers the smallmouth a sound to home in on. (In the absence of light, and even with a subdued light intensity, sound becomes the fish's primary mode of locating its quarry.)

Though they often disagree on other aspects of nocturnal smallmouth angling, most experts agree that a No.4, No.5 or No.6 Colorado blade is ideal for night fishing requirements. The basic rule of thumb here is that a smaller blade will fall more rapidly and will tend to rise more slowly with a steady retrieve, than will a larger blade. Willow leaf and Indiana blades, because of their narrower width, do not displace as much water as a Colorado style.

There is an overwhelming preference for single-bladed spinnerbaits among night anglers. A spinnerbait fitted with tandem blades tends to rise rapidly upon retrieve. Since smallmouths typically inhabit deep-water haunts, anglers strive to keep their lures at the level they expect to find fish. A lure that heads for the surface when retrieved is of little use in this game.

A general rule for selecting spinnerbait colors for night fishing states that the brighter the night the brighter the bait, and the darker the night the darker the bait.

Trailers of either pork or plastic are generally added to most spinnerbaits employed after the sun has dipped below the western horizon. Trailers serve three useful functions. The first and the most important function is to create a bulkier lure, which, since it casts a larger silhouette, is easier for the fish to see. Secondly, trailers are added to slow the rate of descent of these baits. And thirdly, they provide an increased action to the bait.

Without question, pork chunks are the most popular trailers added to spinnerbaits when night fishing.

When fishing in truly deep water, many anglers switch to a smaller pork frog as it will not impede the fall of the bait. To preserve the large size of a deep-water bait without decreasing its rate of descent, trim all of the fat from the pork chunks, leaving only the tough, top portion of the skin. Top nocturnal pork colors in-

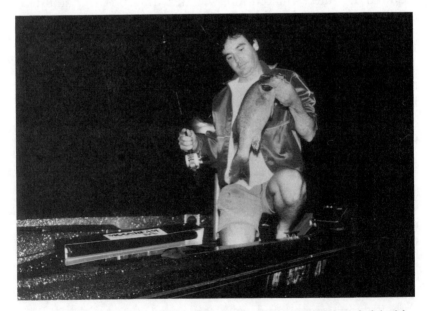

This 4-pound smallmouth was taken at night on a jig. Note the black light to the left of the angler. Wise after-dark bass fishermen never leave home without a good black light.

An Uncle Josh #11 Pork Frog is the best choice as a trailer for spinnerbaits or big jigs like this one. For use with a fly or smaller hair jig, choose the smaller, #101 pork frog.

clude purple, brown, black, chartreuse/black and red/black.

Most devout night fishermen are staunch proponents of black lights. In essence, black lights make fluorescent fishing lines glow, appearing like rope rather than thread. Even if you do not feel a strike, you should have no trouble seeing even the most subtle bite when night fishing under the purple glow of a good black light.

Smallmouths On The Drop

While spinnerbaits are probably tossed more often by late-night smallmouth anglers, some experts put more faith in traditional drop baits. But most anglers do not fish deep enough. Some smallmouths move fairly shallow, but the largest populations remain in relatively deep water.

A jig can be a far better drop bait than a spinnerbait, especially when you are fishing 20- to 30-foot depths, or even deeper in clear water. If you are fishing structure of a more horizontal nature like flats and gradually sloping points, then a spinnerbait is definitely a better choice. But for steep banks, river ledges and channel drops, a jig will work much better.

Experts prefer a jig/trailer combo, which is basically a hair jig,

Experienced anglers never hit the water at night without a black light, flashlights and pliers to straighten spinnerbaits that are mauled by angry smallmouths.

usually made of deer hair (a bucktail), that is then tipped with a pork trailer. Hair flies are more compact than a rubber jig, and many anglers believe they more closely represent the natural forage on which smallmouths most often feed.

A $^1/_4$-ounce fly can be a mainstay, but switch to a $^3/_8$- or even a $^1/_2$-ounce fly when fishing extremely deep structures.

A jig/trailer combo is fished like any other drop bait. Make the cast well beyond the intended structure, and then allow the fly to sink on a tight line until it hits bottom. When the fly touches down, rapidly raise the rod from about a 9 o'clock position to 10 or 11 o'clock, reel in the slack, and let the fly sink (again, on a tight line) until it hits bottom. Raise the fly just a few inches when fishing a very steep bank. On the other hand, you should raise the fly a foot or more when fishing a bank with a more gradual slope.

Maintaining a tight line is of the utmost importance when fishing a fly or a jig. The vast majority of strikes will occur while the lure is falling, and unless your line is tight you will never feel the fish hit. Bronzebacks typically do not strike a fly or a jig with the same fervor that they hit a spinnerbait. Instead, the strike will be a subtle tap, or the lure may simply stop falling. If you are employing the services of a black light (and you should be), then strikes are often detected by a slight jump of the line.

Unusual Alternatives

Though crankbaits and topwater plugs are not typical offerings for late-night smallmouths, they do play a role in this specialized game. A few anglers use a crankbait routinely when angling for nocturnal smallmouths. Throw a deep-diving crankbait over a structure after having fished it with spinnerbaits and jigs.

When smallmouths feed at night, they may move up onto a point or a bank, feed for a short while and move off and suspend in open water just off the deep-water end of the structure. Run a big crankbait off the point or bank so that it swims through the suspended fish.

The use of topwater plugs is rather limited in scope and truly productive for only a few weeks throughout the year, and then only in the clearest impoundments. In the immediate post-spawn period while the bronzebacks are still holding in shallow water, and then again for a few weeks in mid-autumn if you can locate fish holding in shallow cover, a noisy topwater plug will often draw explosive strikes.

Not only is night fishing the most productive way to take smallmouths throughout the summer months, but it is extraordinarily enjoyable as well. The peaceful serenity of a quiet, moonlit lake coupled with the chance to battle a bruiser smallmouth is enough to make night fishing the favorite pastime of many anglers. Wear your life jacket, use a good spotlight, drive safely and enjoy your night on the water!

25

Smallmouths On Rocks

Over the years you may have heard various anglers mention that the key to smallmouth bass fishing is "rock." This is somewhat misleading in that rocks by themselves play a very limited role in influencing smallmouth behavior.

It has been widely assumed that when we fish a new lake, we should concentrate our efforts on areas consisting of rock. The fact is, rock is not the only essential ingredient when it comes to smallmouth fishing, but it is an important part of the whole.

Smallmouth bass normally use some kind of structure to assist in ambushing food. In a great many instances, that structure happens to be rock, but in the absence of rock it could just as easily be stumps or even an old sunken tire. If stumps and rock are also located within a gravel or hard mud bottom, you have found a potential smallmouth "hotspot." The bottom line is, if rock is found in association with other structural features favorable to smallmouth bass, the bass are apt to be there.

Transition areas are also excellent places to look for smallmouth bass. These are places where one size of rock changes to another or where rock changes to gravel or mud. Transitions can be found by looking for these changes on the bank. These areas attract crayfish, and hence, smallmouths.

Like people, bass have very specific preferences. You may have a bank made up primarily of rock that stretches for a mile, but you can bet that the bass will be found in only one or two specific

Fishing for smallmouths on rocks may not be an end in itself. However, when you find rocks in association with the other features smallmouths favor, you may have struck the jackpot.

places on that bank. These places will be the transitions, the points that show a break or change in structure along the bank.

Fish, especially smallmouth bass, associate with different sizes of rock structure at different times of the year. For instance, during the spawn in the spring, smallmouth bass gravitate to gravel and hard mud bottoms. Gravel, and in some instances sand, is the ideal bottom for spawning. Smallmouths instinctively select this bottom because it provides a firm surface for the eggs. If smallmouths were to lay eggs on a silty bottom, the eggs would be buried and not survive. Smallmouth bass will rarely bed in brush, as largemouths do, but they will nest along a log, stump or large rock that serves as protection for one side of the nest.

Fishing during the spawn is quite easy and affords anglers the luxury of using a wide variety of baits without worrying about hanging up on every cast. Fishing these areas is not restricted to just the spawning season since the bass will use these transition points throughout the year both during the day and at night. To successfully fish these areas, concentrate your efforts on the areas in and around the actual point of transition. A crankbait or jig worked across the edge of the transition should produce action.

Transition zones hold fish because the area attracts baitfish, a primary food source for smallmouths. These transition zones are used as pathways to and from feeding by foraging fish. The angler who can successfully identify these areas can eliminate the vast majority of the shoreline.

Marking these specific areas on a topographical map of the lake will enable you to quickly zero in on the correct spot and save you many unnecessary casts on any follow-up trips.

Rock Formations Where Smallmouths Can Be Found

On impoundments where the dominant structure consists purely of rock, transitions still remain a focal point. For example, riprap along the face of a dam is an excellent area to search for smallmouths during the spring and summer months. Even though the entire area may appear to be identical, there will be one place that will hold more fish than others, such as the area where the riprap forms a corner or where rock has slipped and there is a break in the contour of the bank. The most productive time to fish riprap is in the spring and early summer.

Big smallmouths like this one frequent rocky areas to forage on baitfish and crayfish. Subtle differences in the face of a rock bottom will hold both prey and predator.

Smallmouths On Rocks

Transition zones can be represented by changes as subtle as bottom gravel that gives way to small rock, or solid rock that changes to broken rock. Concentrate your efforts in these zones.

Broken Rock Attracts Smallmouths

Gravel and riprap are not the only kinds of rock to which smallmouths gravitate. In fact, during the spawn, very large broken rocks with deep crevices are found in conjunction with feeding smallmouths. During the spring, baitfish and crayfish use the deep crevices as hiding places. While rock plays an important role to these bottom dwellers, it is also important that the rock be surrounded by a mud bottom and that some mud be in the crevices, as well. Without the mud, there will be no crayfish, and without the crayfish, there will be no smallmouths. Crayfish bury themselves in the mud during the coldest months of the year and emerge again when the water warms in the spring. It is when the crayfish become active that the smallmouths take up residence and feed.

During the spring any number of baits, ranging from grubs to crankbaits, will do a good job around rocks. It is important that you bump your bait against the rock for best success. In addition, work the bait along the edges of features discussed above, pulling the bait off the ledges.

Fishing on rock is really no different than fishing any other form of structure or cover. The same baits that produce small-mouths elsewhere will work on rock and the presentations are basically the same. The most practical tip in fishing rock is to fish from shallow to deep as opposed to pulling your bait parallel to the bank. Observe the way the rock lies and try to pull your bait as if you were pulling it down a set of stairs, and you will prevent many unnecessary hang-ups.

Generally speaking, rock does play a part in smallmouth bass fishing but not to the extent that one might expect, and certainly not in the absence of the other necessary features.

26

Suspended Smallmouths

L
et the truth be known, smallmouth fishing can be tough. There are days when cold fronts blow the fish out of the shallows and into deep water where they hug the bottom and barely move. But most smallmouth anglers feel the toughest smallmouth bassin' of all occurs when these fish are suspended. Many bass anglers say that trying to catch suspended fish is rarely productive. Sometimes they are right. But often, they are wrong. Fact: You can catch suspended smallmouth bass—if you understand the right approaches and are not afraid to try some new wrinkles. You may be astounded at just how productive many of these techniques can be!

Why Smallies Suspend

We think of "bass" generally as shallow-water fish. This applies to largemouth bass, but not to smallmouths! As we have seen elsewhere in this book, the smallmouth, especially in Southern reservoirs, is a fish of deep channel structure much of the year. It is also a fish that readily suspends, even when actively feeding. Here are some of the reasons that you will find telltale hooks on your graph showing suspended smallies.

Smallmouths suspend because of weather changes.. This may be especially true during the early spring and winter months. During these times, bronzebacks often move up shallow, especially during several days of stable weather. But when a cold front blows through, the fish often drop back into the first available deep

The thrill of finding and catching suspended smallmouths is hard to match. Suspended fish re-late to baitfish and temperature rather than any physical structure of the bottom.

Suspended Smallmouths

water and suspend. These fish are generally hard to catch in the spring, because they may have been on shallow flats before the front forced them deep. But late fall or winter fish often stay quite deep, and a cold front is less likely to knock them for a loop. If the fish were eight feet deep and the front moved them to 35 feet, fishing will be tough. But if the fish were holding at 28 feet before the front and are now holding at 35 feet, you can find actively feeding fish.

During hot weather, smallmouths suspend within a band of water at their preferred temperature range. A range of 60- to 70-degree water is ideal, but you may have to go as deep as 40 feet to find water this cool in a Southeastern highland reservoir in August. Look for smallies to suspend close to the thermocline during this period.

Smallmouths suspend to conserve metabolic energy. Leading reservoir smallmouth experts know that during extremely hot or cold weather, smallies often suspend close to deep points or river channel structure, areas where schools of baitfish will likely pass through. Instead of chasing the migrating baitfish, the bass suspend and wait for the fish to move through their territory.

Smallmouths suspend when their food source suspends. In reservoirs, when the chain of life is driven offshore by high or low temperatures and wandering schools of baitfish feed on drifting blooms of plankton, smallmouths will suspend close by. In reservoirs where oxygen is plentiful in deep water, and super-deep forage species such as alewives abound, smallmouths might suspend at depths of 70 feet or more!

Smallmouths suspend when they are inactive, but they usually remain close to feeding areas. These fish do not move around much. They will head to a bank to feed, but return to deep water and suspend quite close to the feeding area.

Using Your Depthfinder To Locate Suspended Smallmouths

A good depthfinder is an absolute necessity when you are seeking suspended smallmouths. On good units a fish will show up as a tell-tale "hook", or inverted "V", between the surface and the bottom, usually around 15 to 45 feet deep. Most often you will spot these hooks somewhere near schools of baitfish, which appear as thin-to-thick blips between the bottom and the surface on your flasher or as a cloud-like marking on your graph or liquid

Locating Suspended Smallmouth

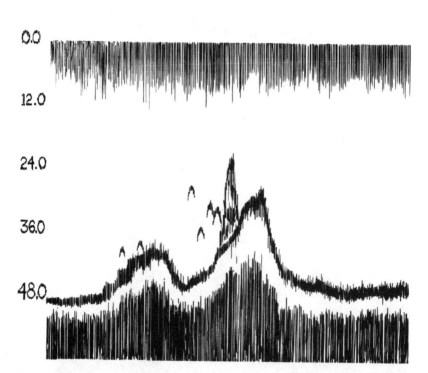

0.0

12.0

24.0

36.0

48.0

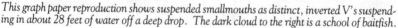

This graph paper reproduction shows suspended smallmouths as distinct, inverted V's suspending in about 28 feet of water off a deep drop. The dark cloud to the right is a school of baitfish.

crystal display. A good depthfinder will differentiate individual fish located within the baitfish school when the gain setting is turned up a bit.

At times, smallmouths may suspend when no baitfish are present on your depthfinder. This does not mean that these fish will not hit, but the bites may be slow in coming. The best electronic signal you can watch for is a ball of baitfish with larger fish close by. Baitfish ball up when threatened by predators. You can bet these fish are aggressively feeding.

The jury is out on whether suspending fish can "hear" or "feel" the pulses of today's high-powered sonar devices. Some anglers have reported cases where they were directly over suspended fish and could not catch a one until the depthfinder was turned off.

Marker buoys, which are very useful in locating and fishing

offshore structure such as submerged humps, may be of little use when you are concentrating on suspended fish. You would be hard pressed to find a buoy with enough cord to reach to the bottom on some of the better areas that smallies use when suspending!

Properly used, your depthfinder is your eye to the world beneath the surface, and nowhere is this more true than when fishing suspended smallmouths!

Vertical Jigging—An Important Technique

Vertical jigging, or fishing with a lure straight up and down when you are over suspended fish, is a method bass fishermen usually employ as a last resort. It works best when fish are suspended in deep water. Depending upon how deep the fish show up on your depthfinder, here are some good lures for this technique:

Jigging spoons from $^3/_4$ to 1 ounce are a good choice. These are plain metal spoons with a single treble hook on the end. Fish them on a wire cross lock snap or a snap swivel (these lures can really twist your line, so using a swivel is a good idea). Use a 6-foot baitcasting rod with a stiff action and 10- to 12-pound line. Lower the lure to the fish zone, or simply make a long cast and let the

Sinking metal lures can be used to vertically jig for smallmouths. Hogeye's Blade Runner is particularly effective for both vertical jigging and countdown and retrieve methods.

Vibrating plugs are thin, lipless crankbaits designed to run with the nose at a steep, downward angle. Most are designed to sink, so they can be run at any depth.

spoon fall back on a tight line, pendulum-style. When the lure reaches the fish zone, engage the spool and pop the lure repeatedly with varying movements of the rodtip. Let it fall back each time on a tight line. Set the hook immediately when a strike is detected or if anything feels "heavy" on the line (bass often inhale a falling spoon).

Metal vibrating lures are great for vertical jigging. Again, use a snap on the bait. Lower the lure into the fish zone and draw the rodtip back quickly to make the lure vibrate and flutter. Then lower the rodtip at the same speed at which the lure falls. Bass usually inhale these lures as they are falling. This is an exceptionally good bait in cold water.

Lipless crankbaits are usually fished shallow for largemouths, but they may be vertically jigged for suspended smallies. Use baits with a metallic flash, such as chrome or gold in clear water. If you lose fish on this lure, try removing all but one of the hooks on the treble. Saltwater anglers use jigging lures almost exclusively with single hooks and they seldom lose fish on the strike.

When lowering your lure to where bass are suspended, it is easy to drop it too deep or too shallow. "Counting down" to estimate lure depth is not always successful because different lures fall at different rates. Baitcasting reels are available with built-in line counters that measure how much line is pulled from the reel. They are an excellent tool. Another option is an inexpensive clip-on line counter. You can find one in almost any mail-order tackle outlet. As a last resort you can simply pull line from the reel in two-foot increments and count it out. Once you hook a fish you can mark the line with a red felt-tip marker.

You can vertical jig for smallmouths almost anywhere they suspend. This method works extremely well when fish are suspended close to deep offshore structures such as humps. When fish are in the 30-foot zone, for example, it is difficult to keep most lures in the fish zone for very long because as you retrieve them they will start to swim upward toward the boat. Vertically jigging, on the other hand, allows you to keep your lure in the fish zone as long as you desire.

Trolling For Suspended Smallmouths

One of the most exciting developments in the world of smallmouth fishing in recent years is the employment of downriggers and other deep-trolling equipment to catch deep-water smallies. For anglers in the Great Lakes area, trolling with downriggers is nothing new, but many southern fishermen had never seen a downrigger before the game and fish agencies of various states began stocking landlocked striped bass in deep reservoirs. Interested anglers soon began searching for ways to catch these deep nomadic fighters and for many, downrigging equipment proved to be the answer. Savvy anglers quickly learned that downriggers could also be used to pluck smallies from deep water. In fact, the method is so successful that the next world record smallmouth is likely to be taken by someone trolling with downriggers!

Fishermen who downrig for smallmouths in the Southeast begin using downriggers in the late spring, when the surface temperature reaches approximately 82 degrees and a thermocline begins to develop. At this time, big smallmouths often hang at the edges of flats, very close to deep channel structure, but usually not much deeper than 20 feet.

You can use a combination of downriggers and flatlines (lures simply fished behind the boat without the use of any device to make them run deeper) at this time. Try lightweight "flutter" spoons, baits Great Lakes salmon fishermen know well. These

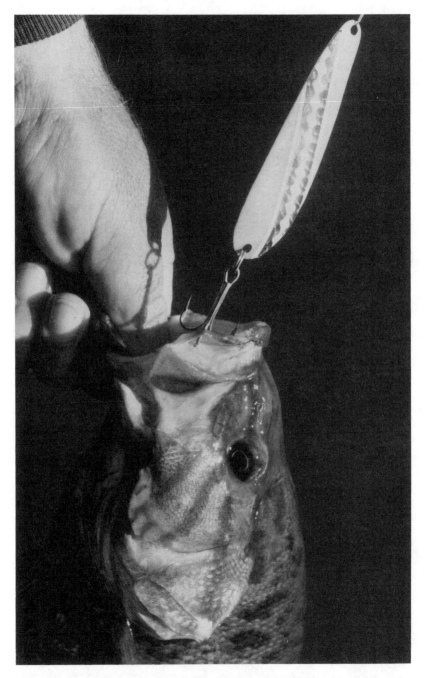

Flutter or trolling spoons are thin pieces of metal that require a weight or downrigger to take them to the desired depth. They do not drop when trolled slowly.

Suspended Smallmouths

lures are virtually weightless, and usually come with single hooks and a bright tape strip added for flash and color. They are designed to be fished behind downriggers. You will also need cannonballs, releases and other equipment. If you have a buddy who fishes the Great Lakes regularly with downriggers, pump him for information. He should be able to help you set up correctly.

Flatline trolling can be highly productive when smallmouths are suspended within 20 feet of the surface. Lures well-suited to flatlining are floating minnow lures, small spoons and crankbaits. In the winter months, small spoons are ideal when fished on a long line.

Deep-diving crankbaits can sometimes be used to catch suspended smallies, but we have our best luck when trolling these lures by rooting them along on slick gravel banks. Bass are attracted to the erratic, crayfish-like motion produced by bumping bottom with these plugs.

The successful smallmouth troller knows that a big bass boat with a V-6 engine can be more of a headache than a help. Big outboards are not designed for trolling and often foul their plugs when run at slow speeds for long periods of time. The best trolling boat is one with a smaller engine (25 to 70 hp work fine). A trolling plate will help to slow the boat down greatly, which is especially helpful when deep-trolling in hot weather for suspended smallies. Lightweight flutter spoons have their best action at these very slow speeds.

Deep trolling is new to many anglers. It requires some outlay for equipment if you wish to do it right. A downrigger can be tremendous on a deep, clear lake, but may cause only headaches on a flatland reservoir with lots of standing timber or deep cover. Your boat may need several rod holders. The best trolling rods are long, with straight handles that enable you to stick them in rod holders.

Live Bait Also Takes Suspended Smallmouths

One of the deadliest and most exciting ways to catch suspended smallies is with live bait, especially large creek minnows, or chubs. Big smallmouths attack these minnows with a vengeance and peel off yards of line when they make their initial run.

First, you need bait. It may not always be available at local outlets and you may have to catch your own. But the extra effort is well worth the trouble if you can capture the right critters.

This angler has nailed a smallmouth suspending in 25 feet of water in a "hollow" between two points. Finding fish with electronics, then getting them to strike, takes persistence.

A standard minnow trap will work fairly well, but it's a slow process. You may have to bait the trap with bread or crackers and leave it overnight. The preferred method is to use a cast net. One accurate toss into a creek may bring you several dozen of the best minnows you ever laid eyes on. Five- or six-inch stone rollers or red-tail chubs are perfect. Keep the minnows cool and well-aerated. A great minnow tank can be made from an old ice chest and an aerator pump powered by a 12-volt battery. With this tank, you can keep bait alive and healthy for weeks.

For a good baitfishing rig, start out with an $8^{1}/_{2}$-foot downrigging rod. This rod has a soft action that will whip a big fish quickly. Use a baitcasting reel with a large capacity spool and a clicker feature. Load backing halfway up the spool (20-pound mono works fine) and then load the remainder with 12-pound line.

To the end of the line, add a $^{1}/_{8}$- to $^{1}/_{4}$-ounce sliding egg sinker (size depends on the wind strength and depth of fish). Below this add a small red bead and below that a small split shot 18 inches above a 2/0 to 5/0 live bait hook (size depends on minnow size). Use a large enough hook with the bigger bait, but not so large that it overrides the natural swimming motion of the minnow.

Suspended Smallmouths

Live Bait Rig For Suspended Smallmouths

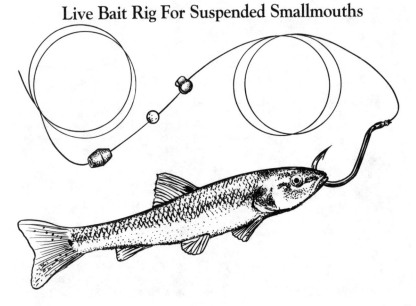

A good live bait rig for suspended fish includes a ¹/₈ ounce sliding egg sinker, red bead and small split shot 18 inches above a 2/0 to 5/0 (depending on size of bait) Kamagatsu bait hook.

The best time to try this method is during the winter months. Start on a deep point. After making a brief survey of the area with your depthfinder, see what depth the baitfish or gamefish are using. You want your minnow to be right at, or slightly above, this depth. Avoid fishing below the bass.

Say, for example, you want to drift your bait 30 feet deep. Pull out 30 two-foot sections of line slowly as you drift with the wind or your trolling motor. The added line will compensate for boat speed or wind velocity. You will find this an accurate method of gauging how deep your bait is running. If the wind is really blowing hard you may have to compensate by pulling out a few more feet of line.

Slow troll the bait with the electric motor on the slowest possible speed to maintain forward motion and keep the boat under control. On some 24-volt trolling motors, you may have to switch over to 12 volts to slow down the bait sufficiently.

If the fish are using the 30-foot zone, you will want to follow this depth contour all the way around the point. Be patient and make several drifts if you feel certain the fish are all there. If you do not get a bite after a reasonable amount of time, try moving shallower or deeper in five-foot increments until a fish nails the bait. When you get a strike, set the hook immediately. Do not let the bass run or it will swallow the hook and you will end up killing the fish. Set the hook immediately upon detecting the strike and you will usually hook the fish in the lip, making a quick release possible without injury to the bass.

Another good spot for drifting bait is in the hollow formed between two points. These deep V-shaped areas often load up with smallmouths, especially during the winter when they frequently suspend 20 feet deep. Dragging minnows right down the middle of these hollows, some of which may be 100 feet deep, can prove very rewarding.

Do not be afraid to venture out into open water when drifting bait. At times, big smallmouths seem to relate very loosely to structure such as points. The point might be three long casts from where the bass are suspending. Schools of big smallmouths will often move well off these points and suspend in deep water, sometimes for days at a time, before returning closer to the bank.

Big Surprises

Once you really get into fishing for suspended smallies, you will begin to learn more about this great gamefish than most fishermen will ever understand. Rather than being a slave to shallow water and cover, the smallmouth is perfectly at home hanging suspended in water 20, 40, even 60 feet deep or more in many bodies of water. The thrill of finding and catching a trophy smallmouth in a situation like this cannot be described. Neither can the thrill of letting one go.

27

Offshore Structure

What do you think of when you think of bass fishing? If you are like most bassers, you daydream of a shallow, coffee-colored lake peppered with lily pads and stumps—the kind of place your old Uncle Ezra would fish in his ancient wooden boat. Yessir, it sends a tingle up your spine to visualize that big topwater plug swishing through the air and landing with a KER-PLOP next to a mossy cypress stump. You can sense the anticipation as you twitch the lure one, two, three times, and then—KA-BOOSHHHH!!! The strike of a lifetime!

How different daydreams can be from reality—if you are a savvy smallmouth fisherman, that is! The fact is, the smallmouth bass is seldom a fish of shallow-water haunts, and it does not care much about cover—certainly not the way its cousin the largemouth does! While a bigmouth bass is perfectly at home wallowed down next to a stump or lurking under a strand of lilies, smallmouths are more attuned to deep water, ledges, humps and drop-offs—places far, far from the nearest shoreline!

There are bass fishermen...then there are *smallmouth* bass fishermen! The best smallmouth anglers, those who have proven themselves by boating giant bronzebacks, know that pounding the banks is seldom the route to glory. These anglers know that fishing *offshore*—sometimes clear out in the middle of the lake—can yield startling results! For NAFC members, mastering offshore structure can be the key to big smallmouths.

Many bass fishermen are reluctant to turn their attention away from the shoreline, but once you do catch smallmouths on offshore structure, you may never want to go back to shore.

Offshore Structure

Hammered To Death

There are two tremendous reasons that you need to turn around and head away from the shoreline in today's world of bass fishing. One: All bass—largemouths included—are much more highly pressured these days. There are a lot of good fishermen out there, and most of them are fishing shallow water. It is easy to see why. Fishermen enjoy casting to an object, be it a brush pile, stump or rock. Indeed, we are taught early on that casting accuracy is the mark of a good bass fisherman. The problem these days is, with so many people pounding the banks, the fish are literally hammered to death in many waters. Most of the bass living in shallow water may have already been caught. Reason two: You will not catch many smallmouths in shallow water. Smallmouths, by their nature, are deep-water fish. Most of the year they prefer depths of 15, 25, or even 35 feet. The largemouth, by contrast, favors the shallows.

So, if you are fishing up shallow and hope to catch a big smallmouth, for all but a few weeks of the year you are kidding yourself. You may not even catch any largemouths in waters heavily trafficked by anglers. The smallmouths are lurking out there over your shoulder...on the points and ridges and humps halfway across the lake!

Deep River

Virtually all the best smallmouth bass guides believe that the biggest smallmouths are not going to be close to the shoreline. Most of the true behemoths, they say, relate to deep river or creek channels in reservoirs, or offshore humps or reefs in lakes.

Those big, offshore fish are almost a different kind of smallmouth. But bear in mind that it is tough out there in deep water. Most fishermen will not put up with it. Here is how you can succeed and land one of those big fish.

Any decent topo map of a reservoir or contour map of a natural lake will clearly show old channels, offshore reefs, humps and breaklines that fall to deep water. In a big reservoir like Dale Hollow in Tennessee or Cumberland in Kentucky, you would be hard-pressed to fish all the best channel structure even if given a lifetime in which to do it! It might be a slightly more reasonable task in a smaller natural lake. Rather than try the impossible task of starting out blind in your search for a trophy smallmouth, think of the deep drops as a vital ingredient in a successful mixture—like the chocolate in a chocolate cake. But you still need other ingredients to make a successful recipe!

Look on your map and note the places where the river channel swings close to a bank, creating a bluff, or where an offshore reef takes a steep drop. Bluffs, or steep drops are probably the one type of structure that receives considerable fishing pressure. But smallmouth experts agree that these steep drops, while good structure for some gamefish, are not really that great for big smallmouths. You can catch smallmouths on steep drops and on bluffs. But day in and day out, anglers who catch lunker smallmouths have considerably more luck in fishing other types of offshore structure, particularly when it is far from the nearest shoreline.

Humps Are Heaven

By far the most desirable offshore structure for big smallmouths is the area where the deep channel or breakline swings in close to a submerged hump. You may know these as high spots, mounds, submerged islands—all the same basic structure. When you find a good hump, you are really onto something.

You can spot humps easily on a lake map, and sometimes, in reservoirs, you can see their tops during a winter drawdown. The ones whose bald tops stick out of the lake in January and February are the ones that will get noticed and fished in the spring and summer when they are under six to 10 feet of water. You have a chance of catching a big fish off one of these, but because they are revealed during the winter drawdown, they invariably get fished more throughout the year. Look for deeper humps, ones that will not show during low-water periods. You may be the only angler on the lake fishing there.

Experience has shown that you cannot rely on even the best map to tell you everything that is going on beneath the surface. When in doubt, spend some time and gasoline running the lake with your depthfinder on to spot any offshore structure.

The best smallmouth humps are within one or two casts of deep water. Experts who fish reservoirs agree that big smallies hold in the channel itself for long periods, then move up onto the hump when they get hungry. A good hump can also be a tremendous spawning area for a giant smallmouth. Why should a fish liv-

Vibrating plugs are a good choice for working the contours of offshore structure. The baits can be run a few feet, below the surface, at mid-depths or along bottom in deep water.

ing its life in the river channel make a trek of a mile or two to the nearest bank to spawn when it can crawl up on top of a 12-foot hump to lay its eggs?

Humps are often long and rather tapered at both ends. One side usually has an abrupt drop into deep water (indeed, the river channel may butt against the hump) while the other may have a more gradual slope. The best smallmouth humps usually have a little "gravy" on them—a couple of big stumps, a little patch of weeds or a few big rocks.

When you locate a good hump, your approach will be greatly determined by the time of year you are fishing. In the spring, smallies are likely to be right on top of the structure, where the sun can penetrate to the maximum to incubate their eggs. On super-hot summer days you might catch some smallmouths on top of the hump at night, but the real bruisers are likely to be holding in the deepest sectors of the structure. In the fall, you might have good luck at the submerged points formed by the ends of the humps. Then again in the winter, the fish could be just about anywhere on the structure, but usually close to deep water.

Humps are deceptive because they look very easy to fish. That is because most anglers consider only the top of the hump when they choose their lures and tackle. True, you can cast a light-weight grub or a deep-diving crankbait and successfully hit the top of a 12-foot hump. But when you wish to probe the 20-, 30-, 35-foot zones—it is a different story. Here, you should consider your tackle first and foremost. If you do manage to get a bite by one of those big ol' fish, what will it take to pound home the hook onto its bony jaw in 20 to 30 feet of water? A light spinning rod and 6-pound line might be enough to stick one of these monsters lurking on a shallow flat, but not this deep. Expert deep-water anglers gear up seriously when preparing to do battle with big smallmouths! A 7-foot, heavy-action spinning rod is one option. Some experts rely on a stout baitcasting outfit, of at least medium-heavy action. Choose a rod with enough backbone to drive the hook point home in considerable depths.

The best lures for fishing deep on submerged humps include weedless jigs, the new "spider" jigs, heavy spinnerbaits, tailspins and jigging spoons. Jigs are the top choice for several reasons. They sink quickly, are easy to work in deep water and they have single hooks, making it more difficult for a big smallie to throw the bait. They also have a realistic action both day and night—a dark-colored jig hopping across the deep reaches of a hump simulates the look and sound of a live crayfish scurrying across the bottom.

When you fish a jig, be sure to use some pork rind as a trailer. Real pork will add mass, making the lure more visible in dark, deep water, and feel highly realistic when a bass inhales the bait. For fishing deep, try a heavy hair or rubber-legged jig ($^3/_8$-ounce to $^5/_8$-ounce sizes are best) tipped with a piece of pork frog. Trim the meat off the head of the frog with a fillet knife or razor blade. This will preserve the overall mass of the trailer but enable the jig to fall more quickly. Less meat on the trailer's head where it meets the hook will improve your chances of a solid hookset.

Choose a jig with a solid hook, and avoid the thin wire hooks you will use in the spring of the year when fishing with small hair jigs and leadhead grubs. A big smallmouth will straighten these out on heavy line! There is one drawback with most heavy jig hooks. They usually have a barb so large it inhibits penetration. You may have to file down the barb with a rasp or grinder. Even the slightest barb is enough to hold the hook solid. You can barely see the barbs on a porcupine's quills with the naked eye, yet they will hold fast, as some unfortunate outdoorsmen can attest.

Spider jigs are excellent baits for fishing deep humps. These lures combine the weight and bottom-crawling capabilities of a standard jig with the soft feel of a plastic worm. They have a circular skirt that fits around the collar of the leadhead made of soft plastic. Should a big smallmouth grab the lure, it will rarely let go because its mouth closes around squishy plastic, not hard metal. With these lures, you can virtually lead a smallmouth around the boat before setting the hook! These lures usually come with large barbs, so think about trimming it a bit when fishing in water deeper than 20 feet. Scoot and hop these sensational lures at various depths on the hump in the spring and again at night in hot weather, and hang on tight!

Deep-diving crankbaits are often too large for smallmouths. Tournament anglers favor these lures for their abilities to catch big largemouths in deep water. Even the deepest divers, however, attain depths of only 20 feet or less, which may be too shallow for big smallmouths. If you are going to try these lures, stick with the smallest ones you can find. Try these diving lures in the fall, especially on the top and ends of the offshore hump.

Tailspins like this Little George can be vertically jigged along drops, or cast and retrieved. You can cover a lot of structure fast with one of these little lures.

A spinnerbait is usually thought of as a shallow bass lure, but you can fish it effectively in deep water. Use a very heavy one, up to 1 ounce, with a short arm and single blade. Attach a trimmed pork frog to the hook. The heavy weight of the lure will let you make a long cast with 14-pound line (minimum). The short arm will cause the lure to helicopter on its way down. Many strikes occur as the bait is falling. This lure can be effectively fished over a deep hump both day and night.

Jigging spoons and tailspins are among the fastest artificials with which you can fish on deep humps. Use a medium-action baitcasting rod with 10- to 14-pound line. Attach a wire cross-locking snap to most metal lures or they will cut your line after a few casts. The jigging spoon is a simple lure that can be fished effectively in 30 feet of water. Cast the lure to your target zone and let it fall on a tight line with the rod at 10 o'clock. When it hits bottom, immediately lower the rodtip and snap it back about a foot, then keep the rod as high as the jig falls again. If you keep hanging up, trim one or two of the hooks off the treble. You can add a spinnerbait skirt of a plastic grub to the hook as a trailer to make the lure more visible in deep water. You can also get right

Coming up! A smallmouth angler hauls on a bass that struck a lure worked along the deep side of an offshore reef. These fish often head straight for the surface and beyond when first hooked.

over the hump and vertical jig the lure by popping it off the bottom repeatedly, a highly effective plan in cold water.

To help you stay on a deep hump, get a set of marker buoys and delineate the four sides of the structure. The drawback of this, of course, is that other anglers may see you fishing the hump and claim it as their own as soon as you leave. The beauty of humps is that not every fisherman knows where they are. Keep a low profile when you find a good one!

How To Fish Deep Points

Another sensational structure is the deep point. Unlike humps, points are an extension of the shoreline. They provide an important interface between the terrestrial world and the water itself. Points are particularly important in deep waters with a shad forage base as big schools of baitfish will move from one point to another following drifting plankton blooms. That is why smallmouths station themselves close to points. Bass use these structures as holding areas. By literally sitting and waiting for a school of bait to pass by, they can conserve their metabolic energy—especially important in very hot or very cold water.

A deep point will often slope off rather gradually into the lake and then drop off suddenly into deeper waters. If you are interested in fishing places that are still untouched in your quest for a big smallmouth, deep points should be on your list. You may see other boats fishing these areas, but if you pay attention, you will note that most fishermen are casting into the shallow areas of the point, often with fast-moving crankbaits. This technique is okay for largemouths and maybe a keeper-sized smallmouth or two, but will seldom produce the lunker smallmouth you are after. The key is to forget any water shallower than about 15 feet and concentrate your casts on the deeper sides and ends of the point. Again, only a few lures will work well in this situation. On a windless day a $1/4$-ounce leadhead grub in a chartreuse or smoke color is an excellent producer.

A grub is a very realistic, subtle lure that is capable of fooling a giant smallmouth. It is an excellent choice in the late fall or winter when the water is 55 degrees or colder. Tight-line the grub around various areas of the point by casting, keeping the rod at 10 o'clock as the lure falls. Watch your line like a hawk. While many anglers avoid using fluorescent lines except when night fishing with black lights, these lines are excellent for fishing with grubs because they are easier to see than clear or green lines against a background of rocks and wooded hillsides. If you see the line pause, twitch or move sideways even the slightest bit, rear back and set the hook hard! Fish the grub on a 6- or 7- foot heavy-action spinning rod with 8-pound line in this situation, and keep your reel well-adjusted so that the drag slips slightly when you pop the hook. In cold water, try a 3- or 4-inch grub with a twist tail.

Often the wind comes up and makes it difficult to feel the grub as it drops because your line had a big bow or "bag" in it. Line-watching is critical when fishing with grubs, so you might as well forget about using them on windy days. Go instead to a heavier lure that sinks fast and resembles preferred forage. Vibrating jigging lures are favorites among many smallmouth anglers. These thin metal vibrating baits sink very quickly and are some of the few lures you can fish easily in 40 to 50 feet of water, which you may have to contend with at the end of a deep point! Many anglers find it difficult to fish this lure correctly. Here is how the experts do it. First, make a long cast using a baitcasting rod with medium action and 10- to 12-pound line. Let the lure fall to the

Great Lakes smallmouth veterans know the benefits of fishing offshore structure. Some scattered reefs on these big waters almost never see a fishing lure—and the smallmouths are huge.

bottom with the rod held at 10 o'clock. Many strikes occur on the fall. If you do not feel a solid thump indicating a fish, draw the rod-tip back sharply from one to two feet and quickly reel while lowering the rod back to 10 o'clock. This will cause the lure to scoot off the bottom like an alarmed crayfish. Repeat the action until cast is complete. Smallmouths really belt these lures! In the late fall and winter, they are some you *have* to have in your tackle box.

Do not neglect the side of deep points. Usually the point will have one side that slopes off more sharply than the other. When you are night fishing in the heat of summer, attack the deeper water first, using heavy spider jigs or the other lures mentioned for use when fishing a deep hump. In the early spring, try the shallower side—big females may move onto this zone early when spawning. But again, do not fish much shallower than 15 feet.

Highway To Heaven

Old roadbeds on the bottoms of reservoirs are regarded highly by most bass fishermen, but again, the largemouth angler tends to fish the shallow areas and leave the deeper parts alone. This means you, the dedicated smallmouth angler, can reap a big reward if you cover this structure patiently with the right approach and the proper selection of lures.

Big smallies will spawn on submerged roadbeds in the spring. When the water hovers around 60 degrees, move out to the 12- to 15-foot zone as you follow the roadbed out into the lake with your depthfinder. A deep-diving crankbait will often pay off, but a surer bet here would be a $1/4$-ounce grub. Fancast to cover both the top and sides of the structure. This will enable you to attract both smallmouths that have already moved up on the roadbed, and bass that are staging on the deeper sides. A little bit of cover is usually present on the sides of a roadbed—brush, stumps, broken rock. This can prove attractive to staging fish.

In the summer, particularly at night, you can reap big rewards by fishing the roadbed in deeper water. Stay on the structure with your depthfinder until you reach the 20- to 30-foot zone, maybe even deeper in a highland reservoir. Use the spider jigs and heavy spinnerbaits previously mentioned and have a ball!

Rock Piles Hold Many, Many Smallmouths!

Rock piles are often man-made in reservoirs, and a good place to find them is near some other man-made structure, such as road-beds, house foundations, etc. In natural lakes they may be found in random locations, so once you find one, etch the spot in your memory. Rock piles in reservoirs are usually a lot smaller than humps, which are natural structures, and hence a lot harder to locate. They may not even appear on most topo maps. If you find a rock pile, you may have located a gold mine. Fish rock piles with crankbaits and jig-type lures. A shallow rock pile is often marked by a navigational warning sign, but these are the ones that will be most heavily fished.

The Best Place In The Lake

When most anglers think of a great fishing spot, they think of a stumpy bank or a weedbed. But when you turn your head around and look the other way, you will realize that your best shot at a giant smallmouth may well be on deep, offshore structure. Take time to do your homework—it will pay off big.

=28=

Smallmouths Under
The Ice

The notion that bass hibernate during the winter has been around for a long time. More than a century ago, in the *Book Of The Black Bass*, Dr. James Henshall cited observations of smallmouth bass in various states of winter dormancy in both upstate New York and West Virginia. Ninety years later, divers in Lake Erie reported aggregations of winter smallmouths numbering in the hundreds, all lying belly to bottom, covered by a layer of slime and apparently unaware of happenings around them.

Despite such observations, it is exceedingly difficult to convince an angler with a limit of smallmouths lying on the ice that these fish are dormant in cold water.

Smallmouths may not be active and catchable at all times during the winter and might just as well be nonexistent once the surface is frozen in some bodies of water. But in many lakes they provide an excellent ice fishing opportunity, particularly at first and last ice.

"Chisel fish" is what one experienced New England ice fisherman calls smallmouths. If the ice is thin enough to make cutting a hole by hand a reasonable proposition, smallmouth fishing can be excellent. On the other hand, if there is enough ice to mandate a power auger, prospects are not as high.

Reading The Signposts To Find Smallmouths
Successful smallmouth ice fishermen in the United States

Smallmouth activity decreases under the ice cap of frozen lakes, but it does not cease. Bass are particularly active, and catchable, at first ice and just before spring thaw.

Smallmouths Under The Ice

have found a number of environmental predictors leading to good winter smallmouth catches.

Winter smallmouths tend to prefer offshore, hard-bottomed flats bordering drop-offs or radical changes in bottom consistency. However, the most reliable predictor of a smallmouth hotspot has to be an abundance of panfish—specifically, small yellow perch.

If a spot is hot for big, humpback yellows it is probably no great shakes for smallmouths, but if nearly every drop of a small tear-drop and grub catches a 4- or 5-inch perch, chances are good that smallmouths use the area too. So strong is this relationship that some anglers use the perch to locate smallmouths. Since yellows are far more numerous than bass and are among the most active fish under the ice, they are usually not difficult to locate.

By peppering a likely area with holes and jigging a tiny ice jig dressed with a grub for a few minutes in each hole, concentrations of small perch can usually be found pretty easily. An abundance of tiny perch will quickly send most ice fishermen off in search of a better area. But the experienced winter bass fisherman realizes that it may mean he is very close to a mother lode of smallmouths. By switching to larger baits once a solid bunch of yellows is located, and systematically checking the fringes of the perch area, he stands a good chance of loading up on big smallmouths.

Finding Smallmouths On Structure

Structure is another factor commonly cited by successful ice bassers. There seems to be a strong tendency for winter smallmouths to relate to offshore structures rather than shoreline connected drop-offs. Also notable is that productive areas usually exhibit a substantial, hard-bottomed flat of some type. Offshore humps, secondary rises off the end of extended points and slightly elevated, hard-bottomed protrusions from a silty lake basin are typical hotspots.

Gravel- or rubble-strewn bottoms are key. The huge boulders that many anglers envision as ideal smallmouth habitat are not particularly attractive during the winter. More subtle cover is likely to hold winter smallmouths. In reservoirs, a moderate amount of stumpage atop the hump is a definite plus. In natural lakes, low-growing, brittle vegetation is often found on the best winter smallmouth humps.

The ideal depth range for structure to top out in is less definite.

Live minnows can be suspended on a tip-up like the one lying on the ice. The tip-up flag signals the angler when a smallmouth has grabbed the bait.

In most artificial impoundments, 15- to 25-foot-deep flats seem ideal, but in natural lakes, depths from 10 to 40 feet have been productive. Smallmouths seem able to utilize a wide range of depths and will settle in the area with the best combination of bottom content, structural configuration and abundant forage.

Once a suitable location is found, you can start checking for smallmouth activity. Key spots are the crest, or shallowest reaching section of the structure, and the edge of the flat adjacent to the primary breakline. Within those areas, specific breaks such as stumps, patches of grass or sharp turns in the breakline will prove to be important.

Dropping your lure or bait in exactly the right location is a must because the fish do little roaming. Miss the right spot by more than a few feet and you may never know if smallmouths are present! It is not uncommon for a single hole to produce a half-dozen smallmouths, while holes a few yards away prove either fishless or produce only little yellow perch.

Thorough coverage of a potential area is of paramount importance and that usually means jigging. Plenty of smallmouths are caught on live bait fished beneath tip-ups, but unless your state allows more than a couple of lines, tip-ups simply will not let you cover enough water to effectively locate smallmouth hotspots.

Jigging Lures Best For Ice-On Smallmouths

The list of artificial lures that consistently catch smallmouths through the ice is not very long. The most productive by far are weighted jigging minnows. Any color will work but gold/black seems the predominant choice. Silver/black or silver/blue lures also work well.

Typically, this lure is fished by dropping it to the bottom and then imparting a fairly slow, long, jigging motion; pausing a few seconds at the top and the bottom of the lure's path. Some anglers like to jiggle the jigging minnow a little as they rest it, before dropping or lifting it again.

The jigging minnow has a reputation of being a "fish dropper." There are various methods used to increase the percentage of fish iced. Some remove the treble hook completely; others substitute a slightly larger one. Whether you modify the lure's hook arrangement or not, be sure to clean off the clear epoxy coating from the barbs of the end hooks and sharpen them to a razor point.

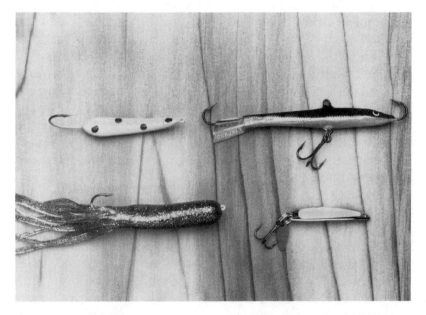

A jigging spoon (upper left) can be covered with a tube jig (lower left) to create an effective lure. The jigging Rapala (upper right) and Swedish Pimple are proven smallmouth baits.

The Cotton Cordell Gay Blade is an effective lure any time of year. When using it for jigging through the ice, turn the front hook set around or attach a treble for better hooking.

In recent years a handful of ice fishermen have been attracted by the success open-water winter anglers in the South have had with blade baits. Northern anglers have begun experimenting with similar lures for ice fishing. Like the jigging minnow, most blade baits hang in a horizontal attitude when fished vertically.

Drop the blade to the bottom, lift it a few inches, and hold it steady for 15 seconds. Reel it up a crank or two, hold it steady again, drop it halfway back to bottom, reel it up another crank, and stop it for a few seconds. Then drop it to the bottom and repeat the procedure. The sequence is down—up a hair—steady. Up two feet—steady—down two feet—steady—up three—steady—repeat. The more rhythmic you make it, the easier it will be to tell when a smallmouth has taken your lure.

Working Variations Of Jigging Spoons

Another category of artificial lures that consistently takes winter smallmouths is jigging spoons. Traditional ice fishing standards will work, but inch-long willow leaf spoons are often more effective. Most anglers dress the willow leaf's single hook with one or more grubs. A variation that seems particularly attractive to

A light, sensitive jigging rod and ultra-light spinning reel make an effective combination for taking smallmouths through the ice with artificial lures.

smallmouths is stretching a panfish-sized, transparent, metal-flake tube grub over a small willow leaf spoon. This version may also be "sweetened" with a maggot or grub.

Once you catch a smallmouth, settle in. They are often bunched tightly at this time of year. You might consider setting a tip-up or two within a couple feet of the hole that produces more than one fish. Expect the action to come in flurries of three or four fish, and then nothing. Leave the tip-up to tend that spot, and begin prospecting again with the jigging rod. Stay close! The fish may have changed location, but it is just as likely that they have temporarily turned off, perhaps as a reaction to the commotion involved in catching a few. In that case, they are likely to turn on again at the same location after an hour.

A final important factor in ice fishing for smallmouths is time of day. Once a prime smallmouth area has been identified, get there at daybreak. There seems to be an almost mystical relationship between big smallmouths and the crack of dawn—a relationship that is not diminished by the cover of ice.

=29=
Smallmouths
In The Weeds

Boulder-strewn ledges, clay flats, gravel-topped humps, stump fields, floating docks—anglers will cast a lure or bait to almost any type of structure in hopes of catching a smallmouth. Any type except weeds. Smallmouths and vegetation just do not go together—or do they?

Despite the smallmouth bass' well-known proclivity for rocky areas and gravel bottoms, anglers who either do not know any better or who purposely choose to ignore conventional thinking make some awfully impressive catches around weedbeds. In many lakes, smallmouth bass do indeed use vegetated areas. It pays to learn to recognize patterns that point to smallmouths in weeds and to develop presentations designed specifically for extracting smallies from their tangled haunts. It is likely to pay off even more often in the future.

Adapting To A Changing Environment
The number of waters in which smallmouth anglers must cope with vegetation is constantly expanding. With civilization and the passage of time, the fertility of water bodies increases and vegetation becomes ever more abundant. The typical gravel- and clay-bottomed smallmouth lake will eventually support some rooted vegetation.

The ability of a lake to support vegetation is a function of its fertility and a natural by-product of eutrophication—the natural

In many lakes and reservoirs, smallmouth bass frequent areas of scattered weeds for both food and cover. Knowing which weeds, and when to fish them, is the key to this overlooked bonanza.

Smallmouths In The Weeds

aging process of a lake. Despite mass media misinformation linking eutrophication exclusively to pollution, every body of water on the planet is undergoing this aging process, some faster than others. The effects of nearby civilization accelerate eutrophication, but it occurs even in the most remote wilderness. In many pristine lakes on the Laurentian Shield, cabbage-topped humps and shelves are now prime smallmouth areas, despite the fact that such areas were virtually nonexistent a generation ago.

As his quarry adapts to its environment, so the smallmouth angler must also adapt. Those who refuse to invest the time to learn and develop weed-fishing techniques will be forced to travel farther and farther from civilization to catch smallmouths. Even now, many superb smallmouth fisheries exist in lakes with substantial vegetation. In fact, some of the best lunker smallmouth fishing is found in such bodies of water since the increased fertility that fuels the weed growth also promotes increased growth rates for gamefish.

Types Of Vegetation Frequented By Smallmouths

Most techniques developed specifically for fishing in and around vegetation were conceived with largemouth bass in mind, but the smallmouth is a different breed and often indifferent to largemouth-based presentations. Not only that, but a good smallmouth weedbed—one that the smallies make regular and frequent use of—might be an area that largemouths use only in a pinch. The converse of that statement is also true. Weedbeds that shout largemouth to the angler—dense pads, coontail, milfoil matted heavily on the surface—do not make ideal smallmouth habitat.

The major difference in the way smallmouths and largemouths relate to vegetation is found in the fact that smallmouths have no great need for overhead cover. When they do enter areas where overhead cover is heavy, it is most often for some other reason. Perhaps their prey moved into the cover and they are following, or perhaps prime spawning conditions coexist with that overhead cover.

While a dense bed of surface-matted milfoil might be largemouth heaven, smallmouth bass prefer shorter varieties of vegetation like sand grass and dwarf cabbage, sparse-growing types like immature curly cabbage and "leafless" species like reeds or

Smallmouths in mesotrophic or natural lakes will use weedlines and flats with scattered sand grass as feeding areas. Offshore humps with weeds are prime smallmouth habitat in many lakes.

bullrushes or, in some riverine environments, eelgrass.

Grass And The Smallmouth Bass

Sand grass is a dominant feature of many northern smallmouth waters. Basically, any low-growing (usually less than a foot high), brittle, thin-stemmed plant that carpets the lake floor in hard-bottomed areas can be treated as sand grass. The problems it presents a smallmouth angler are primarily related to presentation. Many of the most productive smallmouth techniques involve bottom-bouncing or bottom-scraping. Sand grass interferes with any lure that normally contacts the bottom and often sends smallmouth fishermen looking for a spot that's easier to fish.

Since sand grass is brittle and thin-stemmed, it can be fished through or across with only minor modifications in presentation. Thinner line, stiffer rods and less delicate baits provide the answers to many problems. When a light jig being worked across the vegetation picks up a few strands, a sharp "pop" of the rodtip will usually suffice to clean the lure. With thinner and less elastic lines, a great deal of "snap" can be transferred to the lure. The same holds true for stiffer rods. Anglers who fish jigs in sand grass frequently use graphite rods rated for 10- to 15-pound test line coupled with fine-diameter, low-stretch, 6-pound test mono. The

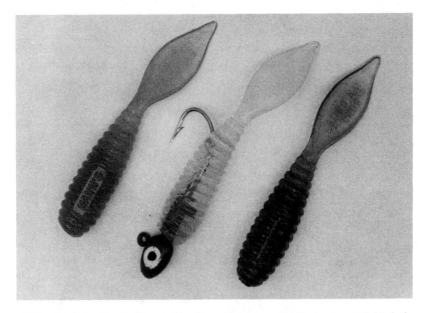

Paddletail jig bodies like this Mann's Sting Ray grub are more durable than long-tailed jig bodies. Use a bit of Super Glue to hold the body to the jig for ripping through weeds.

combination may mean having to learn to fight a fish all over again since all that stiffness and low stretch leave very little margin for error. The technique will, however, give plenty of practice in fighting fish by putting you into effective contact with smallmouths that are being ignored by many anglers.

In conjunction with the light line/stiff rod approach, lightweight, tough jigs are a must. A heavy jig will penetrate too deeply into the grassbed to break free while the typical finesse bait is simply not hardy enough. Live bait on a jig head is too fragile. The sharp, sudden movements needed to keep the jig free of weeds will also rip it free of the minnow or crawler. Soft, plastic trailers usually slide down off the jig's collar, and many popular twist-tailed lures are just too delicate. Try either a flat-tail or offset-boot-type-tail plastic grub. The tougher body and the lack of a thin tail section allow you to subject these jig bodies to abuse that would ruin more delicate grubs. Use Super Glue or a similar product to fix the grub to the collar of the jig head, and you will eliminate the problem of having the lure slide off the collar when you pop it free of the weeds. Then get down to jerking some bass.

Crankbaits also can be productive in low-growing grass if you carefully select one that will just tick the tops of the weeds. It takes a finely tuned sense of feel to keep a plug relatively weed-free in this situation, and you need to ease off as you feel it touch the grass, without letting the plug rise out of the fish's range.

Experience has taught us that when fishing sand grass flats that are either very shallow (less than four feet) or very deep (more than 15 feet), minnow-imitating crankbaits, running just shy of the vegetation, seem to draw the most attention from small-mouths. Between four and 15 feet, crayfish imitators do a better job. However, at these middle depths, it is very difficult to keep the plug free of weeds while trying to intermittently touch bottom.

In low-growing broadleaf vegetation like dwarf cabbage, deep-diving plugs generally offer greater success. The feel of the lure running into the weeds is more easily recognized and your reaction need not be as precise.

Fishing In Tall, Sparse Vegetation

Short-casting a jig and working it on the free-fall until it bumps a clump of vegetation is one way of fishing in tall weeds. A bulky lure is called for here, such as a light (typically $^1/_8$-ounce) living-rubber jig, dressed with either a pork frog or a glued-on plastic twin trailer. The difficulty in trying to work this lure close to skittish smallmouths, however, may limit its application.

Still-fishing in open pockets with live bait is another option. A slip-bobber prevents the float from interfering with casting, and allows effective fishing in depths of up to 15 feet. Again, though, this technique is not without difficulties. Picking out the clearings and low spots in a weedbed from a reasonable casting distance can be tricky, even with polarized glasses.

The most effective way to fish smallmouths in tall vegetation is to work over the top with small baits. Any surface or near-surface presentation that will take smallmouths should work here. Traditional smallmouth topwater plugs and new, soft-bodied stick baits work well. Choose smaller sizes for greatest effectiveness.

Choosing Spinnerbaits For Fishing Around Weeds

When smallmouths are using a weedbed but will not come up for a lure, a spinnerbait is a good solution. Despite the fact that gigantic spinnerbaits will take smallmouths, you will do far better

Weed lures: (top) Baby Slug-Go and Tiny Torpedo, (center) TD-10 and compact spinner-bait, (bottom) jig and Twin Tail, Smoke Grub on jig head and deep-diving shad imitator.

with a substantially smaller lure. Very tiny spinnerbaits, however, are usually too light to effectively penetrate the fish's world on a straight retrieve, and typically carry such a small blade that their most important feature is negated.

One solution is to modify a miniature spinnerbait. Start with a $^1/_8$-ounce single-spin. This lure should feature light-wire construction and a compact frame. Remove the original equipment blade and the swivel (if it is not a ball-bearing type), and simply replace the blade with a larger one. A No. 4 Colorado or Indiana blade will work best. Wrap enough lead wire or solid-core solder around the collar behind the skirt to increase the lure's weight to $^1/_4$-ounce or more. The finished product is a light-wire, $^1/_4$-ounce single-spin lure half the overall size of commercial types. It is deadly for smallmouths and the perfect solution to catching them in tall weedbeds and reeds.

Locating The Fish

Once you have a suitable selection of lures and tackle at hand, finding weed-oriented smallmouths is not much different than locating them in a more traditional setting. Steer clear of surface-matted vegetation, except at first light. At this time, fishing the open edge directly adjacent to heavy cover can be dynamite. Most of the time, however, your best bet is to look past the weeds for locational clues. Generally speaking, vegetation should affect your efforts in terms of presentation rather than location. Remember that, unlike the largemouth fisherman, you are fishing an area in spite of the weeds rather than because of them.

30

45-Degree Banks

One of the underwater structures most overlooked by smallmouth bass fishermen is the 45-degree bank What is a 45-degree bank? Just what its name implies—a bank whose slope is at a 45-degree angle or steeper all the way down to its deepest point.

Why are 45-degree banks so frequently overlooked? One reason is that fish, especially smallmouth bass, use only portions of these banks to live on and feed from, and finding fish on these pinpoint locations is often difficult.

Steep banks are most productive after the spawning period. At this time, smallmouth bass retreat into deep water. Their movement into shallow water is limited only to feeding periods in the early morning, late afternoon and at night. During this period, the 45-degree bank makes an excellent summer residence.

During the spring, the movement of bass is largely in and out, from deep water to the shallows on flats and back into deep water. However, during the summer months, smallmouths still move from deep to shallow, but instead of using the flats, they use humps, drop-offs or 45-degree banks and the movement is largely up and down. Whenever a fish is caught off a hump or 45-degree bank, it is important that you be aware of the depth you were fishing if you wish to repeat the act. As a rule, you can count on the fact that if the fish was caught at a specific level, there will be others holding there as well.

Most smallmouths seem to prefer steep banks to flats during

Some smallmouth anglers find 45-degree banks productive—some do not. These banks are not a smallmouth's favorite kind of structure, but certain elements on these slopes hold bass.

45-Degree Banks

the hottest months because of the immediate access to deep water and the minimal effort it takes to go from shallow to deep. This fact is frequently confusing for the inexperienced angler who assumes that suddenly the fish have quit feeding, which is simply not the case. Rather, they have moved to a more comfortable temperature zone.

Fishing 45-Degree Banks

Fishing this type of structure requires some adjustment in technique and thinking. In contrast to a flat, where casts are made in nearly any direction (since the fish are likely to be on any part of the flat), there are very few random casts made on a steep bank. When fishing a 45-degree bank, your first concern is to locate the depth at which the fish are holding. Do this by working the bait through a wide range of depths. In fact, the most productive method for doing this is to cast at a 45-degree angle away from the boat with the boat positioned parallel to the bank. From this position your bait should work from shallow to deep.

On banks that consist primarily of broken rock, the bottom contour will staircase down. Consequently, pulling the bait from shallow to deep is easier than trying to pull the bait parallel to the shoreline, which will result in unending hang-ups and frustration. Therefore, try to avoid the temptation to throw in front of or behind the boat at all costs.

Bait Techniques

Steep banks can be fished with a variety of baits, although the best producers seem to be the grub, the hair fly and pork rind, rubber legged jig and plastic worms. These baits are especially productive because they can be worked just off the bottom and still remain in contact with the bottom. All of these baits, again, should be thrown at a 45-degree angle away from the boat when the boat is parallel to the bank.

It is important to remember when fishing these banks that smallmouths will be holding at the level most comfortable to them. This does not mean, however, that they will necessarily be in a feeding mode. In fact, it is more likely that they will not. Therefore, the key to catching smallmouths will depend on how close you are able to place your bait to the fish and entice them to eat. Because of this fact, it is crucial that you remain flexible and

Topwater lures will call up bass from the depths on 45-degree banks. Because deep water is so close to shore, bass can hold deep, yet expect to prey on hapless creatures floundering on the surface.

change depths frequently while working the area slowly and thoroughly.

Presenting Topwater Baits

Fishing for smallmouths on steep banks requires a tremendous amount of patience, but there is no stopping a smallmouth bass when it makes up its mind to take a bait. In many instances, smallmouth bass can be brought out of deep water with a topwater bait and 45-degree banks are ideal places to see that happen.

There are two methods that work particularly well in these circumstances. The first involves positioning your boat some distance away from the bank, over deep water, and casting toward the bank. Pull your bait from shallow to deep water. If there are other structural elements that break the bank, all the better.

The second method uses the topwater bait simply as a "tester." Under these circumstances your boat is positioned up close to the bank and you are casting into deep water and pulling the bait into shallow water. You have probably noticed that the topwater bait will be attacked, but frequently missed. When this happens, you can choose to continue throwing the same bait out hoping the fish will come back and hit it, or you can hit the same spot where the fish swirled with a grub or jig and allow the bait to

Cast your lure at a 45-degree angle to the shoreline so that it works shallow to deep, covering a range of depths along the bank you are fishing.

fall. This change in technique gives smallmouths the opportunity to hit the bait as it falls into the area where they are holding. If there is no hit on the way down, allow the bait to rest on the bottom for several moments before moving it. Because you are casting into water that is deep, it will take you longer to thoroughly work the entire area so be patient and do not get into a hurry to move on to the next spot.

Locating Productive Banks

As mentioned earlier, one of the primary reasons fishing steep banks is not so popular is because it is difficult to isolate the most productive banks. There are elements of a productive bank that will help you differentiate it from all of the rest.

Forty-five-degree banks are generally thought of in terms of shorelines that drop into deep water and in most instances they are associated with deep drops. But when some other features come into play, they become much more than just banks. Since there are miles and miles of banks to choose from, the first step in identifying the most productive is to obtain a topographical map of the lake and to study the banks.

Complete Angler's Library

Those banks with the most potential will include:

- Areas where creek or river channels swing along the bank.
- Areas that have flats in close proximity to the bank, conducive to spawning.
- Areas where the banks are heavy in timber. These places will show stumps or will show timber that is still standing in the water.

With the help of a detailed topographical map, these areas can be easily located. The next step is then to go to these areas and look for any 45-degree banks. If you have determined that these banks could hold smallmouth bass, the final step is to fish them and find out if the fish are there.

There are a couple of things to keep in mind when you fish these banks. First, a 45-degree bank that runs a long distance will not hold fish on the entire bank even with all of the above mentioned elements nearby, but there will be several hotspots.

Concentrate on the following:

- A depression or an outcropping that breaks the flow of the bank.
- The point where one type of structure changes to another. For example, from small rocks to large rocks, or from large rocks to gravel. These areas are referred to as "transitions" and are ideal holding areas for bass, especially smallmouths.
- Places where tree stumps are visible at water level and then appear to gradually disappear as the water gets deeper.

A 45-degree bank, in and of itself, is not necessarily a great smallmouth bass habitat, but any steep bank with the right features holds strong possibilities.

Forty-five-degree banks can consist of any type of structure, either rock, mud, gravel and rock or any combination of the above. These banks play an important role in the life of smallmouth bass and should be looked on as such by the serious smallmouth angler.

Targeting
Trophies

31

World Record Story

The giant smallmouth mounting hangs there on the wall of David Hayes' den in Leitchfield, Kentucky. One glance and you know it has to be the world record every smallmouth bass fisherman dreams about. The 11-pound, 15-ounce record has endured since Hayes caught it in Dale Hollow Lake in 1955.

From its underslung jaw hangs a battle-scarred, pearl-finish Bomber. Both are faded with age, but the memories are still vivid as Hayes looks at the lure. A missing belly hook attests to the fury of the fight on that hot July 9 morning. Countless times the unforgettable scene has sequenced through his mind, like a home video replayed on memory's impulse.

Dale Hollow Lake, on the border of Tennessee and Kentucky, is roughly 100 miles from Hayes' home. Hayes and his wife, Ruth, had made plans for a day's outing. By 7 a.m. they were fishing.

Hayes had in mind three points where steep-sloping rocky fingers ran down and disappeared into the clear, clean, deep waters. He would have been satisfied with a nice catch of smallmouths, largemouths, spotted bass or his favorite eating fish, walleyes.

One look at Hayes' boat and rigging and you knew he was not a "catch-and-release" fisherman, but rather a "catch-and-eat" angler whose family enjoyed a fresh-caught mess of fish. The boat was a comfortable 21-foot family craft that had a regular stall at the Cedar Hill Dock. The rod holders on the boat's gunwale marked Hayes as a troller, not a caster.

David Hayes with the world record 11-pound, 15-ounce smallmouth bass he caught in Dale Hollow Lake in 1955. Many anglers believe the record is ripe to be broken.

They arrived at the first point, affixed a fishing rig in each rod holder and began trolling time-proven, big-lipped Bombers that dive deep over rocky shores where the fish hung out during the dog days of summer.

It was not long before Ruth noticed a rodtip take a quick deep bow, and seconds later the drag began to scream, even though it was set tightly. Hayes, who was doing the piloting, put the engine in neutral, grabbed the net and stood ready as Ruth landed a hefty walleye. He reached for it with the net but it was the walleye's day. It flopped free and disappeared into the depths.

Hayes looked over the lure and eased it back into the water alongside the boat to check the action before paying out about 50 yards of line. He then headed the boat for a shale point that had yielded some dandy smallmouths on earlier trips.

At this precise moment, it is difficult not to envision a scene "upstairs" where the gods of fishing get involved in advents like these. It is easy for us to imagine one of the lesser gods looking from Hayes to the head god and saying: "Now?" and the head god smilingly nodding approval.

You see, some world record fish are caught by professional anglers who dedicate their lives to catching that one fish. But most world record fish are caught by anglers who just happen to be in the right spot at the right time, using a bait with magical allure to seduce a world record fish.

Hayes had it all going for him that day as his Bomber descended to the right depth. Moments later the world's largest smallmouth crushed his lure in vice-like jaws.

Hayes heard his reel drag buzz, so he eased the throttle back a tad to slow the boat, went to the holder and lifted the rig to see if the Bomber was snagged on the bottom.

But no snag peels off line with the speed he witnessed, despite the heavy pressure of his thumb on the spool. He shouted to Ruth who was taking a quick nap, and she came running. He kept pressure on the fish and it exploded into the air in an aureate leap that delighted both of them.

After witnessing the size of the huge smallmouth, Hayes decided to keep the boat moving. He was afraid that with so much line out the fish would throw the deep-diving plug if he took the pressure off. He kept the engine running while he maintained a bow in his "rapier steel" rod, as they were called at that time.

After that initial, towering leap the smallmouth headed for bottom and bulldogged it there for several minutes. Hayes maintained bent-rod pressure with a thumb on the line ready to yield yardage if necessary. He still remembered the walleye earlier that shook itself loose because of too much slack in the line.

Like the seasoned fisherman he is, Hayes let a taut line and rod tension tire the fish until he felt it begin to yield line. Reeling and holding, reeling and holding, he coaxed the smallmouth toward the surface where Ruth had the net ready.

He breathed heavily as he finally viewed his all-time biggest smallmouth lying on the deck. He and Ruth knew it was a trophy that would perk up any wall, but the possibility of a new world record never occurred to them. He was thinking how lucky he was to have boated this whopper.

Center Hill Lake, a typical highland reservoir like Dale Hollow, displays the hilly terrain and deep, clear water associated with these smallmouth lakes.

The Bomber was battle-scarred, the belly hook missing, and the remaining tail treble hung in the smallmouth's gill flap. This was just meant to be Hayes' fish, it seemed.

He placed the fish in the cooler, still thinking of it in terms of a larger smallmouth, but not one of record proportions. Tension gone, the pair continued to troll until well after lunch, catching several walleyes and smaller bass.

With plenty of eatin' fish, they decided to call it a day and headed for Cedar Hill Dock. One of the handlers greeted him, asking what kind of luck they had. Hayes replied, "Well, I caught one pretty good smallmouth."

When the handler peered in the cooler to see what "pretty good" looked like, he "came on point" as they say in the hills and remarked, "That's the biggest smallmouth bass I've ever seen!" He then ran to retrieve the scales he kept on hand.

Dick Roberts, then owner of the dock recalled, "I don't know exactly what I was doing when Hayes came in to the dock. But I remember hearing about the big fish and then seeing it. People ran from everywhere and swarmed over the dock like they usually do when a big fish is taken."

He remembers filling out the forms and getting in touch with the Tennessee Department of Fisheries who later sent a biologist to record the details. The fish was certified as a smallmouth bass, 13 years old, 27 inches long and $21^2/_3$ inches in girth. It appeared that the fish had been an adult in the Obey River prior to the impoundment of Dale Hollow Lake in the early 1940s.

An "old timer" and smallmouth disciple, to be unnamed, also remembers the time. When he heard of Hayes' record catch, he wasn't surprised because of an experience on Dale Hollow just one year previously. He had visited the lake for the first time and stopped at Sunset Dock for a noontime snack and to ask about the fishing.

He was about to leave when he noticed a recent picture that stopped him in his tracks. It showed a grinning fisherman holding up a stringer of eight smallmouth bass that weighed 52 pounds! He turned to Lloyd Harrison, the owner and said, "Now there's a man who knows how to catch giant smallmouths. I'd like to meet him and learn how he does it."

Harrison replied, "That's Billy Burns from Lexington, Kentucky, and he phoned to say he's headed this way. If you stick around for a couple of hours, I know he'd be glad to tell you."

You bet the man waited and even had a chance to fish with Burns who showed him his methodology. He says he often recounts this experience for two reasons: one, to show why Hayes' catch from Dale Hollow did not surprise him; and two, to reveal to fellow smallmouth addicts how Burns went about catching bass that averaged nearly 8 pounds!

Burns would cast a big diving plug parallel to the bank over a steep, rocky, fast-sloping shore. Shoving his rodtip underwater to enhance lure depth, he reeled very fast until the extra-big lip of the plug dug into the rocks and hung on bottom.

Using a 20-pound line for strength, he reeled tension into the line until his stiff-action rodtip bowed. Then, grabbing his rod firmly with both hands he braced both feet and ripped the lure off bottom. "Now," Burns explained, "is when those giants grab it. I think the extreme speed tempts them into striking when a slower moving lure doesn't."

"But," he continued with a wry smile, "I don't fish this way any more for two reasons. One, it just flat wears me out over a day's fishing. And, two, I got to thinking that it isn't right for one fisherman to catch in one day more special giant smallmouth than thousands of other fishermen catch in a lifetime." The old-timer tipped his hat to Billy Burns.

Why did smallmouth bass grow to such huge proportions in Dale Hollow? One reason is the rainbow trout fingerlings that the conservation department planted there to see if the species would catch on in these colder waters. The trout did not last, but they certainly made super-rich fodder for the smallmouths in the lake and no doubt added to their growth rate and size.

Will a new world record come from Dale Hollow? Judging by the number of smallmouths weighing more than 8 pounds harvested annually there is a possibility it could happen. Would it upset David Hayes should it happen?

"No," he replied when queried. "One world record fish is enough for a lifetime. I'll let someone else try for the next one."

32

Where Smallmouths Grow Best

Because of the superlative fighting qualities of small-mouth bass, popular demand has brought about transplanting programs making them available in about 90 percent of our 50 states. This means there probably is good smallmouth fishing not too far from your abode.

Throughout many generations, the prime territory for consistent, larger-than-average-size smallmouths has been the Great Lakes region. However, its range has been extended through other sections of our nation where colder waters were created by deep impoundments, especially in the Southeast, Midwest and Southwest.

Let us take a regional look at smallmouth bass hangouts where consistently good fishing has held up over numerous seasons. Remember, smallmouth catching can be cyclic. That is, bodies of water can experience both good and poor years due to numerous factors. So it pays to keep logs with notes on catches and to check with other smallmouth fishermen to see which hangouts are paying off consistently.

Great Lakes

These huge expanses of water have had up and down curves in smallmouth crops but, remarkably, the average has held up. Numerous factors make them ideal smallmouth habitat. Foremost is the cooler and more compatible water temperatures even during hot summer months.

For sheer numbers and size of smallmouths, few waters compare to the warm-water areas of the Great Lakes. Vast expanses of suitable habitat make them a smallmouth angler's paradise.

Where Smallmouths Grow Best

Another plus is the comparatively minor fishing pressure on existing bass populations. Despite heavy traffic from private and commercial fishing crafts near population centers, there are off-shore hangouts that have never seen a fishing lure.

Very important to this ongoing bonanza in smallmouth harvests is the ideal structure common to these lakes. Whereas largemouth bass thrive in weedy, brushy, inshore cover types, smallmouths do best in rocky, craggy, offshore as well as inshore areas.

Here's a rundown on today's better smallmouth spots in the five Great Lakes, plus the "kid" in the group, Lake St. Clair.

Lake Ontario

The St. Lawrence River's moving, fertile waters provide ideal habitat for food chains, spawning and abiding. There is a profusion of bays, cuts, inlets, channels, reefs and shoals available to both shore anglers and boaters.

Historically productive are the famed Thousand Islands that stretch approximately 50 miles from Cedar Island to Outer Wolfe island. This area was only moderately known until professional bass fishermen began holding tournaments there in the 1980s. Their catches were jaw-droppers and the resulting publicity brought thousands of smallmouth devotees to fish these waters.

Hotspots on Lake Ontario proper are: Presque'ile Point, False Ducks Island, Kingston, Jones Creek, Charity Shoal, Main Duck Island, Eel Bay, Bayfield Bay, Amherst Island, Cape Vincent, Battou Channel, Chaumont Bay, Chippewa Bay, Bay of Quinte, Henderson Harbor, Reed's Bay, Grenadier Island, Galloo Island and Sodus Bay.

Lake Erie

Once you fish for smallmouths in the Bass Island area your catches will bear out its name. The smallmouth fishing here has been consistently good over many decades. You have a choice of North, South and Middle Bass Islands.

Throughout Lake Erie you'll find ideal bass structure around reefs, shoals, rocky points and channels. Regular payoff spots on the east end are Cattaraugus Creek, Myers Reef and Van Buren Point. On the west end try Sandusky Bay, Kelleys, Hen and East Sister islands.

Also worth probing are rivermouths, especially those of the Sandusky, Maumee and Niagara rivers. During early summer and late fall months these flowages produce some of the hottest smallmouth bass fishing of the year.

Lake Michigan

Northern Michigan, especially Waugoshance Point, was first brought to national attention by noted smallmouth authority, Byron Dalrymple, who wrote: "If heaven has a smallmouth spot like Waugoshance Point, I'll be content through eternity!"

The straits of Mackinac are ideal wading waters, as is much of the western shoreline. Rivermouths and bays are abundant, including Muskegon, Kalamazoo, St. Joseph, White and Grand River areas. Grand Traverse River and nearby bay waters are cyclical but good.

On Lake Michigan's Wisconsin side, Door County produces good smallmouth fishing from ice-out to ice-in times. Along these rock-bound shores other noted places are Green Bay, Little and Big Bay De Noc, Bailey's Harbor, Washington Island, Detroit Island and Peshtigo Point.

Lake Huron

The colder waters of this lake require more years for smallmouth bass to reach trophy proportions, but those smallies in the 2- to 3-pound range make great catching as well as grand eating.

Michigan's northeastern shore holds many noted hangouts: North Bay, Squaw Bay, Thunder Bay, Oscoda, Au Sable, East Tawas, Point Lookout, Charity Island, Pointe Aux Barques, Sebewaing, Sand Point and Manisou Island.

Lake Superior

Biggest and coldest, Lake Superior's vast expanse is as awesome as a 6-pound smallmouth heading for the clouds after bashing a deer-hair bug. Much of its rocky habitat can be fished from shore.

Fishing is rarely crowded along this lake, even in these popular locales: Lac La Belle, Silver Lake Basin, Portage Lake, Flour Lake and along numerous shores where streams spew forth smallmouth forage.

Maine hosts an outstanding smallmouth fishery, as do many of the states and provinces on the northern fringe of the fish's range. Growth is slow here, but the fish live longer.

Lake St. Clair

Lying between Lakes Huron and Erie, this lake is one of the sleepers for whopper smallmouths. The Detroit River flows from this lake into Lake Erie, providing both food and colder water.

Glen Lau, famed fishing film producer, showed lunker smallmouths, ranging from 3 to 6 pounds, being caught around weeds over sandy bottoms. The leaps were spectacular and the action torrid. This was in the Walpole Island area. Good spots on the U.S. side are Anchor Bay, Big Muscamoot Bay, Pearl Beach, plus the Middle, North and South channels.

Canadian Areas

In Lake Erie's northern stretches good smallmouth catches are registered every year from Pelee Point, Grecian Shoal, Kingsville, Long Point, Bluff Bar, Morgan's Point, Point Albino and Amherst Island. Notable in Lake St. Clair are Mitchell Bay, Stoney Point and Tecumseh.

Productive lakes between Lakes Ontario and Huron are: Stony, Pigeon, Sturgeon, Buckhorn, Balsam, Simcoe, and Cameron. North of Lake Huron are Lakes Nipissing and Wanapitei.

Swinging westward from Lake Superior the record shows these lakes worth a smallmouth trip: Lake of the Woods, Rainy Lake, Eagle Lake, Minnitaki Lake, Sturgeon Lake, Shebandowan Lake, and Sturgeon Lake.

Northeast

While the New England states are homeland to smallmouth bass, Maine has come through with more 4- to 7-pound smallmouths than the others in *Sports Afield's* State Fishing Awards Program. Especially notable are lakes in the twin-county area of Piscataquis and Penobscot, including Lakes Seboeis, Schoodic, South Branch and Sebec.

Mid-Atlantic

Pennsylvania: Pymatuning and Allegheny reservoirs, plus the Allegheny, Juniata, Susquehanna, Delaware, Pine and Potomac rivers.

West Virginia: Lakes Tygart, Sutton, Summersville and Bluestone; and these rivers: Greenbrier, Potomac and Elk.

Virginia: Lakes Claytor, Smith Mountain, Philpott and Anna; and these rivers: Clinch, New, Potomac, James and Rappahannock.

North Carolina: Lakes Fontana, James and Santeetlah, plus the Little Tennessee River.

New Jersey: Musconetcong River and Round Valley Reservoir.

South/Central

Georgia: Lakes Blue Ridge, Nottely and Chatuge.

Alabama: Lakes Pickwick, Wilson and Wheeler, plus the Tennessee and Coosa rivers.

Mississippi: Only Pickwick Lake in the northeastern corner.

Tennessee: Lakes Percy Priest, Center Hill, Dale Hollow, Tim's Ford, Ft. Loudon, Watts Bar, Cherokee, Watauga, Center Hill, Norris and South Holston, plus the Tennessee River.

Kentucky: Lakes Dale Hollow, Cumberland and Kentucky, plus Goose Creek, Kinniconick, Tygarts and Troublesome rivers.

Ohio: Ferguson Reservoir and Lake Erie, plus numerous rivers including Great Miami, Scioto, Stillwater and Paint.

Indiana: Lakes Schaefer, Freeman and Maxinkuckee, plus

Tippecanoe and Pigeon Rivers.

Illinois: Fox, Kankakee, Mackinaw, Illinois, Rock and Kishwaukee rivers.

Iowa: Spirit and Okoboji lakes, plus Cedar, Volga, Iowa and Middle Raccoon rivers.

West/Central

Arkansas: Rivers include Cossatot, Caddo, Ouachita, Little Red, Middle Fork, Buffalo, Kings, White and Crooked Creek.

Missouri: Fine smallmouth river fishing can be had in Eleven Point, Current, Piney Creek, Niangua, Osage Fork, Gasconade, Meramec and Huzzah Creek.

Southwest

Texas: Lakes Belton, Meridith, Canyon, Lyndon Johnson and Texoma.

New Mexico: This state's deep, cold-water reservoirs have responded well as smallmouth habitat, including Navajo, Chama, Conchas, Gila and Elephant Butte.

Arizona: Two lakes, Theodore Roosevelt and Apache, and the Black River yield laudable catches.

West Coast

California: California has done extensive transplanting with good results in these lakes: Pine Flat, McClure, Nacimiento, Comanche, Pardee, Berryessa, Folsom, Oroville, Shasta and Clair Engle (Trinity), plus the Cache Creek and Russian River.

Oregon: Oregon's fast-flowing rivers are a joy to fish, including the Umpqua and its north and south tributaries; Umatilla and Columbia. Also notable are John Day, Brownlee and Prineville/Owyhee lakes.

Washington: Best rivers are Columbia, Snake, Yakima and Okanogan; notable lakes are Sammamish, Washington, Osoyoos, Banks, Moses and Potholes Reservoir.

There is the overview of notable smallmouth waters in the United States and southern Canada. Because of the smallmouth's growing popularity and clout with sportfishermen, further transplanting will take place in many more locales. There is, no doubt, passable smallmouth bass fishing not too far from your bailiwick.

State Smallmouth Records

Alabama	**Owen Smith** caught this state record smallmouth in **1950** at **Wheeler Dam**. (*All weights given in pounds)	10.50 *
Arizona	**Dennis Barnhill** caught the Arizona record smallmouth in **1988** from **Roosevelt Lake**.	7.96
Arkansas	The Arkansas record smallmouth was caught by **Acie Dickerson** in **1969** in **Bull Shoals Lake**. According to an expert Arkansas angler, the record is due to fall soon, possibly by a behemoth from either Bull Shoals or Greers Ferry.	7.31
California	Any time your smallmouth catch tops 9 pounds, you not only have a keeper memory, but also a potential state record fish. California's top smallmouth was caught by **Tim Brady** in **1976** from **Clair Engle Lake**.	9.06
Colorado	**Janie Novak** had a memorable day on **Pueblo Reservoir** when she caught her record-setting smallmouth in **1987**. Chances are this record will be broken by a considerably larger fish, which, by the surveys, are known to live here.	5.50
Connecticut	Angler **Joseph Mankauskas, Jr.**, caught his record smallmouth from **Shenipsit Lake** in **1980**.	7.75
Delaware	Here is a record you stand a reasonable chance of breaking. **Richard Williams** caught his fine smallmouth in **1983** from a **quarry pond**.	4.44
Georgia	**Jack Hall** caught his record smallmouth from **Lake Chatuge** in **1973**.	7.13
Hawaii	Smallmouths were introduced to the Aloha State in 1953, but have not done especially well because of the year-round warm waters. **Willie Song** caught Hawaii's record smallmouth from **Lake Wilson** in **1982**	3.69
Idaho	**Don Schiefelbein** caught his smallmouth in **Dworshak Reservoir** in **1982**. The Snake River, from Twin Falls to the mouth, offers prime fishing much of the year.	7.35

Illinois	This state has a strip mine resource that yields many heavyweights each year. This is where **Mark Samp** caught his record beauty in **1985**.	6.44
Indiana	**Ray Emerick** caught Indiana's whopper smallmouth from **Sugar Creek** in **1985**.	6.94
Iowa	**Rick Pentland** nailed the Iowa state record with a **Spirit Lake** smallmouth in **1979**.	6.50
Kansas	**Rick O'Bannon** caught his winning smallmouth from **Wilson Reservoir** in **1988**. Our files indicate there are record-breaking smallies waiting to be caught in Cedar Bluff and Norton reservoirs.	5.04
Kentucky	Kentucky's state record is also the existing world record (see chapter 31). This record, from **Dale Hollow Reservoir**, has stood since **1955** when **David Hayes** caught it in a reciprocal water bordering Kentucky and Tennessee. Both states share this record.	11.94
Maine	The record in this perennial homeland of smallmouth bass was taken in **1970** from **Thompson Lake** by **George Dyer**. Not only are Maine's rock-bound lakes prime habitat for smallmouth bass, so are numerous rivers such as the Penobscot and Piscataquis. A number of line-class state records are attainable for those eager to break the existing ones.	8.00
Maryland	Maryland's present record was caught by **Gary Peters** while fishing **Liberty Reservoir** in **1974**. The bigger smallmouths are concentrated in the western portion of this state. Particularly noteworthy are Loch Raven where the previous record, an 8-pounder, came from; plus the deep craggy holes in the famed Potomac River.	8.25
Massachusetts	The **Quinebaug River** holds a special place in **Michael Howe's** memory because it yielded his record smallie in **1984**. Additional, ideal homelands for bronzebacks are Quabbin, Wachusett and Ashland reservoirs, and South Waputta Pond.	7.25

Michigan	The Wolverine State offers a wide expanse of smallmouth waters including **Long Lake** where **W. F. Shoemaker** caught the state record in **1906**. This record will be hard to top, but waters capable of doing so are the beauteous streches around Grand Traverse Bay and Waugoshance Point, all the way south to Lake St. Clair near Detroit.	9.25
Minnesota	The Minnesota state record smallmouth was caught back in **1948** by **John Creighton** in **West Battle Lake**.	8.00
Mississippi	Although smallmouth fishing is confined to the northeastern portion of the state, Mississippi does have notable smallmouth fishing. The state record was set in **1987** from **Pickwick Lake** by **Thomas Wilbanks**. One of the unusual aspects here is the ability of anglers to catch both smallmouth and largemouth bass in the same areas.	7.94
Missouri	The current Missouri state record was caught by **Richard Bullard** in **1988** in **Stockton Lake.** We believe the record will not stand for long since tons of heavyweight smallmouths are thriving in the sparkling waters of the Gasconade, Meramec, Current, Eleven Point, and Elk rivers; not to mention Table Rock, Bull Shoals, and Truman reservoirs. It is only a matter of time before one is taken.	7.00
Montana	Although known more as trout country, the smallmouth is listed as one of Montana's top 10 gamefish. The record was caught in **Fort Peck Reservoir** by **Marvin Loomis** in **1987**.	5.69
Nebraska	**Merrit Reservoir** seems to be the main source of consistent smallmouth catches, fed by the booming Snake River. Here is where **Wally Allison** caught the existing record in **1978**. But, you will find good, uncrowded fishing in the lakes bordering Interstate 80 and in the Sand Hill area.	6.09
Nevada	Nevada's food chain is more suited to trout than smallmouth bass. **Gleen C. Deming** caught the record fish in **Dry Creek Reservoir** in **1989**. Steady catches are made in the Carson, Humboldt and Bruneau rivers.	3.50
New Hampshire	New Hampshire lists more than 100 lakes harboring this scrapper. The record came from **Goose Pond** in **1970** and was caught by **Francis Lord**. Lake Wentworth is a consistent producer of husky bronzebacks.	7.91

Where Smallmouths Grow Best

New Jersey	The record shows there are two main hangouts for smallmouth bass in New Jersey: Round Valley Reservoir and the **Delaware River**, where the existing state record was caught by **Earl Trumpore** in 1957.	6.25
New Mexico	The core of New Mexico's smallmouth fishing is primarily limited to the Rio Grande River above the confluence of the Rio Chama River. Also worth fishing is **Ute Lake** where **Carl Kelly** caught the record smallmouth in 1972.	6.55
New York	There seem to be good smallmouth waters all over New York, including the Delware River, West Branch Delaware River, Lake George, St. Lawrence River, Lake Champlain, Lake Ontario and countless small streams and lakes scattered among endless hills and flats. The record smallmouth was caught by **George Tennyson** while fishing **Friends Lake** way back in 1925. This record may never be broken.	9.00
North Carolina	The best waters seem to be confined to the western section of the state and an ongoing smallmouth planting program keeps fishing lively in reservoirs such as Fontana and Santeetlah, plus the New and James rivers. The record is a monster caught in **Hiwassee Reservoir** by **Archie Lampkin** in 1953.	10.13
North Dakota	**Denise Hoger** holds the state record with a smallmouth she caught in **Lake Sakakawea** in 1987. This reservoir seems to be the best bet for lunker bronzebacks despite an abundance of other lakes and rivers.	5.06
Ohio	Ohio's record smallmouth came from the **Mad River** in 1941 (before this magnificent stream was polluted by effluent from a pulp mill). Ohio's rock-strewn streams and reservoirs hold good populations of smallmouth bass, but Lake Erie is the best bet for trophies. The state record was cuaght by **James Bayless**.	7.50
Oklahoma	**Lake Texoma's** colder waters gave birth to the state record smallmouth caught by **Jeff Smart** in 1989. Rivers in Oklahoma yield the most catches, including the Grand, Illinois, Mountain Fork, Little and Glover.	6.44
Oregon	The Oregon record bronzeback came from the **Columbia River** in 1989, caught by **Reuben Klevgaard**. Other good waters include the Snake, Willamette and Malheur (middle fork) rivers.	6.88

Charlie Pence of Franklin, broke the Pennsylvania state record when he caught this 7-pound, 10-ounce smallmouth on a green tube jig in Lake Erie.

Where Smallmouths Grow Best

State	Description	Record
Pennsylvania	This state's record smallmouth was caught in 1990 by **Charlie Pence** in **Lake Erie**. Other good spots include the Youghiogheny Susquehanna and Delaware rivers.	7.63
Rhode Island	Little ol' Rhode Island has some chunky smallmouth bass in a couple of dozen lakes, including Staffords, Ashville, Indian and Blue ponds. The state's all-time biggest smallmouth came from **Wash Pond** in 1977. **Butch Ferris** was the angler.	5.94
South Carolina	Although South Carolina's total smallmouth population is small relative to its supply of largemouths, it still has some lunkers. The **Broad River** coughed up the state record caught by **Gerald Knight** in **1988**.	6.75
South Dakota	**Robert Kolden** latched on to South Dakota's trophy smallmouth in **Clear Lake** in **1988**. Other good holdings are Pierpont Lake, Little Moreau Dam No. 1 and the Missouri and Cheyenne rivers.	5.21
Tennessee	No smallmouth lover can forget the massive state and world record that **David Hayes** caught in **Dale Hollow Reservoir** in **1955**. Other good waters are Center Hill Reservoir, South Holston Lake, Wautauga Lake, and the Nolichucky and Buffalo rivers.	11.94
Texas	The Lone Star state's smallmouth program is progressive and making headway each year. The record here was caught in **Lake Whitney** by **Ronald Garner** in **1988**.	7.72
Utah	Although Utah has tried stocking in numerous waters, it is not ready to be touted as smallmouth country. The record was caught in **Lake Borham** in **1983** by **Roger L. Tallerico**. Flaming Gorge yields minor catches.	6.75
Vermont	**Jean Houle** caught this state's record fish in the **Connecticut River** in **1988.**	7.75
Virginia	**John Justice** had a good day on the **New River** back in 1986. This state lists more than 20 waters, mostly rivers, where smallmouths are caught. Good rivers include the Rappahannock, James and Shenandoah.	7.44
Washington	Washington's rivers are a delight to fish. Not only are they beautiful, they offer big smallmouths. The state record was caught in the **Columbia River** by **Ray Wanacutt** in **1967**. Native anglers believe that mark will fall soon to another river fish.	8.75

West Virginia	Northern West Virginia is a good place to find trophy smallmouth bass. **David Lindsey** caught the record in **South Branch River** in **1971**. Other proven streams are Greenbrier, Elk, Cacapon, Fish and Wheeling.	**9.75**
Wisconsin	When you go after smallmouths in Wisconsin, concentrate your efforts in Vilas Country, which contains nearly 200 lovely lakes. Trophies dwell in Green Bay as well. The record was taken from **Indian Lake** by **Leon Stefonek** in **1950**.	**9.06**
Wyoming	Although it is doubtful that Wyoming will ever become noted as prime smallmouth country, **D. Jon Nelson** managed to catch the state record, in **Southeast Pit** in **1982**. Who knows, a bigger one may be waiting for you!	**4.75**

The Future

33

Pollution's Effects On Smallmouths

Pollution. Where does it figure in the world of smallmouth bass and devoted anglers who pursue this noble species? When we pause to ponder this question, it can leave us feeling lower than a submarine track. But, ponder it we must if we hope to secure future smallmouth fisheries. When we say "pollution" we mainly mean water pollution, because that is where most man-made pollutants wind up...in the water we drink and in the world of fish. And because we live in a high-tech society, the list of potential pollutants grows with the population and its demands.

Acid Rain Means Polluted Waters

Let us begin with acid rain, which most of us hear and read about but give little thought to because we do not readily see its devastating effects on our smallmouth fishing.

The first effects of acid rain could be seen in Scandinavia when anglers were only vaguely aware of it in North America. Twenty years ago, Swedish angler Lennart Borgstrom told of a beautiful smallmouth lake where the fishing was good and the fish healthy.

"Would you believe that five years ago this was a dead lake? Smallmouths couldn't live in it," Borgstrom said. "They died off because of acid rain brought here on prevailing winds from the Saar, Germany's vast industrial valley."

He continued: "We restored it, and maintain it, by dumping

Acid rain, created by the sulphur emissions of coal-burning power plants and other airborne pollutants, may sterilize smallmouth waters hundreds of miles from the pollutant's source.

Pollution's Effects On Smallmouths   353

tons of limestone flour. Without this continuous treatment the smallmouth would perish. America is not yet alert to this threat, but it exists and one day will take its toll."

Time has proved his prophecy. Today acid rain and snow compose runoff waters that have seared smallmouth streams and lakes across America, particularly in the industrialized northeast and on the eastern coast. One study showed that 50% of Adirondack lakes above 2,000 feet are barren of life. Recent tests in Wisconsin revealed damage from acid rain and snow. Numerous lakes and streams are undergoing neutralizing treatments to preserve them.

Where does the acid in rain and snow originate? It's an airborne pollutant, made up mostly of sulfur oxides from gasoline or diesel exhausts, and nitrous oxides effusing from industrial smokestacks burning untreated coal.

Most fishermen are unaware of the effects of acid effluents, but workmen in our nation's capitol have witnessed the heavy damage of acid rainfall on the Lincoln Memorial and hundreds of buildings made of marble or limestone. If not controlled, its effect on smallmouth fishing will be as destructive in America as it has been in Scandinavian countries. What is being done about it?

Countless studies have been made at great expense. Some states have taken remedial steps to control and restore their streams and lakes. Congress has passed laws calling for cleaner exhausts both from automobiles and plants. As fishermen we must support such efforts and pray they will be effective before it is too late.

Unfortunately, acid rain is only one segment of pollution problems affecting smallmouth fishermen. There is a mindboggling array of other threats to our environment including: ineffective water sewage treatment, poor toxic waste disposal, careless proliferation of pesticides, herbicides and fertilizers, and topsoil erosion caused by poor farming practices.

Another frightening source of deadly pollution was sledgehammered to our attention when the Love Canal story hit the headlines a few years back. Here an entire New York neighborhood began showing the frightful effects of poisons seeping into its water and homes.

The deadliest pollutant was dioxin. How deadly? One news source pointed out that if just three ounces of dioxin were dis-

Once a clear-running stream, this water has been clouded by the runoff of agricultural fertilizers and livestock waste. Bank disturbance and erosion have also helped to eliminate smallmouths.

persed in New York City's water supply, it could kill seven million inhabitants. Love Canal was estimated to hold about 130 pounds of dioxin. Another dump site, New York's Hyde Park, is said to hold some 2,000 pounds of this deadly chemical.

Since then, the Environmental Protection Agency has issued some hard guidelines to demand better handling and disposal of hazardous waste products. But, with our nation's three-trillion-plus dollar deficit and budget tightening the order of the day, manpower for enforcement of anti-pollution laws is and will be woefully inadequate in the decades ahead.

Depletion Of Our Water Supply Means Fewer Smallmouths

These foregoing facts on the perils to smallmouth water quality are shocking enough, but there are other threats to our water supply from coast to coast and from border to border—diminishing quantity.

Like many things in life, we humans prefer to ignore rumors or threats until they become real. Then we hit the panic button and demand that things be done to eliminate whatever the said threat might be—hoping that our efforts are not too late.

Here are some factors affecting the quantity of water, a vital resource that we waste in countless ways. As one travels across our nation and views the countryside, we see a growing proliferation of huge, rotary wells used for agricultural irrigation. These pump water from aquifers, our vast underground reservoirs, in tremendous volumes.

The reason for this is that our rainfall is unpredictable in many large farming sections. Insufficient rain means a stunted or lost crop with a resulting loss of income. Oftentimes, a farmer must either install a rotary well or go out of business.

This mushrooming demand for water has caused a serious shrinking in the size of our aquifers, especially the main Ogallala aquifer in the eastern United States. One Alabama farmer who installed a second rotary system five years after installing his first was asked how much deeper he drilled to reach aquifer water the second time. He replied: "Five hundred feet deeper than the first drilling."

This is shocking for two reasons: One, depending on the size of the aquifer, this could translate into millions of gallons of shrinkage in his area. Two, multiplied nationwide it means billions, maybe trillions, of gallons of water shrinkage in our precious aquifer system.

There are other signs of a lessening water supply, some of which may be apparent where you live. When anglers visit smallmouth streams they fished and swam in as youngsters, they are often stunned to see only a trickle of water remaining. And the smaller the volume of water, the less it is able to maintain a healthy environment for fish.

Water Degradation—How Does It Happen?

Another example of water degradation adversely affecting smallmouth fishing is Florida's Kissimmee River. The Corps of Engineers dredged this once beautiful, winding stream, converting it to an ugly, straight-gut ditch for faster runoff and flood control. The farmers loved it because they wound up with more acreage.

Fishermen who formerly caught bass from the meandering Kissimmee ceased fishing it because it was a waste of time. The fish preferred to dwell in the lake. The main reason was water degradation which occurred because the river flowed so fast that there was insufficient time for it to cleanse itself of chemical impurities and certain algae which tend to cause eutrophication, or aging.

A backlash occurred when fishermen hollered loudly enough to be heard in Tallahassee. The Corps of Engineers has since been ordered to restore the Kissimmee River to its former meandering self and, hopefully in time, to its original good smallmouth habitat. One cost estimate is $50 million!

Exactly where do our billions of gallons of water go each day? One survey allocated it this way: 46 percent to industry, 42 percent to agriculture and 12 percent for household usage. So, it's obvious that the two biggest users must have restrictions imposed to conserve water through reuse, instead of wasting it all in runoff or carrying harmful chemicals with it that degrade our lakes and streams. We anglers must also do our share by conserving water now, and not when we are forced to do so because of a crisis.

Everywhere that sizable groups of people dwell across America, we see the crisis of poor water quality and diminishing quantity growing ominously. Water rationing is a way of life in many sectors, and the business of selling bottled water, or water purifiers, is booming.

But, the question that begs an answer is "What can you as a concerned angler do about it?" The following chapter on conservation contains some guidelines.

34

The Conservation Effort

Having spotlighted some of the myriad sources of pollution and causes of a shrinking water supply for our nation, one obvious conclusion is that the buck-passing has to stop, and concerned citizens/fishermen must take action. So easy to say, so hard to do until each of us, or our families, feels the hurt.

As smallmouth bass lovers, we either begin to take individual actions toward a common goal or we will be guilty of passing along to our kids, and coming generations of fishermen, a heritage we have enjoyed but one that is seriously flawed for their prospective enjoyment.

One step that would bring much individual satisfaction and very definite smallmouth fishing enhancement is a movement called "Adopt-a-Stream," which has caught on in a number of states. Concerned trout club members began such projects in the early 1980s.

Suppose one of your favorite smallmouth streams, pits or lakes is showing signs of a decreasing population. One cause could be cyclic because certain bodies of water do have up-and-down years depending on how year-classes of smallmouth fry survive.

However, when the decline continues for a number of years, then it is time for concerned action. The first step is to call a meeting of other concerned fishermen, possibly organize a smallmouth bass chapter. You can get valuable help from organizations like Smallmouth Inc., Edgefield, South Carolina. Smallmouth Inc. is

An angler holds today's trophy in one hand and what may be a future trophy in the other. Tomorrow's smallmouth fishing depends on the conservation measures you practice today.

The Conservation Effort

The days of keeping strings of smallmouths like this are gone—if we want good fishing tomorrow.

in constant touch with smallmouth movements around the nation and can put you in contact with other groups who are in the forefront of smallmouth fishing enhancement.

Another helpful ally constantly concerned with improving our environment is the Izaak Walton League of America, with chapters in every state. Also, for expert appraisal of what ails any body of water, contact the nearest office of your state fish and game department and request the assistance of local fisheries biologists.

Water Conservation And The Smallmouth Angler

Oddly, there is a bright side to the coming water shortage mentioned previously. When that shocking fact grips our nation, you will see a concerted effort in each state to conserve water. One of the ways to stretch the usage of annual rainfall is to build impoundments to hold it for human consumption, electric power, industry and irrigation.

Every dammable stream will be utilized. This will mean millions more acres of water for recreational usage. Also, because water temperature and cover are compatible, your state department will attempt transplanting programs for smallmouths.

The fast-flowing, deeper streams will be looked upon in a new

Smallmouth tournaments are popular in some locales, but the smallmouth also shows up at largemouth tourneys. Vojai Reed caught this beauty at the Bass 'N Gal Classic on New York's Hudson River.

light...how to best utilize this water for the utmost benefit. Obviously, keeping it clean and ridding it of any form of pollution will be the order of the day. And the cleaner they keep our streams, the better they will be as smallmouth bass habitat. Should you see any form of pollution entering a lake or stream, report it immediately to your state conservation department.

Another way you personally can help enhance the realm of smallmouths is to play the role of steward on your favorite lake or stream. When you go fishing, take with you a plastic bag for picking up the trash some unthinking person has left behind. This not only makes it more palatable for you, but for all who love nature in pristine form. And if you observe people discarding unsightly debris, remember that it may be ignorance, because no one ever has enlightened them on the ethic of respecting Mother Nature. Talk with them.

Practicing Catch-And-Release Fishing

And now, let's take a close look at our favorite sportfish, one of God's finer handiworks, the smallmouth bass. It is with a feeling of awe that we peer into those reflective orbs and contemplate what it had to endure to reach maturity.

If 1 percent of the tens of thousands of smallmouth eggs

hatched reach maturity, it's a high survival rate. So many things take a toll, including a multitude of predators, toxic chemicals, degraded water, disappearance of protective cover, diminishing food chains, bacterial infections, fungus and overfishing in crowded waters.

Many smallmouth fishermen are driven by one main desire, to catch a lunker so they can hurry back to the dock to show it off and take pictures. Some fishing programs on television show an equal lack of consideration for smallmouths. The host is in some remote hotspot for smallmouths. Repeatedly, he and his companion hook, fight and land bronze beauties. Then, after showing off his catch the host shows what a good sport he is by callously tossing back the smallmouths. They land with a splat on the hard water, risking serious injury.

Smallmouths deserve better at all anglers' hands. There is more to the ethic of returning smallmouths to the water than just tossing them back. They merit releasing with tender, loving care.

As you hold that unique fish among fish that you have inveigled into taking a lure, enjoyed an exciting battle during which it fought you with every ounce of the fighting blood coursing through its body, remember...there is but one thing you can give it in return—its life. A chance to live on, to delight other smallmouth anglers and provide offspring to keep alive the tradition.

This is especially true with trophy smallmouths. Some biologists say that lunker bass have only 10 percent viable eggs because they're too old for full fertility. While it may be biologically true, there's another factor involved—genetics.

Just as children born of big parents tend to be big as well, so may giant bass beget giant bass. There never has been an in-depth study made to ascertain if this is true, but the possibility alone should cause you to relish returning lunkers, gently and fondly.

Being A Good Sportsman

A lifelong smallmouth angler who will remain unnamed told of an enduring smallmouth memory made while courting his "Childbride" of 53 years.

The couple had been dating about a year, and while she knew he was a smallmouth fisherman, they hadn't talked much about it. They were taking a Sunday drive, and as they passed over a bridge on one of his pet smallmouth streams, he stopped to eyeball a clus-

If you like smallmouth fishing like this, practice catch and release whenever possible. Handle fish carefully. Grab a fish with a liplock, not an overhand grip like the angler on the right.

The Conservation Effort

Conservation groups like Smallmouth Inc. of Edgefield, South Carolina, who distribute boat landing signs and license plates promoting catch and release are helping smallmouths flourish.

tering of tree roots at the base of a sheer limestone cliff. He knew a fullback lived here because he had lost it a couple of times.

At that instant he saw the big bruiser flash at something, possibly a minnow, so he asked her to pardon him while he opened the trunk and extracted an always-ready casting rig. Easing down to the bank he wafted a soft cast to the target, reeled a couple times, and that smallmouth blasted his lure with a vengeance.

The fish headed for the sky and the angler estimated its size at about 5 pounds of bronzed muscle. Then it dashed under those roots and tangled the lure. He could feel it tugging but couldn't move the lure, so it was a stalemate. He knew what he had to do.

It was early April, and still ice was fringing the bank. He asked his companion if she would please just keep her eyes forward in the front seat while he stripped to his shorts. "Why do you need to shuck your clothes?" she asked.

He replied: "It will be hard for you to understand this, but that is one fine specimen of a smallmouth. If I don't set it free it could hang there and die. And I couldn't live with that thought." She shook her head, smiled, nodded and complied.

He swam across the frigid stream, carefully captured and released that admirable smallmouth bass, then shivered back into his wet clothes. Several years after they married and she had become a seasoned angler, she observed: "When you endured that cold water just to release a fish, I knew it was going to be an interesting life. And now that I've learned to admire smallmouths, I know why you were compelled to free that fish."

It is the choice of every smallmouth fisherman to decide for himself whether or not to release his catch. There is nothing wrong with keeping enough smaller fish to treat the family to fresh fillets.

Anglers who have caught more than their share may find it difficult to remember that part of the charm of fishing is to be able to catch and enjoy eating the results of their efforts. But there comes a time in every smallmouth fisherman's life when he begins to view this special gladiator with an awe that borders on reverence.

If you haven't reached this stage it is nothing to be concerned about. This reverence grows with the memories of battles lost and won. May they be yours in abundance!

About The Authors

Editor **Jay Michael Strangis** has fished from Canada to Florida, and coast to coast. He has been employed researching, writing and editing in the field of outdoor publishing for almost a decade, and his work has been featured in many national publications. He serves as Managing Editor—Books for the North American Fishing Club and the North American Hunting Club.

Jay began his fishing pursuits like many youngsters, catching panfish in the lakes and warmwater streams of his native Minnesota. His interests broadened with his travels, and he has fished for all of North America's major freshwater gamefish. Jay has caught and released hundreds of smallmouth bass.

Although he has fished in some of the wildest country in North America, Jay's special interests include the challenge of taking trophy fish on some of his home state's most heavily fished waters. His largest smallmouth to date, a fish well over 5 pounds, was caught on a lake in the Twin Cities metropolitan area.

Chris Altman, who authored the night-fishing chapter of this book, left a medical career to take up freelance writing in 1986. Since then, he has been published in virtually all of the major outdoor markets and now writes regularly for such magazines as *Bassmaster, Field And Stream* and *Southern Outdoors*. He also writes a weekly syndicated column for newpapers in four states and is senior writer for *B.A.S.S. Times*.

Chris has received numerous awards from various national, state and regional organizations for his written works.

Currently, he lives in eastern Kentucky with his wife, Susie, his three-year-old son, Ryan, and a "good-for-nothing" golden retriever.

Chris also contributed to NAFC's Complete Anglers Library book *Freshwater Fishing Secrets*, and has been a contributor to *North American Fisherman* magazine.

Tony Bean of Nashville, Tennessee is one of America's leading experts on the smallmouth bass. Born in Lynchburg, Tennessee, Bean grew up fishing and hunting, eventually becoming one of the South's most successful professional outdoor guides. Tony has fished more than 300 days a year but now spends a large amount of his time doing seminars on smallmouth bass fishing. He has personally caught more than 300 smallmouths exceeding 5 pounds each; his largest over 8 pounds. In addition to writing the fishing on rocks, banks and reservoir sections of this book, he has co-authored another book on smallmouths and has written for many national magazines.

Tony is also a bait and boat design consultant. He is an experienced photographer and has served as consultant on a number of books covering smallmouth fishing across the United States.

Homer Circle, angling editor of *Sports Afield* magazine since 1948 and author of the sections in this book on targeting trophies and the future of smallmouth angling, has fished over much of four continents, questing for and writing about the world's great sportfishes. He is a former president of the Outdoor Writers Association of America and the only member to receive all three of this organization's most prestigious awards.

Homer is also a former commissioner of the Arkansas Game and Fish Commission and is a member of the Fishing Hall of Fame. He has hosted three national television shows on fishing and has starred in more than 50 fishing films, one of which won seven national and international awards. Homer has written and narrated two national radio fishing shows, authored seven books, and his monthly articles have appeared in *Sports Afield* since 1964.

Steve Filipek, who authored the section in this book on smallmouth biology, has spent a large part of his life studying smallmouth bass either with a rod and reel or electrofishing gear in numerous streams and lakes.

A graduate of Colorado State University with a degree in fisheries biology, Steve has worked in the fisheries field for 14 years. This has included experience with the Fisheries Divisions in Colorado, California and Washington. For the last decade, he has worked as a Fisheries Management Biologist and is currently a Fisheries Research Biologist for the Arkansas Game and Fish Commission.

Steve has published more than 25 scientific papers, several on smallmouth bass biology, food habits and the effects of floods on smallmouths. A Certified Fisheries Scientist, Steve is a past president and cofounder of the Arkansas Chapter of the American Fisheries Society.

Tim Holschlag authored chapters on finding smallmouth bass in Canadian Shield lakes and catching spawning fish in this book. Born and raised in northeast Iowa and southwest Wisconsin, Tim spent his youth fishing and exploring the many smallmouth waters of the region. He has maintained an intense interest in these bass for three decades. During this time he has explored smallmouth waters across the continent.

Believing in the need to combine conservation with sport angling, Tim helped found the Smallmouth Alliance, an organization committed to improving smallmouth angling. As president, he contributes regularly to its publications, conducts programs on aspects of smallmouth fishing and participates in club conservation projects and research.

Tim's recent work includes numerous magazine articles, and a book.

Boyd Pfeiffer, who authored most of the equipment and moving water sections of this book, is an award-winning outdoor journalist widely known for his expertise in fresh- and saltwater fishing, tackle and photography. During a 25-year period, he has authored a number of books and hundreds of articles. He served as outdoor editor of *The Washington Post* and has been a contributing writer to a long list of outdoor related publications.

Boyd has received more than 40 major local, regional and national awards for his outdoor writing and photography. He is widely known for his knowledge of tackle and serves as a consultant to fishing tackle manufacturers. He is also in demand as a lecturer and product photographer.

Boyd is a former president of the Outdoor Writers Association of America and the Pennsylvania Outdoor Writers Association.

Thayne Smith, author of the chapter on the use of sonar in smallmouth fishing, is a veteran journalist and photographer, specializing in the outdoor and travel fields.

A full-time freelancer, he is "Boating & Accessories" columnist for the *North American Fisherman* magazine and writes for many of the major hunting and fishing publications in the United States and Canada.

Thayne is active in many writing and conservation organizations in North America. He is a former president of the Outdoor Writers Association of America, Association of Great Lakes Outdoor Writers and Great Rivers Outdoor Writers.

Thayne gained his expertise on the subject of sonar during his years as public relations director for Lowrance Electronics, a company that pioneered the use of flashers and graphs in the sportfishing industry.

Louie Stout is a veteran outdoor writer who toiled as an Indiana newspaper reporter and editor for 15 years before launching an independent outdoor writing career in 1986. In addition to writing the chapter in this book covering mesotrophic lakes, Louie has had work published in numerous national and regional magazines. He is one of the top authorities on bass fishing in Midwestern waters and has won 17 state and national writing awards.

The Bristol, Indiana author also serves as the Sunday Outdoors Editor for the South Bend, Indiana, *Tribune*.

"Smallmouths are a lot like many of my friends who helped me in my career," Louie explains. "They have character; they're unpredictable and highly motivated. Above all, they wake up mad and stay that way all day long."

Don Wirth, who authored the sections in this book on fishing flats, offshore structure, highland reservoirs and catching suspended fish, has been writing about bass fishing for 20 years. He is perhaps best known for his humor series in *Bassmaster Magazine*, "The Adventures of Harry 'n Charlie," but he writes regularly for a number of other fishing publications. He is the author of several books on fishing and boating and is also an accomplished photographer whose photos have appeared on the covers of many publications. His books and magazine features have won numerous awards over the years. As an award-winning video producer, Don's production credits include 3M's "Catching Big Bass" series with Doug Hannon.

Don currently resides in Nashville, Tennessee, close to the world's "best" smallmouth bass fishing.

Rich Zaleski was led to the outdoor writing field in the early 1970s through a love of fishing and an article penned as a favor for a friend. He authored the chapters of this book covering fishing through the ice and catching smallmouths in and around weedbeds.

Currently, Rich has a weekly outdoors column in a local newspaper and is host and producer of a radio show. He also serves as field, state or contributing editor for four magazines and his photographs are popular in catalogs, brochures and calendars.

An active member of the Outdoor Writers Association of America and the New England Outdoor Writers Association, Rich lectures extensively on fishing for warm-water species.

He has also been very successful in competitive fishing. Rich was the North American Bass Association champion in 1985.

Index